Harriet E. Bishop

FLORAL HOME
or
FIRST YEARS OF MINNESOTA

EARLY SKETCHES,
LATER SETTLEMENTS,
AND
FURTHER DEVELOPMENTS

◈ Harriet E. Bishop ◈

HERITAGE BOOKS
2012

HERITAGE BOOKS
AN IMPRINT OF HERITAGE BOOKS, INC.

Books, CDs, and more—Worldwide

For our listing of thousands of titles see our website
at
www.HeritageBooks.com

A Facsimile Reprint
Published 2012 by
HERITAGE BOOKS, INC.
Publishing Division
100 Railroad Ave. #104
Westminster, Maryland 21157

Copyright © 2002 Heritage Books, Inc.

New York, New York
1857

— Publisher's Notice —
In reprints such as this, it is often not possible to remove blemishes from the original. We feel the contents of this book warrant its reissue despite these blemishes and hope you will agree and read it with pleasure.

International Standard Book Numbers
Paperbound: 978-0-7884-2165-5
Clothbound: 978-0-7884-9441-3

TO

HONORABLE ALEXANDER RAMSAY,

FIRST GOVERNOR OF MINNESOTA,

WHOSE SAFE COUNSEL, JUDICIOUS AIMS, AND PRUDENT USE

OF

EXECUTIVE POWER,

ARE THE CORNER STONE OF ITS PROSPERITY,

This Volume

IS RESPECTFULLY DEDICATED BY ITS

AUTHOR.

PREFACE.

THIS work has been prepared at the urgent solicitation of friends, and is designed to exhibit the rise and progress of Minnesota; what it *was* and what it has become; the rapid development of its resources; when, how and by whom the foundations of an unparalleled prosperity were laid; and to rescue from oblivion facts which might be unchronicled by the future historian.

In this volume the aim has been to present the reader with a truthful picture, so far as words can be signs of ideas, of the beauties and rare advantages of this Floral Territory. And the most important object of its publication will be secured if men and women of sterling worth, are, by it, induced to identify themselves with the interests of this youthful empire, and labor to make it the first state in our glorious Union.

CONTENTS.

CHAPTER I.

A Peep at the Past—The Northwest as it Was, - - - - 17

CHAPTER II.

The St. Peter's River—Early Explorers—Menard—His Death—Sufferings of early Explorers.—Claude Allong—Louis Hennapin—Falls of St. Anthony, - - - - - - - - - - - 20

CHAPTER III.

Jonathan Carver—The Cave—Foresight of Carver, and his Influence with the Dakotas—Dr. Hartwell Carver, - - - - - 24

CHAPTER IV.

Early Trading Posts—Wm. Morrison—Lake Itasca not the Source of the Mississippi—Gen. Pike and the Sioux Purchase—Joseph Renville—His Marriage—Dr. Williamson—Louis Provençalle—Mr. Farribault—The Swiss Emigrant's Death-bed, - - - - - - - 27

CHAPTER V.

Fort Snelling—Col. Leavenworth—First American Woman to Tread this Soil—First Marriage—Col. Snelling—Mrs. Snelling—Her Trip to the New Fort—Incidents after Arrival—Improvements at St. Anthony's Falls—Annual Flat-Boat—The Captive Children—Mrs. Snelling's Christian Character—Chase for the Wolf—The First Steamer—Surprise of the Whites, and Alarm of the Natives—Further Additions to Society, - - - - - - - - - - - 32

CHAPTER VI.

Col. Snelling leaves to visit Friends in the East—Incidents and Hardships—Final Return to the Fort—An old Indian—Mrs. Snelling's Visit to Minnesota in 1851, - - - - - - - - 38

CHAPTER VII.

Franklin Steele—The Country as he Found it in 1837—Commencement of Lumbering Interests—Price of Supplies—Mission at Koposia—

[7]

Mrs. Holton, the first Citizen Woman—Dr. Carlie—Mr. Hone—Anson Northup Settles at St. Croix Falls in 1839.—The Marine Mill Built—Endurance and Virtues of Mrs. Northup—Laurels worn by others—Duties of Women in New Settlements, and their importance, - 43

CHAPTER VIII.

Nucleus of St. Paul—Its original Name, "Pig's Eye," whence Derived—Advice when coming West—Information Imparted—Old Catholic Chapel—Improvements Commenced by Henry Jackson in 1841—His Arrival with his Wife—Their First Night—Erection of a Cabin—Its Gradual Change—In 1842 John R. Irvine claims "Ripper Town,"—Isolated Society—Love of Western Homes—A. L. Larpenteur—Louis Robear—Life a Reality, - - - - - - - - 47

CHAPTER IX.

Why I Came to St. Paul—Answered in a Letter of Dr. Williamson—Opposition of Friends—Cheerfulness in the Decision. - - - 52

CHAPTER X.

Review of the Book of Providence—Palmyra—Preservation from Shipwreck on Lake Erie—Friends Prepared by the Way—The Journey—Mrs. Dr. Jones, - - - - - - - - - 56

CHAPTER XI.

The Last Good-by—Fascinations of Nature—Galena—Dubuque—Bold Scenery—Prairie du Chien—Items by the Way—Arrival at Kaposia—Rush of the Indians—Reception by the Missionaries—Kissing the Pappooses—Presentation to the Chief and others—Dreams of Childhood Realized—Native Prayer-meeting—Stroll through the Village—Early Indian Friends—Little Crow, - - - - - - 59

CHAPTER XII.

First Sabbath—Game of Ball—Religious Services—Rejoicing in Darkness—Nature's Charms, - - - - - - - - 64

CHAPTER XIII.

First Canoe Ride—Its Novelty—Landing in St. Paul—The Scene Changed—The Town as it Was—Kindness of the Frontier—Red River train, - - - - - - - - - 67

CHAPTER XIV.

Indian Character as in Books Incorrect—Their Habits—Trials of Missionaries—A Favorite with the Band—Their Attentions—The Hunt—Danger of the Missionary's Son; his Rescue—Dr. Williamson—Why he entered the Missionary Field, - - - - - - 71

CHAPTER XV.

The Indian Dead—Mourning—A Walk to the Deposit of the Dead—A Wanton Act, - - - - - - - - - - 75

CHAPTER XVI.

Canoe Ride to Red Rock—Frontier Welcome—Musketoes—Red Rock Prairie—The Grove Meeting—Emotions Awakened—Homeward Bound—Sea Sickness—A Ludicrous Position, - - - - - 78

CHAPTER XVII.

Greetings of the Morning Steamer—Morning of Joyful Hope—The Mud-Walled Hovels, and the Work to be Performed—Appearance of the Room, and its Duties—The Picture Reversed—Foundation of Educational Interests laid—Substitute for Society, - - - - 82

CHAPTER XVIII.

The first Sabbath-school—Its Organization—Dea. Cavender—Division of the School in 1850—Fourth of July, 1856, - - - - - 85

CHAPTER XIX.

Indian Dance—Breaking Up of their Revelry—The Boy Dancers, - 90

CHAPTER XX.

Novelty of Frontier Life—A Morning Call—Offer of Marriage—A Parallel Case, - - - - - - - - - 93

CHAPTER XXI.

The Sacred Tree—A Heart-sickening Scene—Increase of population—"St. Paul House," kept by J. W. Bass—Dr. Dewey—The Sabbath, 98

CHAPTER XXII.

The Winter—Origin and Organization of the "Circle of Industry"—Efforts to Build a School-house—Its Completion—Illness of the Teacher—Sick Couch in a Canoe—Stillwater—Miss Hosford—School Lands—Other Teachers, - - - - - - 101

CHAPTER XXIII.

Rum's doings—First Ride to St. Anthony's Falls—Incident by the Way—Log Cabin, and Its Inmates—Murders—Dreadful Death—Temperance Society Organized—Efforts to Decoy—Partial Success—Sons of Temperance—Maine Law—The Vote and Victory—Repeal, - 105

CHAPTER XXIV.

First Religious Movements—Religious Destitution—Duties of the Writer—Reinforcements—First Prayer-Meeting—First Church Organization—Correspondence with Dr. Hill—Appointment of a Baptist Missionary—Sundering Ties—Death of Mr. Parsons—Embarrassments of the Baptist Church—Rev. T. R. Cressey, succeeded by Rev. A. M. Torbet—Estimate of the Importance of the Field—Associations—Biographi-—cal Sketch of the Rev. Joshua Bradley, - - - - - 112

CHAPTER XXV.

Visit of Mr. Neill, and his Appointment—Lecture-room was Burned—Presbyterian Churches Organized—New Church Edifices—Episcopal Mission—German Church—Swede Church—Indebtedness to the Home Mission Boards—New England Spirit Prevalent—Institutions of Learning, - - - - - - - - - - - 120

CHAPTER XXVI.

Wisconsin a State—Desire of the People—Mass Meeting, and its Results—Alexander Ramsey first Governor—Rush of Immigration—Improvements at Work—James M. Goodhue, and The Pioneer—Gov. Gorman, - - - - - - - - - - - - 124

CHAPTER XXVII.

Climate—Birth of Flowers—Soil—Spring—Plowing—Autumn the Crowning Season—Captain Pope's Opinion, - - - - - - 129

CHAPTER XXVIII.

St. Croix Valley—First Farmers—Raising Corn—Wheat—Oats and other Grains—Labor, - - - - - - - - - - 133

CHAPTER XXIX.

Making Claims—Claim Making Experience Embodied in a Letter of a Friend, - - - - - - - - - - 137

CHAPTER XXX.

Wild Fruits—Wild Rice—Game—Fertility of the Soil—Pure Atmosphere—Increase of Population—Poem by Mrs. Sigourney, - - 144

CHAPTER XXXI

Lake Minnetonka—Mr. Owen's Visit there—Lines to Minnesota, - 148

CHAPTER XXXII.

A Ride Proposed—The Town we Leave—Scenery—Groveland Garden—Cheever's Tower—St. Anthony—Contrast with my First Visit—Workings of Improvement—The Island—Suspension Bridge—Minneapolis—

Lakes Calhoun and Harriet, and Lake of the Isles—Our Repast—A Stroll and Row—A Cabin and Wood Nymph—Minnehaha Falls—Poem of Rev. Dr. Phelps—Drive to the Fort—Cemetery—Morgan's Bluff—Reminiscence of my first Visit to the Fort—Captain Eastman and Wife—Doctor Turner and Wife—Minnesota River—An Adventure—Mendota—Visit to the Cave, - - - - - - 151

CHAPTER XXXIII.

St. Paul—Its Growth and Prosperity—Newspapers—Gas Works—Warehouses—Lawyers and Doctors, - - - - - - - 163

CHAPTER XXXIV.

The Stranger's Funeral—Young Men's Christian Association—Historical Society—"Whitney's Daguerrean Gallery"—M. C. Tuttle, - 169

CHAPTER XXXV.

A Stranger's Opinion of St. Paul—Company on Board a Mississippi Steamer—Steamboat Arrivals—Average Period of Arrival and Departure—Lake Pepin retarding Navigation—Chopping Through the Lake, - - - - - - - - - - - 172

CHAPTER XXXVI.

Stillwater the Oldest Town—St. Croix—Prescott—Point Douglass—Hudson—The Grave on a High Bluff, - - - - - - 179

CHAPTER XXXVII.

Visit to St. Croix Falls—Wild Scenery—After Visit in Summer—Enchantment of the Scenery—Exciting Skiff Ride—A Circumstance related by Captain Smith—Wildwood Cottage—Exciting Murderous Scenes—Pleasant close of the Visit and Skiff Ride to Stillwater—A Scene in the Street, and its Cause—Wildwood Cottage in Mourning—Death of Judge Perkins—Reflections, - - - - 182

CHAPTER XXXVIII.

St. Anthony's Falls—First Visit there—First Cabin—Falls Islands—Poem by Rev. S. W. Pond, - - - - - - - - 191

CHAPTER XXXIX.

Former State of the Region around St. Anthony—Rise of Property—St. Anthony the Second City in the Territory—University—Steamers built here—Advantages for Bridging—West Shore—Thrilling Adventure of a Young Lady—Peril of the Writer, - - - - 199

CHAPTER XL.

Minneapolis—The Old Mill—Col. John H. Stephens—His Lecture before the Lyceum—Military Reserve—First Court West of the River—Right of Preëmption, - - - - - - - - 205

CONTENTS.

CHAPTER XLI.

The West, where is it?—Enchanting Scenery—Change in the River Scenery, - - - - - - - - - - - 212

CHAPTER XLII.

The Bluffs—An Ascent—A Beautiful Idea—Lake Pepin—Maiden's Rock or Lover's Leap—Winona—Her untimely Death—Her Father's Death—Her Lover's Conversion, - - - - - - 217

CHAPTER XLIII.

Upper Mississippi Scenery—The "Excursion Party," - - - 221

CHAPTER XLIV.

Wabashaw Prairie—Difficulties Concerning the Winnebago Treaty—Wabashaw Prairie in 1856—Winona in 1852—Winona in 1856—Hastings—Visit to Hastings—The Baptist Church—Return—A Pick-pocket—The Smile of Progress—Koposia, - - - - - - 226

CHAPTER XLV.

Scenery above St. Anthony's Falls—Agricultural Resources—Timber—Towns—Manomin—Saut Rapids—"Minnie Mary Lee"—St. Cloude—Waterville—Forest City—Hutchinson—Fort Ripley—Long Prairie—Bell Prairie—Pembina, - - - - - - - - 234

CHAPTER XLVI.

Pembina Hunters—White Traders—James Tanner—Elijah Terry and his Consecration to the Missionary Work, and Tragical Death—Tragical Death of Mrs. Spencer, - - - - - - - 238

CHAPTER XLVII.

Natural Thoroughfares—First Efforts at the Head of Lake Superior—Advance of Settlements—Government Road—Railroad—Superior City—Mineral Wealth of Minnesota—Salt Region, . - - 242

CHAPTER XLVIII.

Red River Caravans—A Novel Garment—A Great Fright—Rehearsals of Adventures—Bishop of Oregon—Kit Carson—Mr. Goodale and his Adventures and Escapes, - - - - - - - - 246

CHAPTER XLIX.

Cameron—Milnor and his Adventures, - - - - - 250

CHAPTER L.

The Indians—Government Policy in Reference to them—Efforts by

Missionaries—Annual Meeting—Indians Opposed to Education—Old Shakopee's Speeches—Strolls among their Teepees, and Degradation there—A Little Sioux Girl—General Character of the Indian, - 253

CHAPTER LI.

Story of the Wakan Man—The Young Indian Heroine—Attachments of the Indian Women—Wrong and Suicide of a Young Woman, - 263

CHAPTER LII.

The Indian a theme for Admiration—Music, and its Power over Him—The Dandy—Old Hock-e-wash-ta, and his Abrupt Entrance into the Baptist Church—Murder of Mrs. Keener—Murder of a Little Chippewa Girl—Propensity for Eating, - - - - - - 268

CHAPTER LIII.

The Winnebagoes; their Removal—Baptiste. - - - - 272

CHAPTER LIV.

The Chippewas and their Language—The Queen—Hole-in-the-Day—Feud between the Sioux and Chippewas—Depredations and Murders—Massacre on Apple River—Scalp Dance—Excitement Prevailing—Governor Ramsey Demands a Treaty—Assemblage of the Tribes—Delay—Final Arrival—Indignity of the Sioux—Courteous Manner of Hole-in-the-Day—His Speech—The Treaty—Hostilities Resumed—His Instincts. - - - - - - - - - - 274

CHAPTER LV.

Explorations of the Minnesota River—First, Second, and Third Enterprises—The Yankee's Trip—Importance of these Explorations, - - 281

CHAPTER LVI.

Treaty Proposed—Red Man's Opposition—Their Removal—Exploring Trip of the West Newton—Our Company—High Water—Advance of Civilization—First Landing Place—Impressions Received—Lake Frances—Miss Hobbs, afterwards Mrs. Owen—Paper Towns—Le Seur—Traverse—Rev. Mr. Hopkins and his Death—Mankato—New Waters—Region of Silence—Little Rock—Trader and Family—Arrival at our Destination—The Lone Indian—Natural Parks, and Glorious Scenery—Reflections—The Tiger's Approach—Wandering Nations—"All Aboard"—Cameron's Grave—Excitement—Dangers to the Boat—Shocking affair at Traverse, - - - - - 288

CHAPTER LVII.

Visit of Dr. Hill to the Territory—Trip through the Minnesota Valley by Land, and its many Incidents—St. Peter's, and its Character and Enterprize—Going Home—The Big Woods—Our Hotel in the Woods—Romps amid Bush and Brakes—The Family—Wood Nymph—Lost—Lame Horse—Last Incident, - - - - - 301

CHAPTER LVIII.

Southern Minnesota—Rev. T. R. Cressey—Missionary in this Field—Soil—Inland Towns—Progress Here as Elsewhere—Earth's Eden—The Panorama—God loves Beauty—The Prospective, - - 313

CHAPTER LIX.

Distance Annihilated—Advantages and Disadvantages—A Stage-coach Story—Robbery, - - - - - - - - - 317

CHAPTER LX.

Love of Frontier Life—A Large Purchase—Change of the Mode of Life—Frontier Housekeeping—Arrangements for Cooking—Gradual Change—Relish of Wild Scenes—Love for Minnesota, - - - - 320

CHAPTER LXI.

Stranger's Inquiry—Recognition of an old Friend—Minnesota in General—Hasty Marriage—Death of Miss Chase, and the Savor of her Piety—Importance of the Board of National Popular Education, - - 323

CHAPTER LXII.

Extract from a New Year's Sermon of Rev. A. M. Torbet—Prosperity of Minnesota, - - - - - - - - - - 333

CHAPTER LXIII.

Conclusion, - - - - - - - - - - 340

EARLY SKETCHES.

CHAPTER I.

A PEEP AT THE PAST.

HAD the same Providence which wafted the Mayflower to Plymouth Rock directed its course into the Gulf of Mexico, and thence up the windings of the Mississippi, into the regions of vast prairies and natural gardens, the forests of New England would be still standing, and no cities, mighty in influence, would have risen from their fall. The red man would still lurk in the dark recesses of those forests, pursuing his game without fear of molestation; and the smoke of his wigwam and council fires would ascend from the ground where his fathers had dwelt and held their council.

Obviously, Providence shaped the means, and the work to be accomplished, though centuries were consumed in man's "rough hewing." The energy and enterprise, born and nurtured on that sterile soil, have no parallel in the world's history; and for their full development, they have pushed on towards the setting sun, and diffused themselves over the "unshorn gardens of the wilderness," while the grand drama of city building was enacting upon the Atlantic coast. There, side by side, arose the church and school-house, and with them men of giant mind, who thrilled the nation with their eloquence. The power of the Press was acknowledged, and the savage was either subdued, or retreated before the light of advancing civilization.

For centuries, the mighty Northwest smiled in unpraised beauty—a befitting field for the enjoyment of celestial beings. The fairest portion of all this beautiful earth has no historic lore, save in some remaining monumental antiquities. The Red Man remained undisputed and undisturbed owner of the soil. His light canoe skimmed the surface of crystal lakes, glittering in the sun's rays, and radiant with reflected floral beauty. The dancing streamlet sweetly harmonized with the gentle breeze and the wood-bird's notes. The graceful swan arched her white neck, the queen of the waters, as she floated fearlessly along. Flowers breathed forth their odors where there was none to admire, and trees of a hundred years grew old and died on the mysterious mounds

> " That overlook the rivers, or that rise
> In the dim forest."

> " The encircling vastness stretched
> Like airy undulations far away,
> As if the ocean in her gentlest swell
> Stood still, with all her boundless billows fixed
> And motionless for ever."

Over these the buffalo roamed in herds that

> " Shook the earth with thundering steps,"

marking a trail to guide the future explorations and surveys of the white man. The untutored savage heard the voice of the Great Spirit in the moaning winds and the deep-toned thunders. He paused from the pursuit of game to render homage to the " wakan " that intercepted his path. The awful war-whoop resounded o'er the bluffs as he pursued his long hated enemy. The reeking scalp was exhibited in the horrid war-dance, and the captive was tortured in the most cruel manner that savage malice and hate could devise.

But in the great plans and purposes of JEHOVAH, a moral dawn appears. The march of empire is westward. On, on it rushes, till the inventive genius of the immortal Fulton has pushed it beyond the Great Lakes; and the wild beasts of the prairie, with the red man, have fled the approach of steam. The iron horse, more mighty than Bucephalus, is neighing far, far beyond, and making the widely-separated Atlantic and Mississippi to meet. Men, indeed, "run to and fro, and knowledge is everywhere increased." Richness and beauty increase as we approach the interior—as we stand upon the banks of earth's noblest stream, surrounded by the flowery plains, the rich, undulating prairies and natural parks of Minnesota, the El Dorado of the world. In the first gush of enthusiasm we exclaim "Eureka! Eureka!"

EMIGRANT TRAIN CROSSING THE PRAIRIES.

CHAPTER II.

FIRST EXPLORATIONS.

The river which gives name to the beautiful territory of Minnesota, was discovered by La Seur, a Frenchman, in 1760. It was known to the world as the St. Peter's, until in 1852, when it was " Resolved by the Senate and House of Representatives, that from and after the passage of this act, the river in the territory of Minnesota, known as the St. Peter's, should be known and designated on the public records as the Minnesota River."

It is a Dakota word, and signifies, according to Dr. Williamson, " turbid or whitish water."

SETTING OUT ON AN EXPLORING EXPEDITION.

The extreme northwest was penetrated by traders and Jesuits, from the Canadas, soon after

SAINT PETERS.

FIRST EXPLORATIONS.   21

> " Our pilgrim fathers moored their bark
> On the wild New England shore."

Of some of these we give brief sketches.

The first white men known to have entered these unexplored wilds, were two French traders from Quebec, in 1654. Their ostensible object was the purchase of furs from the Dakota or Sioux Indians, who then occupied most of the country east of the Mississippi. Their object accomplished, they returned with flattering accounts of the remote region they had visited, and a like adventurous spirit was thereby awakened in others.

Bearing in his hand the standard of his faith to plant amid the wilds, and within the sight of the natives of this region, Menard, a Romish priest, enters the broad arena, *alone*, with his cossack and prayer book. His native enthusiasm, combined with a love for his religion, rendered him a fit person for the enterprise. He was a man of age and experience, and admirably fitted to the toils of the mission. His journey was beset with trials. Such was his scarcity of food, that he was even reduced to the necessity of living on pounded bones, but, finally, he arrived at his destination, on the 15th October, 1660. "For more than eight months, surrounded by a few French voyageurs, and many savages, I dwelt," to use his own language, "in a kind of small hermitage, a cabin built of fir branches, piled on one another, not so much to shield me from the rigor of the seasons, as to correct my imagination, and persuade me that I was sheltered."

On the 20th of August, 1661, while making a tour to visit the Hurons, his comrade made a portage with the canoe, and Menard entered the woods. No traces of him could afterwards be found, and as the Indians have a tradition that the first white man who built his "teepee" among them was murdered, it is probable that such was his fate.

Many years afterwards, his cassock and prayer book were found in a Dakota lodge, and were regarded by the possessor as "wakan," or supernatural.

Menard might have perished from starvation, as this among the early explorers was not unfrequent, according to tradition. An intelligent native, lately deceased at La Pointe, related the following story: "While the natives were dwelling on the island, a party of lads who were spearing fish through holes in the ice, discovered a smoke arising from its eastern extremity, which was then seldom visited. Proceeding in the direction, they found in a rough cabin, two white men in the last stages of starvation. Coasting the lake late in the fall, they had been driven by the ice on the island, and not knowing that any human beings were near, they had almost perished, having roasted and eaten their blankets."

This event saddened, though it did not deter the Jesuits from further attempts to plant missions among the Indian tribes of this region.

Menard was succeeded by Claude Allong, a Jesuit, who acted somewhat in the capacity of a missionary while in pursuit of copper. After spending two years near the head of Lake Superior, he embarked on the Wisconsin River, and after paddling seven days, entered the great "Father of Waters," four hundred miles below St. Anthony's Falls; the first white man who dipped his paddle in the Upper Mississippi, but stopping short of the limits of Minnesota.

In the spring of 1680, Louis Hennapin descended the

Illinois River in a canoe, accompanied by La Salle, who was murdered by one of his own party.

Notwithstanding the terrors depicted by the Indians, Hennapin resolved upon the hazardous undertaking of ascending the mighty stream. He built a more commodious boat, and after a fatiguing and dangerous voyage of nineteen days, arrived at the mouth of the Minnesota River. He was first to stand on "Pilot Knob," and drink in the Eden-like beauty of all the eye could scan; the first to listen to the roar of our far-famed cataract, and to gaze with admiration on its radiant bow, while his glowing soul expanded amid such glorious scenes. He left the marks of his enthusiastic devotion to his church on everything. The falls which he named for his patron saint, he describes as being sixty feet high. From the fact that they are constantly receding, and that within the last ten years they have fallen away several feet, perhaps a rod, it is quite probable, that at that time, they were as high as he asserts (though now scarcely fifteen feet), and, indeed, there is indubitable evidence of this a half mile below.

"Father Hennapin" was kindly received by the several Indian tribes, who had not then learned hostility to the whites, and during his brief sojourn, was surprised by the arrival of a party of French traders. In the month of September following, they all bade adieu to the lovely land, leaving it for others to profit from their discoveries, and become the rich partakers of its golden fruits.

A spirit of adventure was awakened in France by the publication of these "Travels and Discoveries," and many daring adventurers plunged into the heart of the unknown wild, some impelled by the spirit of gain, and others with the mere love of novelty and desire for adventure.

CHAPTER III.

FURTHER EXPLORATIONS BY THE ENGLISH.

UNTIL 1766 these explorations had all been confined to the French; but a restless, roving spirit was in the breast of Jonathan Carver, a true-born Yankee of the bluest stamp. He is supposed to have been, and doubtless was, a descendant of the Mayflower passenger who was first governor of the Plymouth colony, and inherited the adventurous spirit of his ancestor.

As early as 1763 he conceived the design of exploring the northwest, but it was not carried out until June, 1766, and in the November following he arrived within the present precincts of our territory. With only a Frenchman and Mohawk for guides, his heroic nature defied the dangers of the expedition; he ascended the almost unknown river in a canoe, and exulted in the fact of being first of the Anglo-Saxon race to view this grand scenery, to tread this fertile soil, and listen to the roar of the now far-famed cataract.

His winter abode was the cave which bears his name, one mile below the CAPITOL, and now included in the city limits of St. Paul. Carver describes it as a "remarkable cave of amazing depth," which the Indians termed "Wakan Teepee." He says the entrance is about ten feet and the arch within about fifteen feet high, and about thirty broad, the bottom consisting of clear white sand.

He also speaks of a lake, which commenced about

thirty feet from the entrance of the cave, the water of which was transparent and extending to an indefinite distance. Having no means to acquire a knowledge of its extent, he says, "I threw a pebble towards the interior part of it with my utmost strength; I could hear that it fell into the water, and notwithstanding it was of a small size, it caused an astonishing noise, that reverberated through all these gloomy regions. I found in this cave many Indian hieroglyphics, which appeared very ancient, for time had nearly covered them with moss, so that it was with difficulty I could trace them. They were cut in a rude manner upon the inside of the wall, which was composed of a stone so extremely soft that it might be easily penetrated with a knife." Such is Carver's description, and though now it differs very widely from his account, the hieroglyphics are still visible. The utilitarian spirit of the age has converted this cave into a commodious wareroom.

Exploring the country, studying the language, making friends with the Indians, shooting the buffalo, encountering the grizzly bear, &c. occupied the time of Carver during his sojourn.

At one time we find him far up the Minnesota River, camping with the Indians, and wherever his canoe was seen the British flag was flying at its head. It appears from various sources that his visit to the Dakotas was of some service in bringing about a friendly intercourse between them and the commander of the English force at Mackinack. That he acquired great influence over the various bands with whom he mingled, we have indubitable evidence; and had he chosen to remain with them, there is little doubt but he would have been elected chief of the Dakota nation.

2

Carver was endowed with unusual foresight and sagacity, and though the Falls of St. Anthony were more than a thousand miles remote from the nearest English settlement, he was fully impressed with the belief that the extreme beauty and fertility of the region would attract settlers. Yea, he saw, with the eye of faith, an enlightened population flooding the land, which, for their benefit, he partitioned into colonies, with the number and description of each. The broad, beautiful waste he saw adorned with stately palaces, and sacred temples, their gilded spires pointing "where man's heart should oftener turn."

We last hear of him at one of the great councils of the Dakotas, in the vicinity of the "cave." Selecting some of their number for guides, and taking a regretful leave of the remainder, he proceeded by way of Chippewa river and Lake Superior to Mackinack, and thence by the nearest route to England, where he published an account of his "Adventures in the Northwest."

In 1848, Dr. Hartwell Carver visited the region which had been the theater of his grandfather's rich adventures. He came as claimant of the soil—his claims being predicated on a title to one hundred miles square, ceded to the former by the two head chiefs of the Dakota nation. This conveyance of land was claimed to have been ratified by George III. But the efforts of the heirs of Jonathan Carver to hold the same were, and are still, unsubstantiated by Congress; and doubtless the last lingering hope of any *right* to the same has expired in the breast of the most sanguine of the heirs.

CHAPTER IV.

FIRST TRADERS AND MISSIONARIES.

A line of trading posts was established far up the Mississippi, above the Falls of St. Anthony, by Wm. Morrison, in 1802, and he remained a resident of the country until 1826. During this period he was agent for the American Fur Company of New York City, and was the real discoverer of the reputed source of the Mississippi, having seen Lake Itasca in 1804. This honor has been accorded to Gen. Pike, who, under an order of government, visited this region in 1806, and supposed himself to be the discoverer, the two explorers not having met, whereby the mistake might have been corrected. Schoolcraft also unjustly claims this honor, but it is certain that several had visited this point before he had even originated the design of doing so.

We believe, on good authority, that the reputed source of the Mississippi is not the correct one. Capt. Eastman, of the U. S. A., and others having equal facilities for making a correct opinion, with whom I have conversed, assert its origin to be a hundred or more lakes, of which Itasca is one, all centering in one point, to form the mighty stream. This is far more philosophical, and I have no doubt of its correctness.

It was the visit of Gen. Pike, just referred to, which effected the purchase of the beautiful lands east of the Mississippi, included within the limits of our territory. He was eminently fitted for the delicate but arduous task; and but for his influence with the natives, they would probably have made much stronger demonstrations in favor of the British, in the war of 1812, in which this noble and gallant man lost his life.

Some brief notices of early traders come in place at this point, and may not be uninteresting to the reader.

Mr. Joseph Renville was the son of a French trader and an Indian mother, and his history forms a link between the past and present history of Minnesota. He was born upon the soil about the year 1779, at which time it is computed there were not more than six white families residing within the whole of the vast territory comprised in northern Illinois, Wisconsin, Iowa, and Minnesota.

He was taken to Canada by his father when ten years of age, and his education entrusted to a Romish priest. Still, in youth, he returned to his native land, and was afterwards the guide of Gen. Pike to the Falls of St. Anthony, through whose influence he obtained the appointment of interpreter. During a long period he was one of the most important citizens of the territory, employed by Government in various ways, and extending to all travelers great hospitality. He was a warm friend, both to the missionaries and his mother's people. Under his direction, the first corn was planted in Minnesota, and he was the first to engage in raising stock. His post obtained a reputation among explorers, where a warm welcome always awaited them. He warmly welcomed Dr. Williamson, to whom he rendered valuable assistance in the establishment of his missions, and who spoke of him ever afterward with the greatest kindness and respect. He acted as translator of Scripture, being such a natural linguist as to render him eminently fit for an interpreter.

Years before there was any Christian minister in Minnesota, he was married according to the Christian service, performing a journey to Prairie du Chien for that purpose. He also possessed a large copy of the Bible, which was probably the first in Minnesota. This Bible was recently presented to the Historical Society by one of his sons, and while at the Mission-house in Lac qui Parle, whence it was to be forwarded to St. Paul, the house and all its contents were destroyed.

His wife was the first Dakota who joined the Christian church at the Lac qui Parle, and the first to die in the Christian faith. She had become a Christian through the teachings of her husband, before she had ever seen a missionary, and her death was most happy and triumphant.

Mr. Renville held an important office in the church, of which he was a valuable member. His death scene was one of unusual interest, as described by the missionary, and a bright legacy to the Christian church. It occurred in 1856. His children are respected and honored whereever known, the mantle of their father having fallen upon them.

Louis Provençalle, who died at Mendota in 1850, had been for more than fifty years a resident of this country He was a man of strong mind, but of little education. His books of Indian credit were kept by hieroglyphics, and understood only by himself, and the correctness of his accounts was not to be questioned.

In character he was bold and daring. On one occasion a company of pillagers threatened the seizure of his goods, when seizing a firebrand he held it to a keg of gunpowder, declaring his determination to blow himself and them into the air if they took a single article. This had the desired effect, and he was never afterwards molested. His history would make a large and interesting volume.

Mr. Farribault is the last survivor of the original traders, having reached an advanced age, greatly respected for integrity and uprightness of character.

Among the original inhabitants, who built their cabins on the high bluff of the Mississippi, where now smiles the young city of St. Paul, was an old man of Swiss descent, who had strayed from the remote north. His frugal wants were supplied by the gun, and a few culinary vegetables, cultivated with tools of his own make.

Once in a winter ramble, I found myself at the door of his cabin, and my rap was responded to by the French "*Entrez.*" Comfortless, indeed, was the aspect within. Several children were playing in the midst of disorder and dirt. Age and infirmity were the portion of his cup, but his countenance was radiant with joy as I took his withered hand. He had been perusing some worn and soiled leaves of a French Bible, and evinced by word and look the comfort they afforded him; and raised his dim eyes to heaven in token that his trust was there.

He had become an object of interest, and not unfrequently were my feet treading the narrow path to his miserable abode, and never without a profitable lesson to the soul. One bright morning in the following spring, just as earth had drunk up the snow, I was told that he was sick unto death, and I soon stood at his bedside for the last time. A halo of light was about that bed of straw, and rested upon his pallid features, more radiant than the beams of natural light which entered at his small window. With fervor he grasped my hand, and thanked me for coming to see a poor, old, dying man, while the tears streamed down his wan and withered face.

It was a blessed privilege to stand by *such* a death bed. In life he had remembered his Creator, and in death he was not forsaken of him. His home of poverty on earth was about to be exchanged for the "Mansion prepared for such as love the Saviour." "O, 'tis a glorious boon to die."

CHAPTER V.

FORT SNELLING.

FROM Carver passed an interval of nearly half a century, with naught to mark its periods or note its history. An occasional trader, for the love of gain, planted his post upon the Mississippi and its tributaries, marrying, in most cases, amongst the natives, and seeking no other advantages for his growing family, than were found amongst the tribe with whom he dwelt.

The shout of the hunter and whoop of the warrior resounded o'er the bluffs. The noble river remained unrippled, save by the Indian's paddle, until a defence of the frontier was found expedient.

The present site of Fort Snelling was selected, and recommended to the war department, by Major Long, in 1817. In 1819 the first detachment of troops, under command of Colonel Leavenworth, arrived at the mouth of the Minnesota river, and established a cantonment, preparatory to the erection of more permanent quarters.

St. Louis was the nearest town of any importance, and this only in embryo, whence "supplies" were "poled," nine hundred miles in a flat boat, chartered by government for the purpose, the trip requiring three months. The fort was named after its first commandant, and Lake Harriet, a beautiful transparent sheet of water, after his heroic and inestimable wife. The original barracks were of logs, but were rebuilt of stone in 1845–7, a noble and commanding fortification.

The first white woman who trod this soil, was Mrs. Clark, wife of the commissary; the first to endure the fatigues, and enjoy the romance of a voyage on the Upper Mississippi. The water was so low that the men were obliged frequently to wade in the river, and draw the boat through the mud, thus consuming six weeks in the last three hundred miles.

Arrived at their destination, they were obliged to live in the boat, until a shelter and defence from the Indians could be erected. After one month in the boat, added to the time already occupied by the trip, Mrs. Clark regarded it a rich luxury to commence housekeeping in her new log hut, though it was of the rudest kind, "plastered with mud, and chinked with clay."

It was December when they got into their winter quarters, and the fierce winds which swept over the prairies, obliged them to keep mostly within doors. Once in a violent storm, the roof of their cabin was partly removed, leaving no protection for the inmates, and the baby, for shelter, was placed under the bed.

Let it not be understood that Mrs. Clark was long without female companionship; for some four or five ladies had accompanied their husbands, and with all the discomforts of pioneers, they had their social pleasures, and even in their rude, floorless abodes, held their dancing assemblies once a fortnight.

Mrs. Clark left Fort Snelling in 1827. During the period of her sojourn (eight years), one wedding, only, had been chronicled among their number, there having been but one unmarried lady in their circle. The marriage could not be solemnized short of a trip to Prairie du Chien, three hundred miles distant, and being in the winter it was performed on the ice.

In 1820, Colonel Snelling was appointed to the command, prosecuting the work of building with great energy, and filling his station with dignity, and winning golden opinions from subordinate officers and privates.

Mrs. Snelling, true to the noble instinct of woman, would not allow her husband to brave the dangers and privations of the wilderness alone. The cabin of the keel boat in which she was a passenger, scarcely allowed her to stand upright, while the weather was exceedingly warm, and the musketoes were as annoying as in later days. The fatigues and anxieties of the trip were increased by the care of her young children; which, added to the fear of the ferocious-looking savages, numerous on both shores, robbed the young mother of nearly all quiet rest. A few months after their arrival, Mrs. Snelling's fifth child was born. Her sick room was "papered and carpeted with buffalo robes, and made quite comfortable." Two years later, soon after moving into the new barracks, this child sickened and died; the first white child whose demise is recorded.

Soon after the arrival of Colonel Snelling, work was commenced at St. Anthony's Falls, on the west side, a grist mill erected, and other improvements contemplated. The first white woman who visited the Falls, was Mrs. Capt. George Goading. What must her emotions have been, as with a proud consciousness of standing where no other of her sex had stood, she quaffed the full draught from Nature's glorious fount!

The first years in the history of Fort Snelling were monotonous in the extreme. The monthly arrival of a mail, conveyed four hundred miles on the back of a drafted soldier, and the annual arrival of a flat boat, were the chief events to record in the routine of weeks, and even months, and years, save the frequent disturbances among the Indians.

One incident, however, which created no little excitement at the time, is worthy of record. Two captive white children, whose parents, from the Red River settlement, had been murdered by the Sioux, were found by some traders on the St. Peter's River, and Colonel Snelling immediately sent an officer with a company of soldiers, for their rescue. Their ages were eight and five. The eldest could narrate the facts relative to their captivity; and because he cried, on seeing the brains of his little sister dashed out against a tree, and their parents cruelly murdered, he had a small portion of his scalp removed, which was an open sore at the time of the rescue. Still, they were reluctant to leave their captors, who were also loath to give them up. They were kindly received and cared for by the families of the garrison. The eldest died while yet young, leaving happy evidence that religious instruction had not been bestowed on him in vain, and the younger was sent to an orphan asylum in New York.

The Christian character of Mrs. Snelling is worthy of special attention. Highly intelligent and refined, she placed all her accomplishments at the feet of her Redeemer, and quietly, yet firmly evinced the power of the principle that "worketh no ill to its neighbor." The instruction of children was her particular *forte*, and on each Sabbath she convened them for religious teaching, to which is attributable the happy death bed of the orphan captive.

She was possessed of a buoyant spirit, and enjoyed, with a high relish, the rich scenes on which her romantic, ardent nature feasted. From childhood she had been accustomed to equestrian exercise, and here she found enlarged opportunity for its enjoyment. How unlike an amble through a well paved thoroughfare, is a gallop wheresoever one listeth, over the unfenced prairie! The very soul expands, as the atmosphere imparts new life to the system, and the inflated nostrils of the beast evince *his* enthusiasm and joy in untrammeled liberty!

On one occasion, as Mrs. S. was riding with an officer, they descried a wolf, to which, as by common consent, they gave chase. Her bonnet flew off, and with hair streaming in the wind, the bounding steeds flew onward, until they actually ran down the object of pursuit.

At this time, the wolves are represented as so numerous, that their boldness was most presuming; and so nearly starved, that any sort of food left within their reach, was sure to be devoured by them; and it is the more wonderful, that our fair huntress and her gallant attendant, were not devoured by the half-famished animal, than that it should have been borne home by them, a trophy of their heroism.

In 1823, a sound hitherto unheard, broke upon the silence of this remote region. Nearer, and yet nearer it approached, until a moving, approaching object was descried upon the water. The natives placed their hands over their mouths, in token of astonishment, and finally, with shrieks of alarm, fled in terror from the monster. They imagined that the Great Spirit was angry, and had come to seek redress, and therefore, with streaming hair and sailing blankets, they sought to hide from his presence. A sentinel on duty had been first to discover, and announce to the garrison the steamer's approach, and so unbelieving were the people, that they were about to place him under guard, as an insane man, when the

"Virginia," a stern wheel boat, sought a landing. The booming cannon and shouts of welcome rolled forth, long and loud, evincing an unmistaken and hearty welcome from the whole command. These, and the sound of steam, having ceased, a *daring* Indian ventured to peep out from his covert. Seeing no change in the natural world, he cautiously crept forth, and at last approached the object of terror and wonder, and declared it to be a "*patah-watah*" (fire canoe).

The monotony of society was enlivened by social additions, made by this steamer. Wives and sisters had accompanied the new officers who arrived, and the circle of ladies had swelled to ten. Their isolated position might be regarded as unfavorable to enjoyment, but from what we learn of these women, we are sure they had a fount of happiness within their hearts and homes, and from what we have seen, we *know* they had a *world* of rich enjoyments without. Such a life must be experienced to be appreciated. What are all the gay trappings and trammelings of fashion, to home-bred joys; and what comparison have gilded halls and the adornments of art to the great drawing-room of NATURE!

CHAPTER VI.

FURTHER INCIDENTS.

In October, 1825, the family of Colonel Snelling left to visit their friends in the east. Before they reached Lake Pepin the ice was running so rapidly that they could not proceed; it had cut through the cabin of their boat, and the leaks made it very uncomfortable. It must be recollected that though a steamboat had visited the fort some some two years previous to this, it was only an annual occurrence, under charter of government, to convey men and supplies thither.

A log cabin was hastily thrown up at the point where our travelers abandoned their boat, and an express sent back to the fort for sleighs and provisions, as they had nothing but corn, which they boiled in ley, on which to subsist. A second express was despatched, and after two weeks the joyful sound of sleigh-bells greeted their ears. The little boy of Mrs. Snelling ran out to meet them, found ready access to the provisions, and with a loaf of bread in each hand, returned in haste to his mother, exclaiming, as he threw it into her lap, "Eat, mother, eat."

The half-famished group partook of the coarse food with a hearty relish—sweeter to them than the most dainty fare to pampered appetites. They concluded to return at once to the fort, where they were soon joyfully welcomed by their anxious friends, among whom were reckoned some favorite Indians.

One aged and infirm savage, who had always furnished them game, came leaning on his staff. He was sick at the time, and could scarcely crawl back to his lodge, where the next day he died.

In 1851, Mrs. Snelling, having seen much affliction in the loss of husband and children, but still retaining much of her youthful vivacity and buoyancy of spirit, visited this country, after an absence of twenty-five years. She was gratified with the development of its resources, and the progress of civilization, and many a pleasing reminiscence was revived amid these once familiar scenes.

The introduction of steam into this remote region was an important era in its history, not only to the white, but the red man. Men and women, prompted by the love of souls and their Savior, had, in obedience to the command "Go ye into all the world," taken life in hand, and entered upon the great and trying work in this vast arena, of instructing the blood-thirsty savage in the principles of the Gospel, of leading his dark mind to the fountain of life and peace.

In 1830, a Methodist mission was established a few miles below Fort Snelling. In 1835, Rev. T. S. Williamson arrived, with his family and assistants; and several others, about this time, established missions at different points, these being among the first efforts of the Presbyterians in this vicinity. Through the influence of Dr. Williamson, and in accordance with the long-cherished desire of the few Christians at the Fort, the first church was organised, consisting of traders, officers, and their wives, and the missionaries, to the number of 20.

One of this little band, Major Ogden, recently deceased, was a young man of most unquestionable piety, and commendable devotion to the cause of his Master. He became an elder in this church, and delighted to do good as he had opportunity. Remote from civilization, and far from those he most loved, while superintending the erection of Fort Riley, he died, in the vigor of manhood. There is moral sublimity in such a death. Who would not die "the death of the righteous," and whether cut down in the vigor of youth, or in the ripeness of age, be ready for a crown of glory?

LATER SETTLEMENTS.

CHAPTER VII.

FIRST SETTLERS.

MISSIONARIES and traders, as we have seen, were already within the limits of our territory. A few of the French had strayed from the Selkirk Settlement and Canadas, but no actual settlement had been commenced; no efforts made for the future emigrant, or to induce him hither.

In 1837, Franklin Steele, from Pennsylvania, found his way up the Mississippi, and was the first man to commence active, energetic measures for the future weal of our beauteous land, and at that time was probably the only man thus employed between our present boundary on the south, and Pembina on the north, and between Superior on the east, and the Rocky Mountains on the west. He is supposed to have been the first man that "fleshed his axe" in all this wide domain. The same year he commenced lumbering operations on the St. Croix.

It may not be improper, or uninteresting, to state the humble beginnings of a business already so important, and destined to become even more so. His team consisted of a single ox driven before a cart, and a crew of seven half-breeds. His supplies consisted of a barrel of pork, which cost $40, a barrel of flour $11, half a bushel of beans at $4, molasses at $2 per gallon, &c. &c. His operations the first year were principally confined to getting lumber for a mill. Now, some thirty saws are running on that stream, and from thirty to fifty millions feet of lumber are produced annually.

The great sagacity and foresight of Mr. Steele enabled him to make many fortunate strikes, of which we shall have more to say hereafter. His energies have been extended into every department of business, and every effort has been crowned with surprising success; and now, as a business man, as a man of wealth, socially and otherwise, he ranks first in our territory.

A Mission station was commenced by the Methodists at Koposia in 1835, but was soon after given up to the Presbyterians, and a new one started by them at Red Rock. In a short time this also was abandoned, and those engaged in it resolved to become citizens, and were the original settlers of that beautiful prairie.

Numbered with these was Mrs. Holton, who came at the outset of the mission, and no American woman having preceded her, she can be safely accounted the first white *citizen* woman in the territory.

About this time Dr. Carlie built his cabin on the banks of the St. Croix, and introduced *his* wife to the varieties of pioneer life. Not long, however, was he permitted to enjoy his rural home, but was drowned in crossing the lake. His wife still survives, having married a brother of her first husband, who is a physician also.

Mr. Hone, with his young bride, was one of the early arrivals in the country; but his frontier cabin at Point Douglas has been supplanted by a spacious dwelling, and the wilderness around him has been "made to rejoice and blossom as the rose."

Mr. Anson Northup came to Minnesota in 1839. He drove an ox-team through the pathless country from Illinois, and the following year returned east for his family. He built and kept the first boarding-house on the St. Croix, and to him and his inestimable wife is the country greatly indebted, for services rendered during this important period. The coarse lumberman found shelter and a full board beneath their roof, and many a tenderly-reared son, who had seen brighter days in a far-off land, was kindly cared for, and if sick, gently ministered to, by her benevolent hand.

Then was the basis of our present prosperity laid. They lived not in the present, but future, yet the most sanguine ventured not a hope of what their own eyes were so soon to see, of their own and the country's prosperity.

In 1840, Orange Walker, from Vermont, erected the marine mill on the St. Croix River. In 1844, John McKusick, from Maine, built the first one at Stillwater, at the head of Lake St. Croix, and about the same time Mr. Northup built the first public house there. These formed the nucleus of a settlement—the first to attain importance in the Territory. The enterprise of Mr. Northup has pushed him on from settlement to settlement, one after another being indebted to him for its first hotel.

With the heroism of a true woman, has Mrs. N. *done her duty*, amid increasing cares, privations, and hardships, all struggling for the mastery. But prosperity has triumphed, and her name deserves to be inscribed in letters of gold on historic pages, a pattern of patient endurance and virtuous excellence.

Not unfrequently is it that those who "bear the burden and heat of the battle," are unknown and unchronicled. So with the pioneers in infant settlements. The hardships met, the trials endured, and difficulties overcome, are overlooked or uncared for, by those who swell the after-tide of population, and they behold the laurels which of right belong to themselves, gracing the brows of those who have no just claim to them.

And women there are in every such community, whose unwritten lives would make many an interesting chapter in our country's history; without their coöperation the foundations of society could not have been laid. They have toiled early and late to encourage those who were hewing the rough timbers for the beautiful superstructure. Their words of cheer have sustained the heart-sick wanderer, and with unrewarded care, save in an approving conscience, have they watched beside the sick bed of the stranger, and never known fatigue so long as the wants of their households were not met.

Woman, in all states of society, and in all ages of the world, has had a part to perform, an all-important part, known only in its results. The women of the Revolution, though they could not use the musket, and appear on the tented field, could run their pewter spoons into balls, and bid fathers, brothers, husbands, and sons, be firm in their duty as they left for the camp.

So those who were earliest in Minnesota, and who lived more in the future than the present, were indeed blessings to their companions. Even since the writer's introduction into the Territory, it has been said most emphatically that a "unit added to the female population, was virtually of more importance than a whole cargo of the sterner sex."

CHAPTER VIII.

ELEMENTS AT WORK.

Elements, as we have seen, were at work, which, if kindly fostered, would result in great and lasting blessings. The germs of settlements, in two or three instances, had been planted, and hope whispered a prosperous issue.

Upon a commanding bluff of the Mississippi, scattered here and there, were some half dozen decayed and decaying log hovels, chinked with mud, and every way of the meanest appearance, evincing the lack of taste and ambition in the occupants. They were low French and half breeds, and repudiated the forms and conventionalities of the world, of which they knew comparatively nothing.

The appellation of "Pig's Eye" had been given to the settlement, in honor to an important citizen with one eye, which bore a fancied resemblance to the eye of that interesting quadruped. The nucleus of this village was a ten by twelve log chapel, the site of which was marked by the Romish priest. More recently a *christening* service dignified the settlement with the name St. Paul, and .more recently still, "Pig's Eye" has floated two miles down stream, though this point is fast losing its identity among the "additions" to St. Paul.

During my first journeyings westward I was frequently advised to retrace my steps, as "dangers, and perhaps cruel death," awaited my début among the "bloody Indians." One individual in particular, volunteered this advice, who was then *en route* East, from a visit to the falls of St. Anthony, Fort Snelling, &c. and *knew positively there was not such a place as St. Paul* in that vicinity. "But there was," he said, " a miserable little trading post called 'Pig's Eye,' a few miles below, but no *white woman* could live there, though of course that was not the point of which I was in pursuit."

The old chapel, after undergoing sundry enlargements and improvements, to meet the wants of the increasing congregation, was left in charge of the "Sisters of Charity," for school purposes, and a large brick church substituted for worship. The log chapel is now demolished, and an elegant cathedral is found essential to advance the cause of the Papacy.

But to return. No improvements had been made, when, in 1841, Henry Jackson, with his young wife, landed beneath the towering bluff, from one of the half dozen steamers, which that season found their way here. It was midnight, dark and rainy. Not a light was to be seen, and the bluff loomed in the darkness its formidable and forbidding front. The lady had been assured that it was a "right smart chance of a place," and on inquiry, was told it was "further back," and that there was a "power of mud" before she could reach it. They finally attained the summit of the almost perpendicular ascent, and entered the ravine, (which now no stranger and few citizens could find) following a guide through an Indian trail, winding amid dense hazel bushes, over what was then known as "Mount Pisgah," but now as "Baptist Hill," just leaving "Hazel Mount"* on the left, to the only dwelling in that immediate vicinity, a full half mile from the landing.

* The seat of the Pioneer's School, and the writer's abode.

The cabin roof was of straw, over which was a layer of turf; this was so saturated by the rain, that the inmates had been driven from their beds. The genuine hospitality of their hearts enabled them to devise speedy means for the comfort of their guests, as they proffered them their own deserted bed. A quilt, for the absorption of the water, was suspended beneath the dripping roof, and the wearied strangers retired to dream of shower baths in other lands.

The bright rain drops glittering amid the bushes the following morning, were as so many greetings of welcome, and the clouds, too, had passed from their hearts.

The first work of the emigrants was to build them a cabin, and their site was selected on the commanding point, directly above and overlooking the river at Lower Landing, in other words, at the terminus of Bench street. The original room was twelve by fifteen feet, and minus doors, windows, or floor, they "set up housekeeping." A large slab answered for a rug before the bed, and never a wolf dared thrust his head within the blanket which served as a door, though the lady herself often drove them from the premises. Thus, for eighteen months, did things move on, with naught to chronicle, save some slight improvements in the cabin by way of floor, windows, and door, the "latch string" of which was never pulled in.

There was little expectation then that the isolated trading post would soon expand into the busy, bustling city, with all the elements of the great eastern metropolis, and a daily line of well laden steamers be crowding the levee.

Like all things western, the cabin was destined to *grow*, until it boasted of three or four rooms, with plastered walls, while a white "siding" concealed the rough logs—

an effectual deception as to its original state. There was such an air of gentility and comfort in that cozy sitting room, that the impressions of my first visit are more easily retained than expressed. The rustic porch and small windows were shaded by a dense vine transplanted from the "bottom lands," softening the sun's rays as they fell upon the carpet, and subduing any repulsive feeling which might arise.

In the yard a tame fox and deer had their gambols; and prairie flowers, the sweetest on earth, imparting their odors, enhanced the beauty of the scene.

In the autumn of 1842, John R. Irvine "claimed" the beautiful plateau now embraced in "Ripper Town." With his family, frontier life was a parallel to the above history, with the addition of more numerous domestic cares and parental anxieties.

There was a warm sympathy between these families, the exclusive society of the settlement. The children found sources of pleasure at home, in chasing the gay-winged butterfly, and plucking the wild flowers, as they bounded over the prairie and up the bluffs, and their spirits caught the notes of the grove songsters, until they were tuned to the same sweet harmony.

Life had many cares and pleasures, but withal was wedding the souls of the pioneers to their adopted homes. And though I could not then understand the emotions that induced Mrs. Irvine to affirm, that she would sooner go as much farther west, than return to her home in Buffalo, experience has taught me that I can heartily respond to the sentiment.

In 1845, Mr. A. L. Larpenteur married, established himself in business here, and has become one of our most substantial and influential merchants.

Louis Robear, a French trader, was the chieftain of his countrymen, who then composed the greater part of the sparse population of this place.

Such was the limited society to which the writer was introduced in St. Paul, and yet, isolated as it really was, from the living, acting world, not a cloud of sadness or regret ever flitted across her mental horizon. Life was no longer an idle dream; the hours dragging heavily, and with soul-longings for some real purpose. Here was a field to be cultivated; a garden of untrained flowers to be tended, and the heart raised a thank-offering to heaven and cheerfully entered upon its work. But we anticipate.

CHAPTER IX.

WHY I CAME TO ST. PAUL.

THE question, why I came to St. Paul, will naturally arise in the mind of the reader. This cannot be better explained, nor with less appearance of egotism, than by the following letter from Rev. Dr. Williamson, of the Sioux Mission. It was addressed to the Board of National Popular Education, then in its embryo state, and by them placed in my hands.

"My present residence is on the utmost verge of civilization in the northwestern part of the United States, within a few miles of the principal village of white men in the territory that we suppose will bear the name of Minnesota, which some would render, ' clear water,' though strictly, it signifies slightly turbid or whitish water.

"The village referred to has grown up within a few years in a romatic situation on a high bluff of the Mississippi, and has been baptized by the Roman Catholics by the name of St. Paul. They have erected in it a small chapel, and constitute much the larger portion of the inhabitants. The Dakotas call it Im-mi-ja-ska (white rock), from the color of the sand-stone which forms the bluff on which the village stands. This village has five stores, as they call them, at all of which intoxicating drinks constitute a part, and I suppose the principal part, of what they sell. I would suppose the village contains a dozen or twenty families living near enough to send to school. Since I came to this neighborhood, I have had fre quent occasion to visit the village, and have been grieved to see so many children growing up entirely ignorant of God, and unable to read his Word, with no one to teach them. Unless your Society can send them a teacher, there seems to be little prospect of their having one for several years. A few days since I went to the place for the purpose of making inquiries in reference to the prospect of a school. I visited seven families, in which there were twenty-three children of proper age to attend school, and was told of five more, in which were thirteen more that it is supposed might attend, making thirty-six in twelve families. I suppose more than half of the parents of these children are unable to read themselves, and care but little about having their children taught. Possibly the priest might deter some from attending, who might otherwise be able and willing.

"I suppose a good female teacher can do more to promote the cause of education and true religion than a man. The natural politeness of the French (who constitute more than half the population) would cause them to be kind and courteous to a female, even though the priest should seek to cause opposition. I suppose she might have twelve or fifteen scholars to begin with, and if she should have a good talent for winning the affections of children (and one who has not should not come), after a few months she would have as many as she could attend to.

"One woman told me she had four children she wished to send to school, and that she would give boarding and a room in her house to a good female teacher, for the tuition of her children.

"A teacher for this place should love the Savior, and for his sake should be willing to forego, not only many of the religious privileges and elegances of New England towns, but some of the neatness also. She should be entirely free from prejudice on account of color, for among her scholars she might find not only English, French, and Swiss, but Sioux and Chippewas, with some claiming kindred with the African stock.

"A teacher coming should bring books with her sufficient to begin a school, as there is no book store within three hundred miles."

This was the first I had heard of St. Paul, or even of Minnesota, and the impression was at once riveted on my mind that *I must go;* and when, after two weeks of prayerful deliberation, the question was asked, "Who will go to St. Paul?" I could cheerfully, though tremblingly, respond, "*Here am I; send me.*" Every possible obstacle was presented; the difficulties of the almost unknown route; the condition of society; doubts as to a welcome by the people generally; the self-denials to be exercised; the privations to be endured—all of which were to me as so many incentives to persist in my decision. In short, I came because I was more needed here than at any other spot on earth, and because there was no other one of my class who felt it a duty to come.

Friends violently opposed. Those who dare not oppose did not encourage, and *vice versa.* It was evident that all considered it hazardous in the extreme, presuming on, yea, tempting Divine Providence. Only one had said, "*Go, and the Lord will be with you.*" And thus, with no human aid on which to rely, the arm of the Invisible was my support. And though comparatively ignorant of the world and its evils, I went forth to struggle with its waves; to tread the unknown future—a path hitherto unexplored—a thorny maze; but with the certainty that, where thorns abound, roses often bloom, and their sweet fragrance *has* refreshed me when weary, and been a sweet savor unto my soul.

I was happy then; I am happy in the retrospect. Never has a regret for the decision crossed my heart; on the contrary, it has ever been a theme of gratitude that I was enabled to overcome all impediments, and come at a time when no other one would venture.

CHAPTER X.

REVIEW OF THE BOOK OF PROVIDENCE.

The green hills of my dear native state had faded from my view; the dear dwellers at the old homestead were distanced, farther and yet farther, and for the first time I was without friend or kin, with more than two thousand miles to traverse to my final destination.

It is with no ordinary emotions that I review these pages in the book of Providence, where I was led "in a way I had not known." Surely, "goodness and mercy have followed me" since the morn I went forth at the bidding of my Master, to buffet alone the turbid billows of life.

Friends in Palmyra welcomed the strangers, and kindly entertained them on the Sabbath, and again "set them on their way rejoicing." This is the first incident of my journey to record. Never will that reception be forgotten, or cease to awaken grateful emotions. Some of that "eleven" have since been welcomed at the portals of glory!

Desirous to proceed, we knew of no good reason why we should not have passage on the Chesapeake, instead of waiting a day in Buffalo. But we failed in securing it. No reason was assigned, and we impatiently submitted. The fate of that steamer is well known; and friends still weep for the many who then found a grave in Lake Erie.

Unacquainted with the world, and unaccustomed to traveling alone, God prepared the hearts of Cleveland friends to attend me most of the long journey; and but for this I could scarce have accomplished it in safety. Then the facilities of western travel were very imperfect. There was not a railroad beyond Michigan, and staging over the worst of roads was the only mode of conveyance from Lake Michigan to the Mississippi. To obviate this difficulty, we journeyed by steam and stage to Cincinnati, where seventeen hundred miles of river course lay before us.

All spoke kindly of the object, though none approvingly; and many evidently regarded it as a wild chimera of the brain, and disappointment the inevitable result; and it was, indeed, generally believed, as I had been already assured, that I would never find a St. Paul. But there was never an instance when the sinking hope, or a desire to return, predominated in my breast.

Thus far an unseen hand had led me, and caused me most emphatically to feel that

> " 'Tis Providence that shapes our ends,
> Rough-hew them as we will."

At St. Louis, the New York of the West, a combination of circumstances made me a passenger up the river in the same cabin with Mrs. Dr. Jones, of Galena, Illinois. Had there been the lurking of a doubt relative to the way, she was prepared to remove it. Having been twice at St. Paul, she was the first to define its locality. Her picture of it was not the most pleasing, but I had sought for a correct one and found it. Her words of cheer sent the sunshine of hope through my heart, and the meeting with her will ever be regarded as an important link in the chain of providences which marked my way. Time has proved her not a "summer friend," but a woman whose price is above rubies, whose worth and virtues shine with increasing lustre, a blessing to the world, and blessing all within the sphere of her influence. She kindly took the stranger in a strange land to her own home, put in her way the means of obtaining letters to the most important families in the vicinity, thus throwing light and cheerfulness on my, at best, uncertain path.

CHAPTER XI.

CHANGE OF SCENERY.

The time had come when "good bye" must be exchanged with the last of old and tried friends, the parting kiss exchanged with the last relative, to study new scenes and faces, and make new friends. Before turning homeward, they had commissioned the master of the steamer Lynx with my "safe landing" at the Mission of Dr. Williamson. Hope appeared in the distance—a halo of brightness encircling her form. Nature lent her charms to drive away the last lingerings of sadness, and to impart happiness before unequaled.

Hitherto, the character of the scenery had been pleasing, with little variety. Low banks sloped to the water's edge, and boundless prairies, chequered with fields of waving grain, and dotted with fine farm-houses, formed the landscape. Thriving villages and cities of a precocious growth skirted the river banks, while a degree of thrift and comfort I had little expected to see, met the view. The "wilderness and solitary place were made glad" by the fragrance of the rose, which bloomed in beauty amid the verdant thicket.

Galena, the great lead mart of northern Illinois and southern Wisconsin, is located on a river of the same name, seven miles from its entrance with the Mississippi. Here, the tame scenery merges at once into the picturesque and beautifully wild. Streets are cut through almost solid rock, and in some instances the roofs of three and four story blocks are on a level with the street above; everything indicating the indomitable energy and perseverance of the citizens.

Dubuque, in Iowa, twenty-five miles by the river windings above Galena, is surrounded by an irregular line of bluffs, bold and beautiful. This town, also rich in its mining interests, is one of the *fast* towns of the west.

The scenery now assumed a wild grandeur, varying with every view, and affording a literal feast for the eyes and heart. There was scarce an appearance of civilization for three hundred miles, if we except the old French town of Prairie du Chien, in Wisconsin, founded by some traders the same year that William Penn, under the shadow of his "broad brim," founded the city of "Brotherly Love." Here and there, upon the river bank, was a woodman's cabin, and again a claimant's, with a little patch of culinary vegetables in front, with, perhaps, a half-dozen half-clad children sporting about the door, who, on the ringing of the boat bell, would flee like frighted deer.

The Indian "hugged the shore" with his light canoe, or gazed with listless apathy from the bank, where he smoked his red-stone pipe.

"Slowly and surely" progressed the Lynx, and rapidly the hours sped on. All nature had conspired to form a glorious day when we first looked upon "Little Crow's Village," or Kaposia, where our boat headed on the morning of July 16th, 1847. The ringing of the bell occasioned a grand rush, and with telegraphic speed, every man, woman, and child flew to the landing.

To an unsophisticated eye like mine, the scene on shore was novel and grotesque, not to say repulsive; blankets and hair streaming in the wind; limbs uncovered; children nearly naked, the smaller ones entirely so, while a pappoose was ludicrously peeping over the shoulder of nearly every squaw. In the midst of the waiting throng appeared the Missionary and his sister.

A tear drop, which had suddenly formed in the heart, came welling up, but was arrested by a remark of the good humored Captain (peace to his memory), "That the Doctor was doing it up in fine style—he had got the whole village out for an escort!"

Before reaching the lower deck the crowd were thronging the plank and rushing upon the boat, arrayed in the most fantastic manner, and painted according to their fanciful notions of beauty.

I was received by the Missionaries with more than a kindly welcome, as presented by the Captain, with the playful injunction, "*Not to let the Indians scalp me!*" With other sage advice during this memorable up river trip, he had enjoined that *I should "kiss the pappooses,*" and *thereby secure the friendship of the band.* No sooner was I on shore than this *duty* became manifestly obvious—the greasy, smutty face of every mother's child being presented to afford me my initiatory lesson.

It was a moment of no ordinary interest—of calm, undefinable joy, when I entered the humble mission house. The "wild experiment" had become a reality; I stood upon ground which to me had before existed only in the ideal world.

Most of the principal Indians of the band, headed by the chief, followed me to the house, where a formal presentation took place, and I shook hands with each. They were curious to learn if I was a "big knife" (from the States), and why their expected annuities had not arrived, presuming that I must be conversant with all affairs at Washington. I had never felt so keenly the power of eye scrutiny.

Hitherto, mine had been a dreamy life, full of waking visions, with which reality was strangely blended. The shadowy vista of coming years had, from childhood, been crowded with rich imaginings. The Red Man in his far off home was, to my childish fancy, a being of the ideal world. Rarely had I seen a wandering remnant of the race, and I had formed no correct idea of him in his native state—on his own hunting grounds. Now I was on the very confines of civilization, surrounded by all the evidences of savage life. But soon the scene changed. Instead of stalwart men, half divested of clothing, with limbs naked and covered with grease and soot, to protect from mosquitos, there came a few native christian women for a prayer meeting. As I saw these untutored natives reverently bow, and heard their voices, in an unknown tongue, earnestly addressing a Throne of Grace, new but blissful emotions possessed my heart. Such pathos, such humility, such earnestness, I had rarely if ever witnessed. Yet they were few, very few, who found delight in these exercises. The majority of the Indians, still attached to their "wankons," though Gospel claims are urged upon them, choose the way "which goeth down to death."

Towards evening we strolled through their village, called at several "lodges," constructed of bark, and frolicked with the children in lieu of conversing with their mothers. At the lodge of the chief, a skin was placed without the door for my benefit, by his "superior," wife. This the mission lady urged me to accept, lest offence be given.

It is not an unimportant matter in frontier life to secure

the friendship of the natives. True they are ofttimes treacherous, and perhaps generally so, yet I am far from endorsing the belief that there are no exceptions. From the first they were kindly disposed toward me, regarding me with apparent interest, and many a time since have I been glad to welcome some of these my earliest Minnesota friends. The names of Old Betsey and Uncle John, of Harpa and Winona Zee, are familiar household words, and their good natured faces always brought a beam of merry sunshine into the house. And old Hocka-wash-ta was "always sure to be present when least wanted;" as the proverb runs of an evil genius, "no one could say where he was not."

Little Crow, the chief, whose calls were frequent, both at his village and after I had removed to St. Paul, is a tall, handsome man, with no striking expression of countenance. The youngest of seven brothers, all of whom have died by violent hands, ambitious for the chieftainship, attempted the life of his brother, wounding him severely, and he fearing the design would be eventually executed, ordered the younger to be shot. Thus the last but one of the name was gathered to his fathers. Little Crow possesses not the confidence of his band, who regard him as full of malice, intrigue and cunning. He often attended worship at the mission house and manifested some regard for the Scriptures, which he had learned to read.

CHAPTER XII.

FIRST SABBATH IN MINNESOTA.

THE day succeeding my arrival was the Sabbath, and as yet,

> " The sound of the church going bell,
> These prairies and bluffs never heard."

To the poor Indian all days are alike. Only a few had, who learned to keep it holy, assembled at the mission house for worship: a messenger being sent "to invite others to come in," the room was soon full. Some listened with profound attention; others remained in listless indifference, and others quietly dozed in their seats. A few were inclined to laugh, some left, but most remained until the services closed.

Then commenced their favorite game of ball, arrangements for the same having been going on all the morning, which continued for several successive days. The competitors for the prize placed their most valuable treasures upon a pole, which was carried around by two girls to receive the "stakes," and when the last was entered, the game commenced. The ball is thrown and caught by a small circle, with leather bands on one side, attached to a lever two or three feet long. When uncaught, the women fly off in its pursuit, and though they have no other interest in the game, they seem equally engaged with the men. In this game the wives of the Chief were most active. In passing our door one of them was kindly admonished of her sin, and reminded of the sorrow her Christian mother would have to know she was thus engaged. "She knew," she said, "her mother would feel very bad; but she was far away and could not know it, and besides, her boy's father (a term for husband) bade her '*so bad*,' she could not refuse." They literally "strip themselves for the race," and when fully aroused, ascend the bluff with the fleetness of a fawn—with unaffected grace of motion and dignity of mien.

Towards evening two Frenchmen were seen approaching the village. Suspicion was immediately rife with the villagers that they were bringing with them "fire water;" and some of them came in breathless haste, entreating Dr. Williamson to prevent it, for too well they knew its disastrous consequences. As a people, they were intemperate! Yet some had taken the pledge for a specified number of "moons," and did not wish the temptation there. But vicious and venal white men are responsible for the evil: forgetting that for this, "God will surely bring them into judgment."

In the afternoon, religious services in English were held—some half dozen persons coming from almost as many miles distant. And this was my first Sabbath—these were privileges I should rarely enjoy after a few more days! I thought of friends far, far away, worshipping God under *very* different circumstances; but I had no wish to return. I was happy in the rugged path I had chosen, for I felt, that now, life had commenced in earnest. Too long had it been spent in castle-building, with heart yearnings for *living purpose*. True, the future was a blank book, and with what its pages might be filled, how could I divine? But I felt a calm, unwavering faith; a blessed consciousness that an unseen hand was leading me "in a way I had not known," and through "paths I had not seen before." Thus far the "Lord had directed my steps," and I knew that in Him I might still safely trust, and "move forward."

Nature was lavish with her charms, and the study which I had ever *so* much loved, became doubly interesting. I read the open page in a new light, under new impulses, for it was unmarred by the hand of Art. I seemed to look upon the world as it emanated from the hand of its Creator. Here was a solace for sadness; a substitute for society; a companion in solitude. A web of fibres had intertwined itself with my spiritual being, and a cup of nectar was the daily portion of my soul.

CHAPTER XIII.

FIRST CANOE RIDE.

The sun had never shone more brightly, nor the waters danced more gaily in its beams; never the birds sang more sweetly, nor a heart beat more in unison with the scene, than when, for the first time, I seated myself in a canoe, bound up stream, with two Indian girls at the "paddles." Probably my appearance was very ungraceful in their eyes, for they laughed merrily at my awkward sitting, and finally scolded, hinting at the probability of my getting a "ducking;" and there *was* sufficient proof that a well-balanced head was requisite for the safety of the light craft so heavily freighted.

Once under way, the novelty was pleasing in the extreme. The scenery was delightful, and amidst Nature's profound silence, scenes, tragic and comic, that had transpired in "these ends of the earth," were rehearsed by the accompanying missionaries. Soon the mosquitos began to show a "keen demand of appetite," and when, nearly frantic from their attacks, sea-sickness overpowered me, I yielded defenceless to their combined power.

The cry of "Patah-watah" arose from the squaws, and unbelief was changed to certainty by the peculiar notes of "high pressure in the distance," and the little "Argo" soon left us rocking in her wake. When we had passed up the "slough," and made our moorings beneath the bluff, where now stands the Upper Town, the first order of exercise was to place an Indian blanket beneath the shade of a maple, which was my first resting place in St. Paul. A cold crystal spring issued from a rock at a little distance, whence water was brought which had an almost magical effect, and I have always believed that none *so* pure ever came welling up to the surface from earth's centre.

The stranger, or the citizen even, would fail to recognize the scene which lay around and above, as any part of the ground now occupied by Minnesota's thriving capital. The high bluff almost forbade an attempted ascent. The noon-day breeze played joyfully among the huge maples and smaller trees, which effectually shut out the sun's gaze from the dancing brook, as it entered the Mississippi a few rods above. Following an Indian trail, we wound around the base of the bluff, when suddenly we were cheered by the sound of human voices, and stooping, could discern some women washing at the brook. The scene was enchanting. A vague and indefinite pleasure possessed the heart, and my only wish was that some appreciating friend might share the joys which Nature spread before me. How little was realized then, that here the "woodman's axe" was so soon to resound, the surveyor's chain to mark out a city, and the costly dwelling and substantial business block to rise, while numerous steamers should crowd the landing of that canoe, making our streets swarm with life, gayety and business bustle! Two years, and all this change is in progress; six more, and we have the actual reality, as if it were the work of magic. Workmen of every craft have been engaged, and the rapidity with which it is driven forward astonishes even themselves. Every department of business and science has its representatives; and the little fair-haired girl, with her meek blue eyes, who timidly stepped aside to let us pass, and remained half concealed by the bushes, looking more like a wood-nymph than the living personation of flesh and blood, has grown to be a scholar and a belle, as a part of this wonderful progress.

Turning from Nature, what a cheerless prospect greeted this view. A few log huts composed the "town"—three families the American population. With one of these, distant from the rest, a home was offered me. Their's was *the* dwelling—the only one of respectable size—containing three rooms and an attic.

The kindness and attention bestowed upon strangers in the early stages of western settlement, are proverbial the world over; nor are they overrated. A welcome hand, a warm heart, an open cabin, a full board, the best room and best bed—are sure to greet them. Every individual added to the population, adds an important item to its history. In after years, when it has swelled to thousands, hundreds may arrive in a day and remain unnoticed. Each one becomes absorbed in his own interest and is lost in the whirlpool of the rapid influx. Yet the heart beats as warmly as ever, and really bids the same welcome.

A few days previous to my coming, the "Red River train" arrived, an event at that time of semi-annual occurrence, and one hundred and twenty-one ox teams were encamped in the rear of the landing, where now stands the Lower Town. The principal men of the company had found fare and lodging with the few families, while the remainder encamped with their cattle, sleeping as they had done on the route, in their carts or upon the ground. Their cargoes, composed of valuable furs and rare specimens of Chippewa *embroidery*, were taken to St. Louis. These carts are without a particle of iron, but are very strong; before each a single ox is harnessed, and thus in

Indian file had they passed over nine hundred miles in fifty days. Of the Red River settlement we shall have more to say hereafter.

The captain of this caravan had brought with him his wife, a Scotch half-breed, for the first time out of their settlement, and a child of a year old, and a cow was attached to their cart for its benefit. All seemed full of health and life, with no apparent fatigue from the journey.

Such was the crowd in St. Paul, it was thought best that I should return to the Mission, to remain until it had dispersed, and proper arrangements could be made for the commencement of the school.

CHAPTER XIV.

STUDY OF INDIAN CHARACTER.

I NOW found that all my book knowledge of Indian life and character was cursory, and, for the most part, incorrect. The world has been taught to admire him for his noble traits, his manly bearing, and his alleged remembrance of trifling acts of kindness. The latter, it is true, are remembered, but more with the expectation of repetition than a return. Revenge is always sweet to the Indian, though he is a base coward, and each believes and declares every other man of the tribe to be a thief and a liar. They have no confidence in each other, and, of course, do not expect confidence in return. Their habits are disgustingly filthy, and their dress, if such it may be called, extremely unchaste. The men wear cloth leggins coming to the knees, a breechlet of the same, a calico shirt, and a blanket completes their toilet. No hat is worn, but the head is covered with rude ornaments, and a heavy mass of wampum, often very expensive, adorns the neck. In winter, moccasins are worn, but in summer, more frequently, the feet are bare. The women wear the cloth leggins, a short skirt of the same material, and an open "short gown," with the blanket. Frequently the entire rim of the ear is pierced, and adorned with "jewels of silver," or something resembling it.

Instinct, more than reason, is the guide of the red man. He repudiates improvement, and despises manual effort. For ages has the heart been imbedded in moral pollution.

His visits to the mission house are both in "season and out of season." No room is too sacred for intrusion, and the moccasined feet give no warning of approach. Whatever the demand, it is satisfied, if possible, by those who "watch for their souls," and labor for the improvement and redemption of the race. Ah! what devout thanksgiving ascends to Heaven, when one of these children of nature finds refuge beneath the Cross, and grace commences its refining process upon the heart! Humble, contrite, and devout, and the change is visible to all.

The blanket, as worn by the Indian, is a formidable barrier to his advance in arts or agriculture; when this is forever dispensed with, then his hands will be free to grasp the mechanic's tools or guide the plow. It is both graceful and chaste in their eye, and to adopt the white man's costume, is a great obstacle to their becoming Christians; a requisition too humiliating, for they have personal as well as national pride.

Observation and experience alone impart a correct idea of the trials and privations incident to missionary life among the Indians. Rigid self-denial, close economy in expenditures, and isolation from society, are comparative trifles. Parental anxieties, while the plastic mind of childhood is receiving impress from the rude and vulgar, who know nothing of the refinements of the home circle; and finally, a separation from these cherished objects of his tenderest love—these are heavy burdens which oppress the heart of God's servants. It is no marvel to one who has looked upon the field, that parents and children are so often separated, the latter being sent to the States, and confided even to the care of strangers. Parental love, the best good of the child, and the missionary work demand the sacrifice.

In a little time I was flattered into the belief of having become something of a favorite. I was certainly an object of curiosity. The chief showed me special attention, calling often, and shaking hands in a warm, friendly manner. I had ingratiated myself into his favor, by acting upon the advice of the captain, and bestowing attentions upon the child of his favorite wife. The women examined and commented upon the various articles of my dress, and the children would bring me wild fruit and flowers; and one evening, enjoying at my window " the sober twilight gray," two young braves did me the honor of a serenade.

In preparations for their " summer hunt," everything that would produce a sound was brought out, and dancing, drumming, and chanting, and finally a drunken row occupied the most of the night.

After some delay, and not until the sun was high in the heavens, did the canoe fleet put out for the opposite shore, leaving a " deserted village " behind. The horses were made to swim along side. When in the channel, it became evident to us they were drowning, and Dr. Williamson and his little son, springing into a canoe, hastened to the rescue, and saved their beasts, for which no gratitude was manifested.

A few days previously, one of the children of the mission family having gone to the river for water, for convenience stepped into a canoe, and while he stooped to dip the water, it became detached from the shore, and in a moment was moving rapidly down the stream. He being unable to use the paddle, and the male members of the family being absent, his mother and aunt, in great distress, implored the Indian women to go for him; but they only laughed at their fears. At last, upon the thought that they waited for a pledged reward—"Go, I will pay you well," was no sooner uttered, than enough were ready to seize the paddle, and the most dextrous hand soon reached the fugitive canoe, and returned the affrighted boy to the no less affrighted friends.

Since 1824, Dr. Williamson has devoted himself to the Sioux. He was a native of North Carolina, and impressed with the evil of slavery, and to free himself from its curse, emigrated to Ohio. He had an interesting family, and a flourishing practice as physician; but a voice continually thundered upon his conscience, "Go, preach the Gospel" to the red man. His wife, unknown to him, was impressed with the same duty, and all he was, and all he possessed, he laid upon the altar of the Lord. His sister, too, gave up all of earth, and became a valuable co-worker in the unpromising field, but all rejoice in the sacrifice they have made for Christ.

CHAPTER XV.

BURIAL RITES.

Little rude enclosures met the eye in whatever direction it was turned, and these were the resting places of the departed. On the summit of the bluffs, in the rear of the mission house, were many strange looking objects with a small red flag fluttering over each. With a half superstitious dread, I refrained from inquiring, in hopes that accident might acquaint me with their nature and design. A strange, unearthly lamentation, proceeding from this direction one night, disturbed my midnight slumbers. The wail of a lost spirit could scarcely be imagined more horrid. In alarm I awoke Miss W. to learn the cause.

"It is a poor Indian woman weeping at the grave of her son," was the reply.

"Not at those graves just in the rear of the house? The sound, to my ear, comes from a greater distance.!"

"Have you not noticed the red flags on the bluffs, and the bodies elevated on those scaffolds? There the dead are first laid to rest, and thence this 'mourning' comes."

"And are they ever removed from there?"

"Yes, when the days of mourning are past."

"How long does this last?"

"The time may be longer or shorter, according to the violence of grief. The more violent, the sooner over. Therefore, they lacerate their flesh with knives, stones, etc., that they may the more freely and readily weep. They are Nature's children, and Nature, they say, utters sounds correspondent to feeling or suffering. If the limb of a tree falls, its groan is echoed by the surrounding forest. Oh, my sister, who will arise, and help to lead them to the true source of happiness and wisdom!"

It is a new idea, but it strikes me as perfectly accordant with the dictates of nature, and I have ever observed that the most violent grief is of brief duration. There is no bitterness like silent, concealed, suppressed sorrow. Now, is it not better, and more consistent with our duty to the world, that we give vent to the sorrows of the heart; arise from stupor, and gird the soul anew for conflict. " But, tell me, please, how they contrive to keep the dead bodies from becoming offensive?"

"They are wound up in bark, in a manner they understand, enveloped in their blankets, and with much harangue, feasting and the like, elevated to those positions. That they may pursue their favorite employment in the spirit world, their implements of hunting are deposited with them. The red flag is an ensign of dignity or position. In time they will all be consigned to the earth in the family enclosure, and there wait the summons to the judgment."

Until a late hour the wail was continued, and even before it had ceased, I was again in unconscious slumber, dreaming of perilous positions, and the screams of suffering men and women. I awoke with a resolution to attempt an insight into their burial rites, and for this purpose directed my morning walk up the bluff.

The footprints of departed generations, in intersecting trails, led me on. In the deep ravines, dark shadows played, and the wild birds caroled their morning song in the dense foliage. The sun threw his beams aslant the flower-clad earth, but my soul was sad in view of the dense pall of moral night that rested upon those whose soil we trod. The heart instinctively arose to Heaven, imploring the cheering rays from the Sun of Righteousness to dawn upon them.

I found it quite impossible to obtain any further knowledge of their time-honored custom, and convinced that I must remain content with what I was permitted to *see*, I passed on to several enclosures.

At the head of each grave was the sacred stone, and, by many, some little memento of affection, as a small dish of salt, or wild rice, was placed there to appease the evil spirit that might be lurking around. In a thoughtless moment I sent the " wakan " rolling down the bluff. The act recalled my wandering senses, and I half superstitiously dreaded the result of my wanton disrespect for their sacred dead. Visiting the spot a few days later, we found that the wandering shrine had been replaced, and no serious consequences had come upon the aggressor.

CHAPTER XVI.

GROVE MEETING AT RED ROCK.

ONE Saturday evening, while gazing with delight upon the rose-tinted sky, glowing in a gorgeous sunset, the mind absorbed in rich day-dreams of its own creation, a messenger announced that a "canoe awaited my order." It had been dispatched from Red Rock, where a "grove meeting" was to be held the following day. At such an hour no ride could have been more desirable, and going down stream there was no fear of sea-sickness. Our field for admiration was rich and varied, and in the ecstacy of enjoyment we too soon came to the terminus of our ride.

At a primitive cottage of respectable size, overshadowed with ancient oaks, and enlivened on all sides with golden-hued and modest forest flowers, a *western* welcome awaited us, western hospitality was tendered, with a rich fund of western entertainment. Alas! the musketoes! These were serious drawbacks on all social enjoyments; but most affecting the "new comer," an "old settler" being little temptation to them. When their bites became no longer endurable, there was a resort to the "smudge," and thus alternating between musketoes and smudge, unable to decide on a preference, every approachable portion of the body received their mark, and the eyes were useless from the smoke.

Happily, the days of musketoes, in the older portions

of the country, have passed by, and are remembered only as among the things that were.

Red Rock Prairie, three miles below "Crow Village," now Koposia, on the east side of the river, takes its name from a large red stone there, formerly worshiped by the native, or rather a shrine at which he worshiped. A red stone, whether such by nature or paint, is "wakan" (sacred) wherever found. Formerly the Methodists had a mission station here, which was abandoned after a few years, while those employed as farmers, mechanics, and teachers, remained enjoying the privileges of first citizenship.

No longer is the bark "lodge," or conical teepee, seen upon this beautiful prairie, and here their council fire is for ever extinguished. Here, from within a circuit of thirty or forty miles, about the same number of persons assembled on Sabbath morning, where the bread of life was to be broken. Ah! how little do Christians, in lands where the Gospel banner is fully unfurled, with their costly temples dedicated to God's worship, realize their high and heaven-born blessings! How little do they know the privations, toils, and self-denials of those who remove the rubbish, "break the fallow ground," and sow the first seed for the spiritual harvest!

One Methodist minister, and one retired Presbyterian missionary, preaching occasionally, were, at this time, all who proclaimed the glad tidings to the citizens of Minnesota. On this occasion, the first-mentioned, with the Sioux missionary, officiated. The little assembly was quiet and attentive, for it embraced most of the *true* worshipers dwelling in the vicinity.

A sacred awe seemed to inspire those green old trees as they wafted the hymn of praise which rose from that band, seated on rough boards in front of the speaker's stand; an offering not less acceptable for being presented in "God's first great temple!"

Language is too sterile to give full force to the newly awakened emotions of that day. Shadowy visions of the future flitted before me, brightened by such buoyant hope that I would not have resigned my isolated position for a sceptre and a crown.

Nature, already in her loveliest robes, had donned an additional glory, and with heart tuned to the measure of her glad song, on the following morning I embarked on my return.

For a little time my soul drank in the beauties of the scene, quaffing larger draughts at every view. But, alas! every pleasure has its alloy, and as if to admonish me that earth is nowhere heaven, I was soon wholly occupied with the miseries of sea-sickness.

The power of speech being well nigh gone, in compliance with my signified wish, the prow of the canoe was turned to the shore, and we landed on the margin of a dense thicket. Around, wildness and beauty reigned, each striving for supremacy. Flowers were rejoicing in their own loveliness; vines, which in other lands adorn the mansions of the rich, here clung to the trunks of giant trees, or were interwoven with brush and bush, forming beautiful native bowers.

My position was ludicrously novel, and spiced with a degree of romance not altogether repulsive, and had I not been divested of the power, I should have indulged in a hearty laugh. But upon the thought that a hungry wolf or bear might chance to pass, I signified my wish to proceed; and supported on each side by two anxious cavaliers, both of whom insisted on carrying an umbrella, although the density of the foliage precluded the possibility of a sunbeam's approach, we "worked our passage" through the thick "undergrowth," and after a walk of a mile, were truly gratified to rest at the "mission lodge," feeling, of a truth, that another rich page was added to our chapter of adventures.

4*

CHAPTER XVII.

ENTERING UPON DUTY.

THE arrival of a steamer at the time of which we write was not of daily, nor weekly, nor scarcely of semi-monthly occurrence, and the sound of its high pressure in this land of silence would reach the ear at a distance of eight or ten miles. The sun had just looked over the bluff, and was peeping in at my window, when the welcome sound greeted my ear. I had been anxiously waiting to return to St. Paul, where "all things were now ready," but had shrunk at the remembrance of seasickness from a canoe-ride *up* stream. Joyfully did I hasten my toilet, and await the "Argo." Now day had dawned, not only in the natural world, but in my life, and a golden sun heralded a triumphant progress. Its first tintings on the eastern horizon disclosed the faint outlines of the future; but its onward course revealed objects more and more beautiful. The dreams and yearnings of my childhood had now reached the dawn of fruition, and Hope was by my side to tell of coming scenes.

It seemed to me the trees had never worn so rich a foliage, nor the flowers smiled so lovingly, as when again I trod that grass-grown street, and received the spontaneous greetings of the youthful crowd—a welcome to their homes and hearts! Nor were my emotions less pleasing when I "learned to stoop," and entered that memorable mud-walled log hovel, a primitive blacksmith's shop, where those young minds were to receive impressions for immortality.

ENTERING UPON DUTY.

Some wooden pins had been driven into the logs, across which rough boards were placed for seats. The luxury of a chair was accorded to the teacher, and a cross-legged table occupied the center of the loose floor. Such were the evidences of transforming power, where the moulding of iron was to give place to the moulding of mind. As a "light shining in a dark place," I saw two fair childlike faces amid the dark, forbidding group convened within those decaying log walls; but another, and yet another, was added to brighten this oasis in the desert of life.

To procure means for ablution was one of my first duties; and in due time a portion of the unnatural darkness disappeared, and revealed a skin tinted with other than native American blood. A full rehearsal of duties of that room might offend the delicate ear, and we withhold the details. Soon, all was bright and joyous. Our domicile was converted into a rural arbor, fragrant evergreens concealing the rude walls, with their mud chinkings, and even the bark roof. A friendly hen, unwilling to relinquish her claim, on the ground of preoccupancy, daily placed a token of her industry in the corner, and made all merry with her loud cackle and abrupt departure. Snakes sometimes obtruded their heads through the floor, rats looked in at the open door, and dark faces were continually obscuring the windows. An old pitcher, minus the handle, received the rarest specimens of wild flowers, from which our "center table" exhaled a generous perfume. In front, and at our feet, flowed in silent majesty the Father of Waters, with two beautiful green islands reposing on its bosom, which have since been named Raspberry and Harriet* Isles.

* This name is from the author of this work.

Why should I pine for halls of science and literature, when such glorious privileges were mine—when to my weak hand was accorded the work of rearing the fabric of educational interests in the unorganized territory—of establishing the first citizen-school within its undefined limits! True, since the erection of the fort there had been a garrison-school, taught by the chaplain, under pay of government, and praiseworthy zeal had been manifested by the laborious missionaries in their labor of love among the red children of the plains ; and in one or two instances a few weeks of teaching had been performed in families ; but nothing of this sort was permanent. Now had commenced a work which was to continue so long as there was a youth to educate, and when the hand that laid the " corner-stone " should have been for ages mouldering in the dust. There was not a spot in earth's broad domain that could have tempted me to an exchange. True, I was far from former friends and home, contending with a rough world, but it was *not heartless*. The law of kindness ruled every heart, the avenues of which were not closed by vice. In health, my wishes were anticipated, so far as limited means would allow; and when acclimating sickness fell upon me, I was watched with anxious eyes, kind hands bathed my burning cheek, and smoothed the pillow for my aching head.

Society was, indeed, limited, but nature supplied the deficiency. With her I held sweet council, and feasted upon her rich charms. Vigils were prolonged beneath her stately trees, and converse with flowers in their own pure language. The Mississippi, glittering with her thousand diamonds when " the silent moonbeams fell," inspired the soul with new enthusiasm, and thus life's bitter waters were changed to sweet.

SIOUX-PUPILS.

CHAPTER XVIII.

THE FIRST SABBATH SCHOOL.

The duties of the first week in school were over, and books were deposited upon the rough shelf. The open Bible, from which we had just read, lay upon the table. The eyes of all were upon their teacher, awaiting the closing exercise. She trembled, in view of her responsibility and the proposal she was about to make. She had assumed voluntarily a position fraught with momentous consequences, however it might be viewed by the world. She was the only professing Christian in the community, and religious teaching had been wholly neglected. No sacred house of prayer and praise witnessed the assembling of the people on the Sabbath. Though disposed to allow every one to enjoy his own opinion, provided he interfered not with others, the inhabitants of St. Paul were, in the main, scoffers at religion. For a single-handed and lone female to occupy a distinct and decided position in such a community, was no trifling work. Her actions would be misunderstood, her words misinterpreted, and the devices of Satan would beset her on every hand. Do you wonder that she trembled, and found no strength in herself, and that, but for an invisible presence, she would have shrunk entirely from the new duty.

"Children," said she, "I remember when I was a very little girl, and went to Sunday school, that I read in a little book of a young lady who went to visit some friends a long way from her home, where the children had never heard of a Sunday school. She invited them to come together to form one, and they soon learned to love it very much; and she, too, was very happy in instructing them; and a great deal of good resulted from it.

"Even when a child I often wished for a similar position, but I did not then expect it. While I am with you I wish to do you all the good I can, and therefore wish you to obtain your parent's permission to come here next Sabbath, and *we* will have a Sunday School. Will you come?"

The children looked at each other inquiringly, and one little girl, with meek blue eyes, timidly asked—

"What is Sunday school?"

"Is it not," says another, "where they study the Bible, and learn of the Saviour?"

"And would you not like to know more of the Saviour, and be one of the school?" said the teacher.

"O! very much, and mother will be glad to have us come," said one.

Another said she "would come if the priest would let her." The boys preferred to go fishing, but finally consented to come for one hour. A lesson was given out, an interpreter engaged for those who needed, and we tremblingly awaited the approach of the trial Sabbath.

The day proved dark and rainy; but there was a gleam of pleasure in the eyes of the seven children who composed the *first* SUNDAY SCHOOL in St. Paul. With no ordinary delight the teacher saw that some special preparations had been made, for the soiled and torn dress of the day previous had been carefully washed and mended. One half-breed woman was present as visitor; and we *know*, that however unpromising the prospect, one heart throbbed with happiness inexpressible. It was a day of peace and joy, and I occupied a position which I would not resign for the most exalted on earth. (July 25, 1847.)

The following extract from the records of the "First Baptist Sunday School" in St. Paul, is from the pen of its worthy Secretary, E. G. Barrows, and is a faithful portraiture of the commencement and surroundings of the first effort:

"The beginning of our Sunday School—the first Sunday School *established* in Minnesota*—was made by Miss HARRIET E. BISHOP, on Sunday, the 25th of July, 1847. The school was commenced in a little log hovel, covered with bark, and chinked with mud, previously used as a blacksmith's shop. It contained but one small room, about ten by twelve. On three sides of the interior of this humble log cabin, pegs were driven into the logs, upon which boards were laid for seats. Another seat was made by placing one end of a plank between the cracks of the logs, and the other upon a chair. This was for visitors, in case any should straggle in. A rickety cross-legged table in the center, and *a hen's nest in one corner*, completed the furniture.

"There were *seven* scholars that day—three white children and four half-breeds, and one visitor, a half-breed woman. It was necessary to have an interpreter. A large half-breed girl was found who could speak English, French, and Sioux.† The second Sunday there were but *four* scholars; a circumstance which looked discouraging. An interest was awakened on the subject, and the third Sabbath the room was filled. There were about twenty-five children, besides a number of visitors

---
* The first permanently established.
† All of which were then spoken.

who came to witness the novelty of a Sunday school; for, be it remembered, at that time, not only Sunday schools, but *Churches* were unknown in St. Paul.

"Here the school was continued until November, and then removed (with the day school) to a small frame building on the bluff, near the lower landing. Through the winter, the school was sustained by the personal efforts of Miss B., who, notwithstanding the severe cold, walked every Sabbath morning from her residence, near the American House (nearly a mile), to this little building, made a fire, and waited for the half-frozen little ones to come, and when they were sufficiently warmed, taught them the same precious and beautiful truths that *we* learn in *our* Sunday school, without fee or reward, except the blissful consciousness of doing her duty.

"To Miss B. belongs the credit of commencing and sustaining, for a year, unassisted, a Sunday school in a then almost unknown wilderness, and she is still among us.

* * * * * *

"In the summer of 1848, Deacon A. H. Cavender came to reside in St. Paul, and afforded much assistance in these arduous labors. He was the first superintendent, and has ever since been identified with its progress and prosperity.

"In the autumn of 1848, the school was removed to the new school-house, the first in the Territory, and here continued until the fall of 1850, when it numbered nearly seventy-five members. Other denominations had, in the meantime, come in and taken an interest in this work, among whom were Rev. E. D. Neil, Presbyterian, and Rev. B. F. Hoyt, Methodist. Churches had been organized, and a division was decided upon. Presbyterians and Methodists formed separate schools, leaving the Baptist school in possession of the school-house and a small library, and something over one-third of the scholars.

"Our house of worship was completed in the fall of 1851, and thither the school removed. * * *

"It has been our purpose to sketch the *beginning*, that when our little streamlet shall become a broad and flowing river, the curious may trace it back to its humble fountain."

In 1850, the Sunday school interest was revived by a visit to the Territory of Rev. Dr. Babcock, agent of the American Sunday-School Union, and schools have since been springing up all over the land, nor can their importance be overrated.

In strange, but pleasing contrast with the Fourth of July, 1848, was the Fourth of July, 1856. On the latter day the various schools of St. Paul, comprising more than five hundred scholars, wearing floral wreaths and printed badges, formed, with the citizens, a procession of more than a mile in length, and headed by a brass band, wound through the principal streets to "Great Brook Grove," where public exercises were conducted in the most satisfactory and approved manner. The speakers' stand was decorated with flowers, and a table, sumptuously spread, groaned beneath its burden. When summary justice had been done to the eatables, the grove rang with merriment, and hundreds of youthful voices testified their unrestrained joy on the occasion. All this we saw, where, on the first-mentioned day, the wolf was howling over the still smoking embers of the red man's council fire. In view of all these changes, we could not but exclaim, "It is the Lord's doings, and marvelous in our eyes."

CHAPTER XIX.

INDIAN DANCE.

"Come quick, and see an Indian dance," shouted half a dozen eager, bright-eyed, rosy-cheeked little girls, rushing into my room.

It needed no repetition, and " all eager I hastened the scene to behold." "But, what? where? where are they?" I inquired, as I saw nothing unusual—nothing answering to the descriptions of an "Indian dance," of which I had so often heard.

"Why, down there among the trees; don't you see them?" they exclaimed, pointing at the same time to where the brook wound its way amid the dark foliage; and there, dodging among the trees, in hasty preparations for something, were scores of half nude forms.

"You don't call that a dance surely?"

"No, not yet; but they are getting ready for one; you see they are painting themselves; they'll come up pretty soon. You see they use the water for a looking glass."

Finding it was only the *preparation* for a "dance" that I had been called to witness, we returned to discuss a waiting dinner, leaving the dancers to complete their toilet. Soon the focus of attraction was a circle of these fantastically painted and gayly ornamented beings, seated in their own peculiar manner, with feet crossed, and in the center stood their chief, Shackopee, making a speech. He was enthusiastically cheered at the termination of each sentence by the usual guttural "ugh ugh."

A rich, full intonation gave an eloquent flow of sound,

and his powers of oratory stood confessed, though the language was not understood. His design, however, was to stimulate his band to deeds of virtuous daring and hatred to enemies; and he closed with an assurance to the whites who stood around, that they sought not for whiskey in the " begging dance " about to commence, but food and clothing, though they would not refuse a little wine!

I passed on to the school-room, where order was scarcely restored when a train of one hundred and fifty stalwart men drew up directly in front, forming the ring for the dance. It was truly an imposing scene, in which the weaker sex were not allowed to join. No "woman's rights principles" tolerated there! But they seemed fully to participate in the enjoyment, and rejoice in the privilege of spectators. Moving round and round, each man strikes his heels into the earth, which is soon beat firmly, the limbs and muscles all keeping time with the deep guttural sound and the muffled bass drum. At well understood intervals, each strikes his hand upon his mouth, sending forth shrill notes, which once heard are never forgotten, though no language can convey a just idea of them.

Now, as by common consent, with no apparent signal, they draw off in a straight line, passing on to the next prearranged point; so continuing during the day, and on some occasions for days, or until their strength is exhausted. Presents of blankets, flour, and pork, of considerable value, are often made them, which the performers divide among themselves.

On this occasion, the dancers were in the acme of excitement, and presents were fast accumulating, when a voice came booming across the river, bidding them cease their pleasures and prepare for revenge. A company of Chippewas had come upon their deserted village, and a brother and son had been killed, and the scalps carried off in triumph, the informant having "alone escaped to tell them." Alas! what consternation seized them! There was an unceremonious hurrying to and fro, with strong desires for revenge legible on every countenance. Curses and bitter threats were heard instead of shouts of hilarity, and the women, who could not engage in the revel, were now flying through the street, panting to draw the reeking knife from the heart of a Chippewa, and exhibit the scalp as a trophy of victory.

The warriors and braves hastened to the deposit of canoes, and dextrously plied the paddle for up-stream, leaving the old men and women to make their way home, thirty miles distant, as best they might. The whole affair proved to be a bold but successful intent to break up the scene of revelry.

The "begging dance" was afterward, until the removal of the tribe, of frequent occurrence in our streets, being quite a lucrative business to the performers.

One of the most novel and ludicrous performances of the kind I ever witnessed was by a company of some fifty boys, from ten to fifteen years old, under the tutelage of old Hock-e-wash-ta. They were in the gala of "full dress," or rather *un*-dress, and were not the most submissive to discipline. The mouth of the old decrepit, deposed chief was drawn to a "broad grin" as he gave orders and witnessed the progress of his refractory pupils. In spite of scolding and coaxing, the boys would frequently fly off at a tangent, and the tin-pan music failed in its harmonizing design. Oh! how my heart pitied these poor boys, untrained in the ways of virtue, and inured from infancy to vice; while nought but the ball, the dance, the dive, or the chase, could arouse them from the lethargy in which their minds were sunk!

CHAPTER XX.

AN OFFER OF MARRIAGE.

THE first year of pioneer life was full of novelty. A charm seemed to pervade my whole experience. True, a cruel thorn would sometimes pierce my unpracticed feet, but it had been hidden by a sweetly-fragrant rose, and a healing balm was applied by an unseen hand. Not the shadow of a "cloud as big as a man's hand" fell upon my heart, however dark my path. Sickness prostrated; but kind hands smoothed the pillow, leaving no actual want unsupplied. If there be truth in the lines,

> "Man's inhumanity to man
> Makes countless thousands mourn,"

it was not yet applicable to the people of Minnesota, who abounded in

> "The patience of hope, and the labor of love."

And it must be borne in mind that St. Paul was a small trading post, giving yet no sign of its unprecedented growth. The council-fire of the red men was but just extinguished on the east, and was still brightly blazing on the west side of the river. Our village was almost daily thronged with them, where they frequently encamped in larger numbers than the entire adult male population of the territory. Tragic scenes were often enacted by them when intoxicated and provoked by the fraud and impositions practiced upon them by the unprincipled whiskey seller.

A drunken Indian is the most loathsome, fiendish being that ever wore the "image of his maker." Alas! we can scarcely believe humanity could be so fallen, even in the savage state!

The Indians are flattered with attention, and often become exceedingly obtrusive and presuming, where it is bestowed. From my début in St. Paul, they had regarded me with a curious eye, and bestowed upon me the appellation of Woa-wan-pa Wa-ma-don-ka Wash-ta (good book woman). Among the many who honored my "teepee" with a call, was one of unusually commanding appearance, and of proud, graceful, and dignified bearing. His profuse ornaments were exhibited for special admiration, and a smile, a pleasant recognition, or a cordial shake of the hand was always ready. Early one morning, having been unusually careful in making his toilet, so that in his own eyes he was perfectly irresistible, he called upon me.

Besides the ordinary costume of calico shirt, cloth "leggins," and "breechlet," and the blanket which, in careless negligence, gracefully enshrouded his person, he wore a huge brass bracelet scoured to unwonted brightness, and a bear's claw appended to his numerous silver ear-drops, an additional number of finger-rings, and a heavy mass of wampum about his neck, while a new ribbon of scarlet flannel ornamented his long, braided, black hair, from which waved two pea-fowl feathers, and his embroidered "leggins" were fastened with high-colored bead-wrought ties.

His deep, sonorous voice sounded in the outer room, and by a glance at the aperture of the door, as it stood

AN OFFER OF MARRIAGE. 95

ajar, his graceful movements were visible as he loaded his massive red-stone pipe with "kinnekriknick," and proceeded to light it. This pipe was highly polished, curiously wrought, and so heavily inlaid with lead that, when used, it was rested on the ground.

An unusual brightness lurked in his eye as he drew a whiff or two through the stem, three feet long, and richly and ingeniously wrought with highly-colored porcupine quills, and then passed it until it had made a circuit of the family—a reassurance of peace and friendship. During this preamble, a pair of eagle eyes were constantly peering into my sanctum; and I was about to close and secure the door, when, with the silent movement of a cat, he threw it open, proffered his hand in morning salutation; with a careless, easy grace, took a seat directly in front, and, with those same eagle eyes scanning me through and through, commenced a spirited and animated "talk"—of course in an unknown tongue. The expressive pantomime bespoke the importance of the subject. The good lady, knowing the trepidation of her boarder, came to the "rescue." Departing from the customary manner of wooing, he said, "Say to Woa-wan-pa Wa-ma-da-ka that she must be my wife." In vain it was urged that he had one, and ought not to have another. "All the band have as many as they can keep, and I have but one," was his reply. "She shall have the best corner of the lodge, and the dark squaw shall pack the wood and water, plant and hoe the corn; white squaw may ride by my side in the hunt, and the other shall carry the game, set the 'teepee,' and cook the food and hush the pappoose, while *white squaw eats with me.*" Arguments irresistible! To be permitted to *eat* with my lord! to be *first* in the lodge! But then, to have another claiming even a menial's fare as a right, and regarding mine as *her* lawful lord and master, might, and doubtless would, awaken the "green-eyed monster," and I was incorrigible. "Then when she is dead," said he, for he declared she was dying with consumption, and could not possibly live more than two or three "moons;" but at last, finding that no arrangement could be made, he begged "a dollar to buy a new shirt," and with a haughty, defiant air took leave. The next time I saw Oseola, he was howling in loathsome drunkenness, like a fallen beast, unable to rise, having sought a position for my especial benefit; and he was frightful to gaze upon, but too drunk to fear. After this, his visits became frequent; but in manner he was insolent, seeking to annoy where he could not intimidate, expressing his contempt for squaws in general, and "white squaws" in particular. The last time I saw him was just before his tribe took up their march towards the setting sun. He came with the same wife who, six years before, was so near the "spirit-land," supposing, no doubt, that the past had become oblivious to "white woman."

A similar, though more persevering course of wooing formed a chapter in the experience of my associate, two or three years later. A young warrior had seen and been pleased with her, and perhaps encouraged from some attention she thoughtlessly bestowed, made frequent calls at the house. Unacquainted with Indian character and customs (for she had been but a few weeks in the West), she one day gave him a ring, in hopes that he would be less troublesome. Mistaking her design, he, in return, presented her with a trifling ornament he had worn, which, being accepted, was to him a tacit "engagement;" and, through an interpreter, he told her that he would return and take her to his lodge the next day. She, however, thought no more of the matter until he came indeed to claim his "squaw," and urged his right with all the eloquence of words and pantomime. The second day he returned with five or six young braves, prepared to take by compulsion what was his by right; and, but for timely interference and explanation, the consequences might have been serious.

CHAPTER XXI.

PROGRESS.

It was by the family of J. R. Irvine that I had been first welcomed, and in whose house I found a *home*. The reader who has visited St. Paul will hardly believe that theirs was so recently the only dwelling in Upper Town, or that the site of the spacious "American" near that dwelling was then a dense swamp of hazel bushes, and that the ground of the superb "Winslow," and all the fine buildings around it, was covered with huge forest trees. The brook, which rippled in the deep shade, is turned into lead pipes, and has forgotten its ceaseless song of yore. The trees have disappeared beneath the woodman's ax, and the countless throng thread the graded streets where for centuries they had stood.

One hallowed tree the ax has spared, for beneath its shade we laid to rest the youngest pet-lamb of the family, and we almost fancy we hear the "angel whispers" among the flowers on that little mound.

It was a lovely morning in spring, when one little one "kissed mamma, good bye," lisped it to her sisters, and went home with one of her neighbors. There, in an ecstacy of glee with a sportive kitten, she seated herself in a pan of glowing coals. O! ask me not to depict that scene! In less than two weeks of suffering, heart-sickening to behold, Heaven received the treasure.

> "Death found strange beauty on that cherub brow,
> And dashed it out."

"What would'st thou, mother, for thy darling?
Could'st ask a greater boon than Heaven's bliss?"

The autumn of 1847 had brought some acquisitions to the society of St. Paul, so that the American population consisted of six, instead of three, families. A few neat frame cottages were erected, and a log-cabin, with three rooms, speedily grew to the spacious "Merchant's Hotel," and in it Mr. J. W. Bass opened and kept the first regular public house. His young and accomplished wife, with a fund of good sense and native dignity and grace, presided over her department with wisdom rarely exceeded, and established the fact that a frontier log-cabin can be as deservedly popular as the Irving, or Astor. The testimony of those who knew her then is, that she shone no less the star of her household than when, at a later day, she was surrounded by all the luxuries of wealth and fashion.

With the other arrivals of this season was that of Dr. John Dewey, brother of ex-Governor Dewey, of Wisconsin. The community hailed him with joy, for hitherto they had laboured under much inconvenience for the want of a physician. He was a young man, just graduated from Albany Medical College, possessing skill in his profession. Thus, provision was made for the healing of bodily maladies, but who should attend to those of the soul? Each alternate Sabbath a motley throng gathered from far and near at the cross-surmounted building, where the deluded, ignorant people were instructed to avoid, as a pestilence, the Protestant Sunday-school, and in the midst of such innovation to be more zealous for the "*true faith.*"

Will there ever be a church built here? will faithful

gospel watchmen ever stand upon this ground? and will there ever be here a people who shall fear God?—were the frequent and anxious inquiries of the heart. And shall the rum-traffic ever cease? and will there be *even one* man who shall dare stand up boldly in defense of temperance? These were mental interrogatories to be answered in due time. I now learned an important lesson—that we are not to look for the "*full corn in the ear*" as soon as the seed was sown.

CHAPTER XXII.

THE FIRST SCHOOL-HOUSE.

THE first winter closed in upon us. No longer were we to be greeted by the semi-monthly ringing of the steamboat bell, for the river was fast bound in icy fetters. Books were the companions that enlivened the solitude of our evenings. The social pleasures of the vicinity were merged in a weekly ball for those who enjoyed what, according to the report of the parties, was little else than, in western parlance, a "whiskey hoe-down." What rational, social pleasure can we devise that shall elevate the moral tone of society?—was the theme of discussion, when Joseph R. Bowron, of St. Croix, proposed that a "Ladies' Sewing Society" be instituted, to aid in the erection of the proposed school-house, and for our encouragement, generously pledged $10 for a commencement. Accordingly, the "St. Paul Circle of Industry" was formed, with eight members, and several gentleman as visitors. These little circumstances were important in the early history of this glorious country; and we remember, with an allowable pride, that the *first* payment on the lumber for the *first* school-house was made with money earned with the needle by the ladies of this "Circle." It was no marvel, then, that *they* should feel a deep interest in the work, or that some should solicit subscriptions where men had failed of success; or ride to the Fort for the presentation of so important a consideration, and the securing of $50.

The specified object of the building was the accommodating of the school, church, court, occasional lectures, elections, and, in short, all public gatherings; with the expectation that an expenditure of $300, on a building twenty-five feet by thirty, would be all that would be required for at least ten years. We had not a precedent in the past for a guide, nor warrantable faith for the future. The foundation was laid, the superstructure reared, and with intense interest we watched its tardy progress, in joyful anticipation of the time when we should exchange the mud-walled hovel, with its bark roof, for the new commodious edifice. But constant exposure from those damp walls, and at the bedside of a dying child, prostrated my physical energies; and when, just one year from my arrival, the building was declared *finished*, I was on the bed of lingering illness; so that for many weeks thereafter the echo of my footfall was not heard within those walls. But the desired object was attained, and the way was thus far prepared for educational interests to move forward.

In this emergency it was the desire of the Rev. Dr. W. who had ever exercised a father's care towards me, that I should be taken to the Mission, and though I at first demurred at being taken in a canoe, his kind words soon overcame the objection, and "old Betsey's" services were secured. Green boughs were placed in the canoe, covered with an Indian blanket, a refreshing cordial prepared for the way, and the good man's umbrella shielded my fevered brow from the sun, as I reclined upon this primitive couch. The words of comfort and hope which he spoke were as cooling water to the thirsty traveler in a desert land. He drew my attention to the tender vines, clinging for protection to the stately trees beneath which our craft was gliding; and "so," said he, "should we cling to our Father's arm." All things around us spoke in exalted strains of the love of "Him who made them," and I could not feel sad; my heart responded to the cheerful scene.

A few weeks of careful nursing, and a trip to Galena, fitted me to return in comparative health to my endeared home and labors, where I found valuable accessions to our society; and with a new impetus and double zest, I entered upon my duties in the *new* school room.

Stillwater, (nestled beneath the evening shadows of a high bluff on lake St. Croix,) at this time the declared metropolis, had made early application to the Board of National Popular Education for a teacher; and after nearly a year's delay, obtained, though for only a brief period, the valuable services of Miss Amanda Hosford, who soon after became Mrs. Moss—a well educated and accomplished lady, from my own Green Mountain State. With becoming zeal the citizens addressed themselves to the erection of a school-house, which, though commenced many months later than ours at St. Paul, was completed but a few days after it. By the efforts of the lady teacher, a bell was soon pealing its clear tones from the belfry. An educational interest, never more to flag from this period, was awakened in Minnesota, and the light of Christian education began to irradiate its moral atmosphere.

One of the earliest acts of Congress, in reference to this Territory, was the providing for the education of all classes of the population by the appropriation of two sections of land in each township. And thus, as we may hereafter see, has the little seed expanded into the mighty tree, while many find a generous shelter beneath its extended boughs.

In the spring of 1849, Miss Mary A. Scofield joined our feeble band of teachers, and was for a year associated with the writer at St. Paul. A second school-house was built, and ample means provided for the instruction of one hundred and fifty pupils.

The law, organizing district schools, took effect in the autumn of 1850, and a school was first opened under its auspices by Mr. D. A. J. Baker, an accomplished New England teacher, whose peculiar tact rendered him an adept in the greatest, the noblest of all employments.

FALLS OF ST. ANTHONY

CHAPTER XXIII.

RUM'S DOINGS.

ALAS! the demoralizing influence of ardent spirits. Nature had beautified our domain, but intemperance was laying waste its beauty, robbing the domestic circle of its charms, making paths of quicksand for the feet of young men, and more than brutalizing the poor ignorant native! The *bottle* was the unfailing attendant on *every* occasion and stood confessed the *life of every company.*

My first visit to the Falls of St. Anthony, a few days after my arrival in St. Paul, was made in company with most of its *first* citizens, conveyed in such vehicles as could be found, or on horseback, as we could best accomplish it. I was enjoying greatly my first impressions, as we rode over those pathless prairies and "openings," when one of the horsemen approached our wagon and called for the bottle. I knew that we were well supplied with refreshments, but had no idea that this constituted a part, and novice as I was, expressed my surprise, remarking "it was the first time in my life that I had ever been in a company where it was used."

"Then," replied the gentleman with great suavity, "you are entitled to the first drink," at the same time presenting the bottle.

"No sir, thank you, unless you deliver it into my sole charge."

"That could not be done," and of course a hearty laugh was raised at my expense by the repartee of the gallant cavalier.

At the Falls was a tiny log cabin, occupied by a lone widow and her son, whose white disheveled hair evinced premature age; and the secret was solved when we saw her accept the proffered glass and quaff it to its dregs. We were not surprised, a few months later, to learn she had died of delirium tremens.

Cargo after cargo of whiskey was discharged upon the dock during the season of navigation, which found its way to the lumbermen of the pineries, the soldiers at the garrison, and the lodge of the red man. Men would boast of receiving five dollars a pint when it was *scarce* and money plenty, immediately after the receiving of annuities; and thus, as they said, they would make quite a little fortune from a barrel. On one occasion several Indians of different bands had been indulging freely at one of the stores, and a drunken affray ensued on the ground, which was immediately fatal to one of the parties, and resulted in the lingering death of the other. Some of the whites had, by stratagem, secured the tomahawks at the commencement of the quarrel; but a concealed knife entered the heart of an assailant, and his antagonist himself was stabbed in the back. While the latter survived there were constant rumors of a civil war, which would have been inevitable but for his death, or his deliverance to the murdered man's friends, who would have tortured and finally killed him—the only condition of peace. Said the father of this young man, when he came to the missionaries for condolence, "My son was a brave man, and so has gone to the Good Spirit; yet my soul feels very sad—it weeps all the time; I must lay him to rest; I want him to rest well; it will take a large blanket to cover him." And in compliance with his wish a winding sheet was furnished, while his wail of eloquent sorrow, "Me charke! me charke!" was continually heard.

On another occasion a shocking murder was committed at the door of a dying woman, at the midnight hour—an hour when the Indian is never out, unless under the influence of "fire water," which the white man has sold.

An evidently excited group was one morning gathered around an ox sled, visible from my school-room window. An object strangely human lay upon the sled. In a few moments there came a message from the lady of the house of which he was an inmate, saying ——— was dead, and that she begged my immediate presence. Alas! one look and all was told. He had frozen to death under the accursed influence; had been found upon the prairie and brought in as described. His brain crazed, he had wandered, probably not knowing whither he went, and "died as the fool dieth." Gentlemanly, affable and intelligent, of fine address and noble mien, he yielded to the debasing appetite, and fortunately left no affectionate wife or loving children, blighted in spirit by his dreadful end.

Will not *this* death move the people? was the soul's inquiry, which met no response, and hope well nigh expired. Winter had yielded up his throne,

"The stormy March had come at last,"

but with bright and gladsome smiles which seemed to mock at my doubts, and contrast strangely with the moral darkness around us. With joyful surprise, I soon heard, for the first time, inquiries respecting the constitution and pledge of a Temperance society. The interrogator "had never seen one, but he and others had resolved to be no longer slaves to appetite, and to form themselves into a band for mutual strength and encouragement." Permission was granted for the occupancy of the school-room, and on the morning following the first meeting, a fine drawing, indicative of the evening's resolutions, greeted my vision from the black-board. The picture exhibited a company of revelers assembled, where wine and wit were wont to flow, emptying the contents of their glasses, tipping over the decanter, and turning with joy to a fountain "sparkling and bright," which they had just discovered. It was a noble example to the youthful Territory, when the young men at St. Paul thus rose in moral strength to wipe away her reproach.

Pursuant to arrangement, Rev. Mr. Gear, chaplain of the garrison, delivered the first temperance address in connection with religious services, when a society was duly organized, March 9, 1848. Thirty signatures were the same evening appended to the pledge.

The banner of temperance was now unfurled in auspicious breezes. The drunkard was reclaimed, and young men were saved from following in his steps. But the destroyer of domestic peace—the murderer of the soul, could not sleep. Efforts were made to win the drunkard back to his cups; to overthrow the resolves of the young; to entrap the unwary; and, because this could not be done by *strong* drink, the temptation was presented in the form of light wines and beer, that this pampering of appetite might draw men back to their "wallowings in the mire."

"Come in here and take a drink of brandy," called a rum-seller, to one who had been "saved, so as by fire," from the drunkard's grave. The words were powerless, and he quickened his step.

"Come and have a drink of beer, then, plenty of that yet; mighty pious notions you are getting into your head. *Come, be a man.*"

"I shall not do it; I want none of your brandy or

beer;" and the enticer, crest-fallen, turned to enter his store, as I approached the steps from an opposite direction. A gang of idlers leaned upon the counter, whom the now polite dry-goods merchant pushed aside, fearing, perhaps, he might also lose a lady customer; but I left that store with a mental resolve never to enter it again.

Persevering efforts are generally successful. The beer soon created a thirst for something stronger: and not many months had elapsed, ere one and another had fallen never more to rise. Among them was the merchant above mentioned, who, after leaving our community, in a drunken fit, crushed an infant, by dashing it on the floor. Another, the president of our society, a year or two later, when intoxicated, fractured the skull of a fellow-laborer, who was in a like state, and who survived but a few hours. The murderer was arrested, tried before the first judicial court of Ramsey county, and acquitted on the ground of justifiable homicide. This acquittal resulted, in truth, from the skill and eloquence of his attorneys, Messrs. Rice and Ames, natives of the Green Mountain State.

Such were some of the fruits of the sale of ardent spirits amongst us, and the reward of those who thus lead their victims down to death! But good had been achieved, though unprincipled men sought to overthrow it.

In the spring of 1849, a division of the Sons of Temperance was instituted, with twenty charter-signers, and not long after the Territorial Society was organized, followed by the "Temperance Watchmen." These, each, have done a great and noble work; but though they have laid "the ax at the root of the tree," the monster, with its thousand heads, still lives.

"*News from Maine,*" is wafted on the breeze, and fires the soul of every true lover of his race with new enthusiasm, and rouses to new effort. *We must have the* "MAINE LAW." Mass meetings were now held, stirring speeches made, and sermons preached on the subject from every desk in the Territory. The Legislature met. The petition of five hundred women and eight hundred men, praying for the law, was sent in. The contest between the followers of Bacchus and the cause of temperance was severe, and was finally referred back to the people.

The first day of April, 1851, was bright and glorious. Every voter was at the polls. A day of more general commotion had not been known in St. Paul; the ladies were at the "Sons' Hall," where a free sumptuous entertainment was prepared for all who would come and partake. Each guest was required to leave his autograph, and over three hundred names were entered. With what emotions both friend and foe of temperance awaits the countings of the "YES" and "NO." The sun has set, courier after courier arrives at the capital, and, hark! the bells are ringing! Six bells are announcing VICTORY! VICTORY! VICTORY!

The most honorable of the rumsellers closed their business before the first of June, when the law was to take effect. Rum shops were closed on the Sabbath, and every where the magical workings of the law were felt and seen. Seizures of liquors were made when landed upon the levees, and the prospect was fair for the complete prevention of the traffic, when one individual who had invested all his means in a cargo of liquors, which was seized on its arrival, encouraged by bad men, determined to test the constitutionality of the law. The result was a decision, by Judge Hayner, favorable to defendant, which involved the county in a debt of several thousand dollars, and aroused the slumbering energies of the advocates of strong drink. These efforts placed a majority of this stamp in the ensuing Legislature, and the consequence was, a repeal of the wholesome law.

Now came the reverse. On the night of the repeal, a large steamboat bell was mounted upon wheels, and attended by scores of miserable beings, went booming through the streets of the capital, proclaiming death to the temperance principles, and loud hurrahs for the movers of repeal.

Year by year each party becomes stronger and stronger. Men there are who fight valiantly for TRUTH; but still the blight of this greatest of human curses exists. Rev. A. Sabin, Baptist Minister, and Member of Congress, from Vermont, once, in my hearing, illustrated another theme, by a reference to his father's farm, more famous for Canada thistles than any other in the State. The owner labored diligently to root them out; still there would be thistles, and yet it was a *good* farm, for it gave his widowed mother a maintenance; had supported himself and his children, till all had gone from him; and, said he, "it is a good farm still, though the thistles are not all rooted out yet." Who will say that by those persevering efforts to root out the thistles, it was not made a better farm than it otherwise would have been? So will Minnesotians continue their efforts to root out the nefarious traffic from our midst, and the RIGHT *will eventually triumph.*

CHAPTER XXIV.

RELIGIOUS EFFORTS.

THE *first* religious movement in the Territory was by the Methodist Rock River Conference in 1844. Delegated by that body, Rev. Mr. Hurlbut was first to ascertain the spiritual wants of this country, and sound the Gospel trumpet through this sparsely populated region. He could do little else during the brief period of his appointment than "prepare the way," and leave "fallow ground" for others to sow the seed and reap the harvest.

His successor, Rev. J. G. Putnam, had been one year in the field, when the writer entered the territory; and he, with the exception of missionaries and the chaplain at the Fort, and one retired missionary, was the only evangelical minister "in all the broad domain." His widely remote stations forbade a frequent visit to each; and the reader can form some idea of the destitution, from the fact, that during my five months' sojourn in St. Paul, I listened to but one sermon. The Sabbath school was the only religious gathering; and here, after the formation of a Bible class, we were acustomed to read a tract or sermon, while, for one year, the writer remained the only professing Christian resident in St. Paul, and not another voice was audible in prayer, in that Sunday school. The responsibility of discharging the combined duties of superintendent, teacher, and almost, of minister, she might not and dared not lay aside; and thus, amid encouragements and discouragements, hopes and fears,

REV. A. M. TORBET

sunshine and shade, she worked on, wishing, hoping, praying, that God would put it into the hearts of some of his children to "come over and help" to cultivate the promising garden.

Early in the summer of 1848, Deacon A. H. Cavender, Baptist, and Rev. B. F. Hoyt, a Methodist local preacher, arrived in St. Paul, and became at once valuable and efficient workers. The latter, constrained by the love of souls, occasionally broke the "bread of life" to the listening few. When the "number of disciples" had increased to five or six, though their membership was in three Christian denominations, on November 9th, 1848, a weekly prayer meeting was established.

Early in the winter of 1849, a Methodist class was organized by Rev. Mr. Close (now in Oregon), and about this time Hon. H. M. Price, since our delegate to Congress, made the liberal offer of two hundred dollars and ten town lots, towards the first church edifice. This church accepted the offer, and the following spring was laid the corner-stone of their brick house in Upper Town.

With the establishment of the prayer-meeting, came the resolution to maintain some form of religious worship on each Sabbath, and so blessed was this resolve, that, except on two occasions, we were not without the living teacher.

In the winter of 1848, Rev. Mr. Gear held monthly and finally semi-monthly, service in St. Paul, with no reward but a consciousness of *doing good*, in thus laboring for the benefit of his fellow men.

Near the close of the year 1848, a simultaneous correspondence commenced between the writer and Rev. B M. Hill, D. D., Corresponding Secretary of the Baptist Home Mission Board, under circumstances so singular that we could not but believe that the hand of the Lord was in it, and that *His* Spirit directed the matter. We supposed ourselves to be strangers to each other, one asking for a Home Missionary to be sent to this inviting field—the other seeking information, and desiring to know if the Home Mission Board could do anything in this direction. The result was, the appointment of Rev. J. P. Parsons in February following, who entered upon his duties in May 1849, the first resident minister in St. Paul. On the last day of the same year, "The First Baptist Church of St. Paul," composed of twelve members, was publicly recognized in a new and unplastered schoolhouse, where its services were held through the ensuing year. About this time the union prayer-meeting, which had been cherished as "the apple of the eye," by its originators, was sundered through denominational interests; and though we heartily rejoiced in the religious advance, which created the necessity, it was a painful experience to those who had first wept over the barren soil, and prayed for more laborers in the vineyard.

In 1851 Mr. Parsons went east, to raise funds for the completion of the church edifice in process of erection. He met with general success, and was returning with an amount adequate to the liquidation of the church debt, when he was robbed, it is supposed, of his money and effects; and his death on board a Mississippi steamer, six days before it reached the port of St. Paul, has veiled the entire matter in a mystery, which will probably never be removed. The new house was first opened for his funeral services, in which nine ministers participated.

The embarrassments of the feeble church were now extreme. It would not have been surprising, had a paralysis, fatal to its continuance, fallen upon it; but an

Almighty arm upheld it, and it struggled on, resolved in the strength of ISRAEL'S GOD, *to do what it could.* The "Ladies' Sewing Society" was an efficient auxiliary, and their unwearied exertions, combined with the praiseworthy efforts of the other sex, relieved the church from debt in the winter of 1855.

In the spring of 1852, Rev. J. R. Cressey took the place of the deceased pastor, and labored for two years with great zeal and efficiency, the church in the meantime doubling its members.

In November, 1854, he was succeeded by Rev. A. M. Torbet, a "*workman thoroughly furnished unto every good work,*" who still continues to labor in word, deed and doctrine. His efforts were blessed to the salvation of souls; and during the first six months, the church tripled its numbers, though so constantly dismissing to other churches, that it has been, with propriety, styled a "religious forwarding house."

The religious and denominational interests of the Territory have advanced in a corresponding ratio. In September, 1852, the "Minnesota Baptist Association" was organized at St. Paul, comprising six churches, with less than one hundred communicants. In 1856 this body was convened at Minneapolis, a town which had no existence when it was formed, and eight new churches were received, making the whole number seventeen. A report then and there adopted, read: "Your committee have no disposition to overrate the importance of this field of labor above other States and Territories, but they will venture to say, that, from the moment when the Corresponding Secretary of that Society (the Home Mission), and a solitary Baptist member in the city of St. Paul (who is now present), were both seated, unknown to each other, opening a correspondence upon the subject of Missions in the Territory, to the present time, there is no field that has developed more rich results according to the labor performed. That time is no more years back than the number of churches received into this body at the present session, and yet in it some twenty to twenty-four churches have been organized in this Territory, many of them at no small cost of labor and means to the Missionaries of the Home Mission Society. And in a Territory which has probably *doubled its inhabitants this year*, there must be still other points springing up which will have their churches and will require their missionaries. Ours is no slow growth in other respects, and it must not be one religiously. This Territory needs many more able bodied men, who will enter the missionary ranks and labor for the good of souls and the glory of God. A large and rich harvest invites the man of God to toil and sacrifice."

The "Southern Minnesota Baptist Association" was organized in August, 1856, with four churches and a membership of over one hundred. In view of all this change, we can only say, "What hath God wrought!"

Rev. Joshua Bradley, who came to this Territory in 1850, when it was almost a wilderness and when St. Paul was almost unknown, with the design of following out the great object to which his valuable life had been devoted, viz., the establishment of a seminary of learning in this new land, died, rich in faith, November 22, 1855, aged eighty-four years. "His name stands connected with seventeen academies and colleges, which he had either been the means of founding or fostering into a healthful existence; and thus, in the hands of God, he has been the instrument of assisting to lay broad and deep the foundations of our national learning." He was ever abundant in good works, and during the several interims of pastorate vacancies in St. Paul, the desk was supplied by "Father Bradley," as he was affectionately styled by all who knew him. Mr. Torbet, in a sermon on his death, says:

"His whole life has been devoted to the work of popular education; yet he has in no instance compromised his character and standing as a minister of Jesus Christ.

"Wherever he went, however, he labored in the cause of education; he was conscious that it was but a secondary work to that of commending the Gospel to his fellow-men. His first business in life was the ministry of reconciliation. And in this he was a man of faith, and full of the Holy Ghost, with power. Revivals attended his ministry in many places where he went to build institutions of learning; and many of his pupils he induced to devote themselves to the Gospel ministry. The number of indigent young men whom he has assisted, instructed, and prepared for the ministry, in both our own and other denominations, will probably never be known, until the revelations of the Judgment. Many of them have been fed from his table, clothed from his wardrobe, and taught from his lips.

"When I speak of him as a man, I would say that he was endowed with great executive ability, more than ordinary refinement of taste, good reasoning powers, was remarkably upright in all his dealings, and possessed of strong, good common sense. I may speak of him as a divine of sound practical theological views, liberal feelings, great kindness of heart, ready to sympathize with and comfort the afflicted, and point the sinner to the Redeemer, having an unbounded interest in everything that pertained to the good of men in this world, and their glorification in the next. He had a deep and abiding sense of the worth of Christ, and delighted to commend him to his fellowmen as their salvation and all their desire. During his life he preached more than seven thousand times.

"When I speak of him as an instructor of the young, I may say, he had few equals. His blandness of manner, and simplicity of address, made the young always feel at home in his presence, and fitted him to communicate instruction as few other men ever could do. He was eminently successful, and many of his pupils will to this day attest his faithfulness.

"As a father, he was uniformly kind and careful, though his children were taught obedience; and he ruled his own house well.

"As a husband, he was conservative, and knew how to appreciate the mutual blessings of that time-honored and most tender relation. He has had two wives, and children by them both. The children of her who is left his widow were buried in the morning of life; but he has left one son and a daughter by his first wife to mourn his loss.

"As a Christian, Father Bradley was a perfect and upright man. He possessed strong religious emotions, and loved all who in reality had a spiritual knowledge of the Saviour of sinners, of whatever denominational cognomen they were. His end, therefore, was peace. He had inducements to die, and his language frequently was—"I long to depart, and be with Christ, which is far better." The morning that he died, he broke out and sang the first verse of the hymn

"'O, how happy are they
Who their Savior obey.'

When the first stanza was sung, his tongue became stiff in death, and he could neither sing nor converse more. He died as a Christian, entered into his rest, a loss to the church, a loss to the community, a loss to friends, a loss to sinners—but a gain to heaven, a gain to him."

I have made these brief extracts from the sermon, as many of his personal friends are yet living, and, besides, it is a record of a *good man*, whose works cannot die. He had for several successive years served as chaplain in the legislature, remarkably retaining the vigor of mind and muscle, until a year or two previous to his death. He preached his last sermon in March preceding his demise, during the illness of the pastor. Emphatically, the "luster of his eye was not dimmed, nor his natural force abated." "None knew him but to love him." "Blessed are the dead who die in the Lord!" and may the living, to use the language of the text on his funeral occasion, "mark the perfect man, and behold the upright, for the end of that man is peace."

CHAPTER XXV.

RELIGIOUS PROGRESS.

IN April, 1848, Rev. E. D. Neill visited the territory, spent one week, preached on the Sabbath, surveyed the ground, so far as his limited time would allow, and became impressed with the vast importance, present and prospective, of the field. He sought and obtained the appointment from the Presbyterian Board of Home Missions, and entered the field in July following—the second resident minister in St. Paul.

Until this time, the school-house had been the only place of worship. In a few weeks from his arrival, Mr. Neill had completed a neat little lecture room, in which his family resided while his own dwelling, the first brick house in town, was in process of building. The following January, a New School Presbyterian church, of nine members, was publicly recognized.

It was no trifling affliction to the youthful town when this lecture-room, eight months after its erection, was burned down. But, like many other trying events, it proved a blessing in disguise, for in its stead, and from its ashes, rose the substantial brick church on St. Anthony street, near the spot where once stood the hovel, of immortal memory, in which the first efforts in behalf of education and religion in St. Paul were made.

In 1855, a branch from this formed the "House of Hope" church, and located in the extreme of Upper Town, retaining Mr. Neill for pastor; and in 1856 the first church obtained the valuable services of Rev. James Mattocks, from New York. Prosperity has smiled on this branch of the Church since its foundation, and the people of God have learned " not to despise the day of small things."

In the autumn of 1851, Rev. J. G. Riheldaffer, Old School Presbyterian, entered the field at St. Paul. A vacancy by death in the pastorate of the Baptist church, left the house open to him half the day and evening for the first six months, after which he removed to the courthouse, meanwhile using his powerful influence and energies to " build a house to God." This is a fine edifice, in a commanding location, and was dedicated in 1854. An efficient school is connected with this church, and taught in the basement of the building.

In the summer of 1850, an Episcopal mission was established at St. Paul by Rev. Mr. Breck, a man of indomitable energy and perseverance, assisted by Revs. Messrs. Myrick and Wilcoxson. A church and mission-house appeared in an inconceivably short space of time, and abundant success has attended these self-denying efforts. At the commencement of this mission, a few hundred dollars were invested in real estate, which is now valued at $50,000—a perpetual fund to the denomination ; a precedent which it might, perhaps, be well for others to adopt.

A German Methodist church was organized, and their neat little chapel appeared in the summer of 1852. A Swede Lutheran church was built in 1854 ; and a Swede Baptist missionary has been successful, both here and elsewhere, in itinerancy.

In 1856, the Methodists built a second edifice, large, commodious, and finely-located, in Lower Town. Everywhere have they grown in numerical and spiritual strength commensurate with their noble and indefatigable efforts.

All evangelical denominations are here represented, and the "Man of Sin" holds a powerful numerical sway. But the unhappy "*isms*," which so distract the harmony of Zion, and often mar even the sweetness of social life at the East, have not crept into our territory. God grant they never may!

To the Home Mission boards of the various denominations are all indebted for an early supply of Gospel ministers. Truly, these are of divine origin, and to them we owe, under God, our present religious prosperity.

Churches have been gathered in almost every infant settlement, and the cry is still "Come over and help us." Children are gathered into the Sabbath schools; the Bible and tract distributor, the Sunday school agent and colporteur are abroad; and societies for the good of each community are formed. A country rich in nature's gifts is spread before us, fast developing an enterprise, intelligence, and progress, unprecedented, and of which, perhaps, more from past observation than faith, we may say, it is destined to become emphatically "Immanuel's land."

The reader must have learned by this time, that the interests of education and religion were among the first to receive attention from the settlers of this territory, and as we have heretofore said, the church and school-house were planted side by side. A few years have accomplished, in Minnesota, what required centuries in New England. Eight church-bells ring forth their Sabbath morning peals, inviting the population of the Capital to the sanctuary of the Most High, where talents, eloquence, and pious fervor, beautifully harmonize, to attract simple men to the cross of Christ.

The legislature of Minnesota has incorporated three important denominational institutions, viz., "Hamline University," Methodist; "College of St. Paul," Presbyterian; and "Minnesota Central University," Baptist. The first, located at Redwing, opened in 1855, is already in a flourishing condition; the second opened its primary department in 1856, and all of these will soon rank among the first institutions of our country.

CHAPTER XXVI.

ORGANIZATION OF THE TERRITORY OF MINNESOTA.

THE entire North-western Territory had been under the jurisdiction of Wisconsin previous to *its* admission as a State in 1848. After much agitation the St. Croix river was determined upon as the lower portion of the north-western boundary.

The people not embraced within the State organization determined to assert their right to be represented in Congress, and the subject was agitated by various meetings called for the purpose. A call for a convention was signed by twenty individuals, and was responded to by sixty-two delegates from different parts of the territory, and a petition to Congress, for representation there, was signed by every member of the body. In October of the same year, John Catlin, secretary of Wisconsin, and governor *ex-officio* of Minnesota, issued a proclamation for the election of a delegate to Congress, and Henry H. Sibley received the almost unanimous vote of the people. The struggle to obtain a seat was a severe one, and to his influence are we indebted for a territorial organization in March, 1849, with liberal appropriations for organizing and sustaining its government.

Alexander Ramsey, of Pennsylvania, a man every way worthy the trust, was appointed governor, who, by wise counsel, judicious management, and a prudent course, made even his political enemies to be at peace with him. None ever filled the "Chair of State" with more dignity.

HON. ALEXANDER RAMSEY.

ORGANIZATION OF THE TERRITORY. 125

This was the glorious birthday of our territory; the great epoch in its history. Immediately the tide of emigration set in this direction. Tradesmen of every craft came with the swelling tide; professions were crowded; every dwelling was put in requisition, and, indeed, whatever would afford a shelter. No longer did our citizens wonder whose might be each strange face, for strangers literally crowded the *one* street of the metropolis of Minnesota.

The demand for enlarged accomodations resulted in the appearance of the "American," and "Central House." Streets were opened and buildings went up as by magic. The sound of the hammer ceased not day or night. Instead of a semi-monthly mail, with one letter only, the contents of the mail bags were estimated by the bushel, on its tri-weekly, and, finally, daily arrival. New life was diffused into every element of society, and onward rushed improvement with rapid strides.

Among the early arrivals of the season came James M. Goodhue, who brought with him a printing press, prepared to issue the "Minnesota Pioneer," the first enterprise of the kind in this new territory. His office was an unfinished carpenter's shop, quite open, and the first number of his paper appeared 17th April, 1849.

The natural advantages, resources, and beauties of this new country, delineated by his racy pen, presented great inducements to immigration. That James M. Goodhue was a true friend to the territory, devoted to her interests; a man of strong mind, of decided character, and great energy, are undisputed facts. He was true to his friends, severe upon his enemies, and indifferent to none. Cutting sarcasm was his peculiar forte. His editorial career terminated July, 1852.

In 1853, Governor Ramsey's term of office having expired, Willis A. Gorman took the executive chair, under the appointment of President Pierce. The interests of the territory have been safely guarded, and he has done much to advance the superstructure to its present beauteous proportions, the foundation of which was laid by other hands.

We are quite sure that no territory ever had so precocious an infancy, and are equally sure, that no executive officers have done more to produce so desirable a result, than have the first two governors of Minnesota. The names of Ramsey and Gorman will live and be honored long after they shall have passed from earth. May their names be registered in the Book of Life, and the plaudit "*Well done good and faithful*," secure them admission into that city "Not made with hands."

FURTHER DEVELOPMENTS.

CHAPTER XXVII.

CLIMATE OF MINNESOTA.

The climate of Minnesota is one of its *greatest* attractions. For healthfulness it is unsurpassed. Elevated on the continent above all miasmatic and malarious influences, it is subject to none of those bilious diseases so common in lower and more southern portions of the West. The atmosphere is bracing, exhilarating, invigorating, and pure.

The severity of our winters has, doubtless, deterred many who would otherwise have sought homes in its lovely vales. But experience teaches all that they have nothing to fear from this source.

"It is true, that the cold is here more intense than in the Eastern States in the same latitude; that is, the thermometer often indicates a lower degree of temperature than is there experienced. * * But that the winters of Minnesota are far pleasanter, and that the human system is less affected by the cold here than at the East, is a fact generally admitted by all whose experience enables them to form a correct judgment. This is attributable, in a great measure, probably, to the dryness of the atmosphere, and, in part, in consequence of the system becoming habituated to the change, or acclimated, and capable of enduring a greater degree of cold without inconvenience, than in a damper atmosphere."

The extremities do occasionally suffer the bitings of frost, while the individual is scarcely sensible of cold; and therefore one needs to be well prepared for the season," and he has nothing to fear or suffer. In a more southern latitude one might chill to death without freezing, while here we would freeze without chilling. On one occasion, during the earlier period of pioneer life, my feet became badly frozen during a ride of eighteen miles, on an unbroken road without a house. I was sensible of no material suffering, and yet, such *was* the actual state of my physical system, that I have ever regarded the exercise of digging myself from a snow drift, into which the overturned sleigh had plunged me, as the means of saving me from freezing to death. My nose, too, suffered similarly on another occasion, yet the fact was unnoticed, until it was exposed to the heat of the fire. These extremes of cold are rare, and winter here is, on the whole, a very pleasant season.

Snow usually begins to fall about the middle of November, or the first of December, and until the first of March we have steady sleighing, with no general thaw; and rain rarely falls. The average depth of snow is about ten inches, and it seldom drifts to cause any inconvenience. The highest winds are in the spring, when, though not very cold, they are frequently very disagreeable.

The reign of winter is suddenly resigned, and, without a frown, spring hastens with rapid pace, and earth seems literally to drink up the snow; and the floral train commences to deck the earth. On the "sunny side" of a ravine or bluff, the delicate spring flower announces the awakening of vegetable life, while yet on the "shady side," the formidable snow bank is wasting away. When the ground is fairly bare the roads are usually dry and dusty. Except in few places, mud is almost unknown.

"The soil is of such a nature that it absorbs the water

almost as fast as it falls; and after the heaviest rains, two or three days are quite sufficient to put the roads in the best possible order. How great this advantange is, can be best understood by those accustomed to the impassable thoroughfares of the States below us, during several months of the year."

The spring in Minnesota, with the advance of vegetation, is quite as early as it is several degrees south of us. Immigrants from below often express their surprise at finding vegetation here farther advanced than at four hundred miles south.

"Plowing may usually be commenced as soon as the snow is off the ground. In some seasons it is commenced in March; but ordinarily, little is done before April. Vegetation is quick and rapid, and grains requiring the longest time to mature, are always out of the way of frost.

"Some few excessively hot days are experienced in the summer, the mercury running as high as ninety, and even above one hundred, in the shade. But even then, the nights are rarely oppressive, a cool breeze usually prevailing, and modifying the temperature so as to render it delightful; and a comfortable night's rest is always obtained."

Autumn is decidedly the crowning season. "The glorious Indian summer, from four to six weeks, presents a feature which no other part of the Union can boast in such perfection. Nothing can surpass the splendor of the forests at this season, or the mild, pure, delicious atmosphere. It is worth a journey across the Atlantic to enjoy a Minnesota Indian summer." Fall rains are uncommon, and the wheeling is fine, until the snow falls on dry, hard, and smooth roads.

In illustration of our delightful autumns, I am now,

October 9th, clad in summer dress, and actually oppressed with heat; and such has been the uninterrupted temperature, thus far, through the present season.

I am aware, that if the whole truth *could* be told—if a faithful picture of the matchless beauty and natural advantages of this "goodlie land" could be drawn, it would appear to the world as the work of imagination, rather than reality. The more we know of the country, the greater our admiration, and the more intense our enthusiasm.

Captain Pope, in his Government Report, has the following strong but reliable language: "It is impossible, in a report of this character, to describe the feelings of admiration and astonishment with which we first beheld the charming country in the vicinity of this Lake (the Ottertail); and were I to give expression to my own feelings and opinions in reference to it, I fear they would be considered the ravings of a visionary, or enthusiast." In reference to the country in general, he further says: "I have become so much interested in the country, and so fully convinced of the rapid progress it will make in wealth and population, that it would not only be a high honor, but a deep gratification to me, should I be so fortunate as to be selected for the purpose of continuing the explorations yet to be made within its borders. Without being too sanguine or enthusiastic, it appears to me that no State or Territory in the West presents so many, or such remarkable advantages to the farmer or manufacturer; and I am well convinced that those who may be induced, by the perusal of this report, to emigrate to the Territory of Minnesota, will find their anticipations more than realized, and will be rather disposed to condemn me for having said too little than too much."

CHAPTER XXVIII.

NATURAL RESOURCES.

THE St. Croix Valley was earliest brought into note on account of its lumbering interests; and skirting the western banks of the river and lake are many fine and well cultivated farms. As we pass along we wonder if this region *was* so recently the home of the red man, and the lurking place of the wild beast!

Messrs. Haskell and Norris are entitled to the credit of pioneer farmers in Minnesota, and in this valley, the delta between the Mississippi and St. Croix rivers, their farms were located. "They first demonstrated the fact that our lands are equal to any in the West for the production of cereals, a fact which was denied not only by non-residents of the territory, but by individnals among us."

The erroneous idea has extensively prevailed, that "Minnesota is too cold to raise corn." "The total absurdity of this idea has been so fully and effectually exposed, that it is now rarely or never urged by men of ordinary intelligence. Minnesota will, within a few years, be one of the most extensive corn-growing States in the Union. Both soil and climate are perfectly adapted to the growth of this cereal. The ordinary yield on well-cultivated fields, is from fifty to seventy bushels per acre.

"Wheat is also a staple production; some fields having produced over forty bushels of winter wheat to the acre. But spring wheat has been extensively raised; and if the ground is properly prepared, never fails to produce bountifully. From twenty-five to thirty bushels per acre may be considered the average yield. It is never liable to rust (so far as we know), the dryness of the climate being a guaranty against that mischief. The grain is plump and heavy, and makes a flour nearly, if not quite, equal to wheat produced further south. Its cultivation has been rapidly on the increase, although the demand has more than kept pace with the supply.

"Oats are also extensively raised, and have proved a certain and profitable crop. The average yield is estimated at about forty bushels to the acre, although as high as sixty are frequently raised. They are, perhaps, as profitable a crop as can be raised, as from the immense quantities required for feeding in the Territory, a ready-cash market is always at hand, at high prices. They are seldom less than fifty cents a bushel, ranging from that to a dollar, and even higher on some occasions.

"Barley and buckwheat are both good crops, although the former has not yet been cultivated to any great extent in the Territory. In regard to roots, no country in the world can surpass this, either in quality or yield per acre.

"In short, as a vegetable and grain-growing country, there is not a State or Territory in the Union that can surpass Minnesota, nor is there a country where farming is now more profitable.

"The demand for labor in Minnesota is very great, and no person who is willing to work need here be unemployed. Wages are high for all kinds of labor, especially for mechanics whose trade is connected with building. Ordinary journeymen carpenters get from two dollars to two and a half per day—first-rate workmen, three dollars. The immense amount of building going on is likely to sustain these prices for some time to come.

"Lumbermen usually get from twenty-five to thirty dollars per month. Farm hands get from twenty to twenty-six dollars and board. Sawyers, millmen, and shingle makers, get from one to two dollars per day, according to skill and experience.

"Girls, for doing house work, get from one and a half to three dollars per week—average about two dollars and twenty-five cents. The supply is not equal to the demand, as this class of girls who come to Minnesota always have numerous advantageous offers of marriage, some one *or more* of which they are generally sensible enough to accept.

"Vast quantities of lands are to be obtained at Government price, though none of much value near the principal towns, or bordering on the great thoroughfares, excepting far up the Mississippi. This is one reason for the high rates of wages; for a person can 'make a claim,' put up a shanty, break and fence a few acres, and if he choose, sell out in six or eight months for from three hundred to a thousand dollars, or even more, according to location. Of course, this is much better wages than can be obtained by the month, with, perhaps, less hard labor and hardships; and for every hour's labor he bestows on his 'claim,' he will reap a munificent compensation, whether he preëmpts to make a farm for his own use, or sells his improvements to some other.

"Another reason for the continuance of high rates of labor is found in the immense immigration. Farm houses are to be built all over the territory, and hundreds of new towns are springing up, many of which are to become cities of importance within a few years; hence mechanics need have no fears of lack of profitable employment."

CHAPTER XXIX.

MAKING CLAIMS.

The manner of making "claims" is probably not fully understood by people in the East. The design of the law is evidently to favor the actual settler. It allows him, on the making of certain improvements to the amount of fifty dollars, such as building a house (or cabin), which must "have a floor, window, and door, with lock upon it," and breaking up the "fallow ground," to pay for it in advance, at one dollar twenty-five cents per acre. A quarter section of one hundred and sixty acres is all he can "preëmpt." The chief benefit to the actual settler above others is, that he may secure himself a home and farm, and retain the use of his two hundred dollars during the two or three years that may elapse before the land comes into market. A "claim" unoccupied, unless preëmpted, is liable to be "jumped," as is frequently the case in a protracted absence of the original claimant. In many instances, the quiet claimant has been driven from his cabin, or had it torn down over his head; and if out of the reach of law, has been obliged to submit to the strongest party.

Whenever the land has been surveyed, and a day of public sale appointed, it is offered to the highest bidder; and when competition runs high, it frequently exceeds the minimum Government price, one dollar twenty-five cents per acre, at which price the lands left are subject to private entry.

An account given by a friend of mine, embodying his experience in claim-making, may afford amusement, as well as instruction, to my readers.

Of delicate personal appearance, and evidently tenderly reared, one would hardly expect to find him enjoying the "rough and tumble" of western life. His story runs thus: On a bright spring morning, he and his friend equipped themselves "for the woods," and started out *on foot* in pursuit of a claim, or claims. Their path lay over rough cart roads, upon which, he says, "We took our first lesson in walking on logs over mud holes, and in the absence of logs, in exploring their depths." This was in the "big woods" of Minnesota, and before evening they had stood upon the shores of Lake Wakansica; had admired its surroundings, and gone back five miles to the house of the nearest settler to spend the night, "tired to death with twenty miles' travel." But as our friend has figured somewhat in the literary world, and especially immortalized himself in his correspondence with the "Knickerbocker," in his "Bachelor Suggestions," of "Baby Cars," my readers will be better satisfied with the production of his own racy pen. He says—

"This settler was an honest Hoosier, who had brought his wife and three children 'from back in Indyanna,' to reside on the bank of a pretty lake, 'and get shet of the ager.'

"They lived in a rude log cabin, sixteen by eighteen feet, plastered with mud, and with a huge fire place and mud chimney pushed out at one end. This one small room served as kitchen, parlor, bedroom, pantry, cellar, and all other purposes. The furniture was equally rude, there being but one chair with a back to it, and that quite rickety. For seats, there were a large trunk, two stools, and two empty boxes. We ate a hearty supper of pork and potatoes, and bread and black molasses. Milk and butter were unknown luxuries. There were two beds—the settler and wife occupied one, myself and chum the other, while the children made a bunk on the floor. This was our boarding house—these our fare and sleeping accommodations, till we had erected our first cabin, with a weary walk of five miles at each end of the day.

"The next day we selected and made our 'claims' of one hundred and sixty acres (or less) each, conforming, in our land marks, to the United States' survey, and commenced clearing. We labored under many disadvantages; but after awhile got a 'set of house logs' chopped—about forty—and with the help of two men, raised the frame of the first house on the borders of Lake Wakansica.

"The logs are notched at each end, upon the under side, 'saddled' or ridged upon the upper, and piled up cob-house fashion, to the height of the eaves. Then longer logs are laid for the roof to rest on, and the 'ribs' placed transversely upon shorter and shorter logs till the ridge is reached. These ribs serve the purpose of rafters, upon which the roof, usually of "shakes,' or short boards, split from a straight-grained oak log, is nailed or secured by 'weight poles.' The places for doors and windows are sawed out afterwards. The crevices between the logs are closely 'chinked' with bits of wood, and then plastered with mud. The floor is generally made of 'puncheons,' or split logs, hewn smooth upon the upper surface.

"After we had got up the frame, and the roof partly

on, we proceeded to obtain blankets and provisions, and a few cooking utensils—all of which we had to carry on our backs for five miles through the woods—and moved in.

"Our beds were of boards—'soft side up.' At first it was like sleeping on the floor of a piazza, with the front gate open; but we built a rousing fire, slept well, notwithstanding, and didn't take cold. We progressed slowly, being but stripling pioneers; erected the other cabin, and gradually made them comfortable. The fire place and chimney were of wood, thickly plastered with clay mud. The window of each had to be brought from town. The doors were made of puncheons, hewn on both sides, 'cleeted' together, hung on preposterous wooden hinges, and secured by formidable wooden latches, hewn and fitted with an ax. We were our own architects, builders, masons, cooks, and laborers, and had to labor hard at various kinds of work without the necessary tools.

"Our *cuisine* was somewhat extraordinary, and much more meager in its appointments than that of the principal hotels. Potatoes, ham, bread, and coffee, graced our *board*, in its best estate. When the ham gave out—as all hams will in the woods—salt pork had to supply its place. The coffee failed, yet there was plenty of very good lake water to supply its place. The bread also failed, yet we had pork and potatoes. Finally, the last bit of pork was cast remorselessly into the frying pan, and we were reduced to potatoes and salt.

"In order to have as great a variety as possible, our cook (of whose merits modesty forbids me to speak) served up potatoes boiled, potatoes fried, potatoes broiled, and potatoes *raw*. Thus we had four kinds. Of the cooking department, and its appointments, as intimated above, it will not do to enlarge. Suffice it to say, the cooking is done 'as well as circumstances will admit.' Ravenous appetites make up for great deficiency in skill. We cordially recognize the well-known principle, that 'fingers were made before forks,' and are astonished to find how many uses a jack knife can be put. Some wooden bowls, paddles, and bark dishes, were obtained from deserted Sioux '*teepees.*' Rough wooden spoons were whittled out, with which soup could be eaten as readily as peas with a two-tined fork. We disdained most of the luxuries of life, its formalities and etiquette, for obvious reasons. Allow me, here, to recommend roughing it in the woods as a certain cure for dyspepsia. No sane man could have seen us, amateur backwoodsmen—who modestly think ourselves tolerable judges of good living—seated on a log, voraciously munching at a slice of fat pork in one hand, and a hot potato in the other, and for a moment doubt this.

"The weather was unpropitious. For two weeks it was like Niobe, all tears; or as our own backwoods neighbor expressed it, in a less poetic strain, 'I allow it has been right smart rainy for a powerful spell.' At last the sun shone brightly, and we rejoiced.

"For three weeks we labored on, making improvements on our claims, which consisted in building the log houses above described, and clearing or cutting off some of the timber adjoining.

"We had browned our faces, torn our clothes, kicked our boots, hose and toes to pieces, and bruised, burned, blistered, and blackened our hands out of all beauty and comeliness. I doubt if our best friends could scarcely have recognized us in our tattered and torn, unshaven and unshorn, barbarian condition.

"Now, our houses being completed—the hard work of which we are getting tired—the shabby condition of our wardrobe—our anxiety to hear how the outside world is getting on without us, and especially the alarming fact, that there remain only potatoes enough for one more meal—all conspire to induce us to leave for a 'few days.' So we pick up our 'traps,' strap them on our backs with thongs of elm bark, cast a lingering look over the beautiful lake, and to the tune of

"'I can't stay in the wilderness;
I'm going home,'

depart in search of civilization, of news, of friends, of letters, and of business.

"All this seeming hardship is not without its enjoyment. Did you ever build a house? I do not mean that you contracted for the erection of a magnificent stack of bricks; but that you built, say, a snug little cottage, which you planned, contrived, and took pride in fitting up according to *your own* taste. And if so, didn't you rather like it? So there was a satisfaction, even in working at my little log house. It was *mine*, and I owned every log in it. I wish you could see and admire, if not the snug cabin, certainly its beautiful and picturesque situation. It stands on a high plateau of level woodland, where the tall old trees are arched together over the exuberant growth of verdure, and flowers of white, blue, and yellow, and the thicket of wild currant and gooseberry vines, like some old untrained English park. In front is the blue expanse of the lake, stretching away into the wilderness, its picturesque outlines broken here and there by jutting headlands and bold promontories.

"Fish and game are plenty in and about the lake, and squirrels and singing birds throng the woods. 'Deer sign' was often seen, but only once did we catch sight of the deer fleeting in the forest. Occasionally, at nightfall, we set fire at the roots of some huge hollow tree, dry as tinder, which soon become a roaring tower of flames, and thus we obtained a splendid pyrotechnic exhibition at our very doors.

"One day, sauntering along the shore of the lake, I noticed a suspicious, sharp-pointed drift log among the rubbish. Closer investigation discovered it to be an Indian canoe, very ingeniously hidden by the Sioux. So I off with coat and boots, and after an hour of brisk labor in removing leaves, moss, sand, and water, was enabled triumphantly to 'paddle my own canoe' in search of pleasure and fish."

The foregoing is in keeping with the reports of all who go out "to make claims;" the same spirit of romance and fun characterizes all, and all undergo the same initiation, in kind if not in degree, to a wild wood life. Many, from preference, devote an unnecessary amount of time to the construction of their cabin homes; others enjoy most the rare sport of deer-shooting, duck-shooting, grouse-shooting, and trout-fishing; and, with a relish unknown in any other circumstances, they partake of their rustic meals, while soul and body gather health and refreshment. There is, truly, a strange fascination in this wild life, which needs but to be tasted to be enjoyed.

CHAPTER XXX.

PRODUCTS AND ADVANCE OF MINNESOTA.

WILD fruits of every variety are the spontaneous productions of the soil of this territory. Plums, grapes, and cranberries grow in abundance—the latter forming an important article of commerce. Immense quantities were shipped from St. Paul in 1856. Cultivated fruits, so far as tested, succeed well; and there is no doubt but this will prove as good a fruit-growing country as New England.

Wild rice, which is far preferable to the southern rice, grows in the smaller streams, which the squaws whip off in their canoes, and with slight preparation it is ready for use.

Wild game is abundant. Ducks, pigeons, grouse, quails, and prairie hens, are everywhere tempting the hunter, and the finest venison is brought into market in large quantities. Even buffalo meat, pemmican and buffalo tongue are delicacies to be obtained at some seasons, the latter possessing the most delicious richness of all meats. Pemmican is the dried, pounded meat of the buffalo, packed in bags made of its hide, with the melted tallow poured over, until it is fully saturated. This will keep for years, and is much used by the Red River people on their long tramps, and by them brought into market.

The inoffensive prairie wolf, and an occasional bear, lurk within our borders, though they are fast becoming extinct, or following in the wake of the red man.

With a soil which encourages the husbandman with an abundant reward, a home market, and cash in hand for all produce, there is no portion of our great republic which presents to him a more inviting field than Minnesota; and its resources in this particular have been appreciated. Fine farm-houses overlook most of the crystal lakes, and well-fenced farms, waving with grain, smile in abundance. If it be true, as asserted by some, that the soil is less fertile than in more southern latitudes, it is sufficiently productive for all practical purposes.

The chief advantages of this over more southern latitudes, is the purity and tonic influence of the climate; neither ague nor other bilious diseases prevail here, there being nothing to engender them. Life receives a new impulse. If the aged become not young again, much of the vigor of youth is restored; and though we do not claim to be exempt from death, we surely enjoy better health while we do live than in the Eastern States. Stagnant water, the most fruitful source of disease, is unknown; even our swamps are formed from springs, and the water in them is wholesome and pure. The undulating surface furnishes ample drainage for the water, which reappears in numerous beautifying lakes.

In Governor Gorman's message to the people, in 1855, he asserts that the population in that year had increased forty thousand; and the increase of 1856 is even greater, for it is authentically stated to have more than doubled in this year, and may be safely estimated at two hundred thousand. When we see the rapid strides Minnesota is making towards the highest position as a State, and that even now she might ask for admission into the Union with no fear of denial; when we regard her moral and physical power, her unprecedented resources, we cannot but predict for her a great and glorious destiny. Who can doubt that she is to shine the brightest star in the galaxy of our republic?

We may not inappropriately introduce here the lines from the pen of the gifted Mrs. Sigourney, who has paid a pleasing tribute to

MINNESOTA.

We've a child out at nurse where the waters run clear,
And the Falls of St. Anthony ring on the ear;
And there, where the breezes are bracing and free,
She's as healthful and happy as baby can be;
"*Mens sana in corpore sano,*" you know,
Is a treasure to all who are pilgrims below;
And we, with the wise Dr. Brigham, have thought
That "*corpore sano*" was the first to be sought:
So she runs at her will in the fresh open air,
And takes simple food, and is vigorous and fair.

No toys at Coutant's or Bonfanti's she buys,
Nor at Stewart's for candies or sugar-plums cries;
But plays on the greensward her gambles so rude,
With a huge-timbered doll that her woodmen have hew'd;
Trots away to the bluffs on her own sturdy feet,
Or sings with the birdlings in harmony sweet;
Marks the "Father of Rivers," majestic and deep,
Or sinks in the shade of her forests to sleep.

We've been very much prospered in basket and store,
And have brought up with care thirty children or more;
And our neighbors across the Great Waters, they say,
Regard them with envy, as surely they may;
Still we hope, in her case, some improvement to make,
Since the wisest of parents may sometimes mistake.

Her sisters are doubtless a wonderful band,
The joy of our hearts, and the pride of the land;

Yet a few of the elders, from strictness of rule,
Were sent, we're afraid, rather early to school;
And, perchance, though the teachers had excellent sense,
They developed the brain at the body's expense;
Then some from the heat of the climate are frail,
And others with fever and ague are pale;
And others, alas! have gone mad, we are told,
From the bite of a dog, with a collar of gold.

Now, dear Minnesota, we wish you to shun
The faults into which your progenitors run;
Nor rush after wealth with a perilous speed,
Since the strength of republics lies deeper, indeed;
In the mines of the heart, and the ore of the soul;
In the virtue, and peace, and the patience of toil.
So be pleasant and honest, and keep, as you grow,
The pure rural tastes in your bosom of snow.
We shall hear from you, child, over mountain and wave,
Your nurses will write us how well you behave;
Let no bad report your felicity mock—
Here's a kiss for you, darling, the pet of the flock!

CHAPTER XXXI.

LAKE MINNETONKA.

This country is beautified with innumerable lakes, which abound in the finest fish; and, with their woody shores, are very inviting to the angler and sportsman.

Minnetonka (deep water) is the largest lake yet discovered within the limits of the territory. Its location is between the Minnesota and Mississippi rivers, about fifteen miles from the Falls of St. Anthony; and it is about sixty miles in length. To Simon Stephens is *attributed* the honor of its discovery, in 1852, when he made the first claim on its fertile shores. Since then, the entire region has been entered and occupied, and towns have arisen on its banks.

Mr. Owen, editor of the Minnesotian, who was one of the early visitors there, says:

"The mere discovery of Lake Minnetonka by white men dates probably as far back as Father Hennapin, but the discovery and knowledge of its vast resources and extent are the work of this year. That a lake, or a series of lakes, lay off in this direction, was known to all the old Indian traders, and we have heard them frequently speak of the fact. But until an exploration commenced early last spring, by Messrs. Tuttle and Stephens, it is evident that nothing like a correct idea of the topography of this region was entertained."

Mr. Owen, after giving a glowing description of the scenery, and many amusing incidents of the trip, adds: "We saw no prairie anywhere near the lake; but occasionally, a few rods from the shore, were basins of from one to five acres devoid of timber, and thickly grown with grass, known in the Western States as 'red top,' or herd's grass, which here grows wild to the height of four or five feet.

"It is said the belt of timber is at least two miles wide all around the lake, getting better as you go back from the shore, having for its outer margin a heavy growth of very large white oak, and sugar maple being a secondary growth. Then the country breaks into the most beautiful and fertile prairie, extending to the Minnesota in a southern direction, and to the timber bordering on Crow River on the north. We have here, taking the entire circuit of the lake, a body of as fine timbered land as the Great West affords, one hundred miles in extent, and two in width, with a navigable lake in its center, and the best of prairie forming its outer boundary. What an enviable home for the thrifty and affluent agriculturist!"

If our life be spared ten or twenty years, we feel well assured that here, where now roams in his native pride the red Dakota, where the camp of the explorer is disturbed at night by the howl of the hungry wolf, and where the only sound of life upon the expansive and solitary waters is the scream of the affrighted pelican—will spread to our eyes well-improved and highly-cultivated farms; herds of fat oxen, sheep, and horses; mansions of wealth, ease, and luxury, with well-reserved and tastefully-arranged groves and lawns surrounding these homes of luxury and comfort; beautiful and thriving villages at intervals along the shores; and out upon the waters the shrill steam whistle will call to the pier the business man and idler, as the boat rounds from these jutting headlands and prepares to land. All this we shall see, if the common age of man be allotted us.

The shores of Seneca and Cayuga, in New York, are only *now* what these *will be* in the time we name. Yea, and in less than one fourth the time we have seen the approximation to this perfection; and before the writer of the above had numbered more than half " the common age of man," he has seen it. These are no chimeras of the brain, but actual and convincing realities. Churches have been planted, schools established, and all the elements of society are vigorously at work.

Lake Minnetonka has its outlet in a small stream, which, after a few miles, gathers again into that beautiful chain, so celebrated by all visitors, Lake of the Isles, Calhoun, and Harriet. These discharge themselves into a beautiful creek, which meanders through the loveliest of all prairies, and in one grand leap creates " Minnehaha Falls," and then laughingly enters the Mississippi about six miles below the Falls of St. Anthony.

> Far away in the west, where the " Big Waters " rise,
> And the fair verdant earth meets the blue-vaulted skies,
> Where the graceful fawn gambols o'er flowery plain,

MINNEHAHA.

Or flies from the swift-wingèd arrow in vain;
Where the wail of the red man is caught by the breeze,
As the graves of his fathers in sadness he leaves;—
On scenes that are fairer the sun never shone,
'Tis our land of adoption, our chosen bright home.

Here anthems of Nature, sonorous and clear,
In Falls of St. Anthony ring on the ear;
And "Minnehaha," with a laugh and a leap,
From her green mossy bed sings a lullaby sweet;
And the records of nations are writ in the soil
Where their cities have stood, and the white men now toil.

CHAPTER XXXII.

THE DRIVE OF ALL VISITORS.

COME with me, kind reader, and have one of the most delightful rides that this or any other land affords. It is one of the loveliest of our autumn days. The air is as balmy as June, and Nature is dressed in her richest robes of green, slightly tinged with gold and brown. St. Paul is all astir. The streets are thronged with country wagons, loaded with produce; the business man passes on, with a brisk, determined step; the merchant at his counter is *very* busy, for the ladies are all out shopping, if we were to judge from the array of silks and ribbons in the streets; the lounger is, as usual, taking his ease about the doors of the detestable saloons; in short, "everybody is out," and when *we* are once out of the crowded street, inhaling the pure prairie breeze, we will not "look behind us, nor tarry in all the plain."

Ascending the bluff amid suburban residences and woodland scenes, we emerge into the finest landscape ever spread out for the enjoyment of mortals. You are astonished at the thrifty farms and substantial buildings you see upon the way, and are half in doubt whether you are in the real or ideal world. You find it difficult to reconcile your mind to the fact, that this region has not been settled for ages. Flowers of gold and crimson are blooming along the way; and as we have started out on an excursion for enjoyment, let us draw it from every source.

Groveland is an appropriate name given to the midway

portion between St. Paul and St. Anthony. Let us wind around to the opposite shore of this miniature lake, and revel for a short time amid the flowers of "Groveland Garden and Nursery." Isn't it a fairy-like spot? Surely our friend Ford, the proprietor, has displayed a refined and cultivated taste in the arrangement of his grounds and the innumerable variety of flowers and plants! Then he makes his plans for utility as well as beauty. His nursery embraces nearly every variety of fruit grown in the East, and his vegetable garden is excelled by none.

Proceeding a mile or two further, amidst uninterrupted beauty, you get the first distant view of the Falls. How different from my first view! Then Nature reigned supreme. No noisy mill vied with the roar of the cataract; no bustling village stood upon the ground. Still the charm is not all dissolved; beauty lingers amid the ruins that art has made. We wind along upon the high bank, so high that our heads almost become dizzy in looking into the shallow stream.

Cheevers' tower, ninety feet high, overlooking this beautiful region, embracing woodland, bluff and plain, streamlet, river and lake, comes now in our way, and we must ascend, or we shall miss one of the rarest views.

Now we will drive through some of the principal streets, where all are busy, all astir; and next we will go over to the Island. The foot-bridge has been washed away, but this rude wagon-bridge is more secure. What a change! How I longed at my first visit to the Falls to stand upon this Island, but the waters foaming amid the chaos of rocks prevented. When the dam was built and the water turned to the West of the Island, I sprang from rock to rock, delighted in accomplishing what I had so ardently desired. The wildness of Nature was then undisturbed. A year later I stood on the spot again, having reached it by a foot-bridge, thrown over for convenience, just above the Falls. A snug little cabin had been built, and here we dined on the wholesome Yankee dish—"pork and beans." Now consider the changes in a few brief years. Improvements of all kinds have been made, rural residences have appeared, and mills of various kinds are mingling their jargon with the water's cheerful roar.

See you that shanty poised on the edge of the Falls? What are those men so busy about? If our nerves are sufficiently strong to walk a plank over the boiling surge, we will go out there. Look aloft! or your head will swim, and then—for a ride over the Falls. They are making shingles by steam. How fast they turn them off! We must not, however, tarry longer in the vain effort to see how near we can come to breaking our necks and fail. But these huge old rocks! how I love them, with the bright waters foaming around them!

Our horses must quicken their steps, or we shall be obliged to shorten our calls. Back to the main land, a drive of half a mile on Main street, and another bridge takes us to Nicolett Island, which contains about forty acres, a most delightful spot for summer residences. About the middle of the Island, "a small bluff rises some ten or fifteen feet high, with a slope rounded as if by the hand of art, which seems to be waiting for a handsome mansion."

The suspension bridge, built at an expense of seventy thousand dollars, connects this island with the west shore; a noble superstructure, exhibiting the enterprise and progress of our young Territory. This brings us to Minneapolis, a beautifully located young town, fast ripening into maturity. Our steeds seem inspired with new life as they inhale the prairie air, and unimpeded, our wheels hurry over the smooth road to the Lakes. We alight on the banks of Calhoun. It is high noon; our appetites are whetted by the bracing air, and our spirits are exuberant. We wander off to the grove, arrange our table upon the grass, and partake of its luxuries with the keenest relish.

Our repast over, we go to the water, where plenty of skiffs and fishing implements are kept for the use of visitors. Out on the lake, the fish are dancing about us and then diving deep, and we watch their graceful movements in the water, so transparent that we can count the pebbles at the depth of twenty feet.

Again we are on shore. A walk of a quarter of a mile brings us to "Lake of the Isles." How invigorating the breeze! and how cheering the prospect! One could almost dream life away in this sweet retirement, enjoying the sparkling of the waters and the play of the graceful shadows of the many isles!

Now for a stroll on the shores of Calhoun. The Fairies are beckoning us onward, and the scene inspires the soul with a new love for earth and its beauties. Is this the Fairies' abode, where not a ray can penetrate the dense foliage; or was it built for the resting of visitors? A wood nymph is gliding gracefully through that open space —no, she is human, for she carries in her hand a basket of fresh vegetables. Her address is unaffected and lady-like. A smile of satisfaction plays upon her features when we express our admiration of her home and its rural charms. We feel assured that peace and sweet contentment abide beneath that roof, with love, the crowning virtue of the wildwood cabin or city mansion. On these pleasant wooded shores it would be our delight to linger, skipping stones upon the unruffled surface of the lake, gathering flowers from its banks, or reposing beneath those ancient trees!

Again in our carriage, we are rolling over a continuation of the same prairie, in haste to see "Minnehaha!" Lake Harriet is necessarily left at the right. You must be content with its cognomen at your side. We cross the old bridge built by "Uncle Sam's boys," long before the first claim cabin was erected on the soil.

Turning to the left, our driver reins up his prancing steeds, and we alight. "Why," say you, "do we stop here?" Come, and I will show you; but first listen to the melody of waters! The "ha ha" greets your ear, but no "Minne" meets the eyes. How beautiful the name, for it is a wild, *wild* laugh you hear. We part the foliage, and, standing upon the brink of a chasm seventy feet deep, we behold the laughing waters, the whole width of the stream, making the bold leap. Nature speaks, and you are silent; but admiration is enthroned on the delighted countenance. Cling to the shrubs and look well to your feet, for we must go underneath the fall. An eastern visitor, in relation to this, says: "Who wonders that the child of the forest, ushered into existence within hearing of the falling waters, should have named it 'Minnehaha.' Gaze at it long as you will, walk under and behind the falling spray, and look at the sky through the waters, and then, if you do not laugh, say that 'Minnehaha' is a misnomer." Like the "rose in the shower," in the lesson of our childhood, we emerge from the spray, "all dripping and drowning." Look out for your neck, and we will descend to the rapids. By dint of holding to trees, we prevent ourselves from stepping to the bottom at the outset. A small patch of blue is above us; the towering banks, with their gold and green foliage, are on the right and left; a perpendicular sheet of white spray is spread out before us, and behind us the roaring, tumbling stream hastens to the Mississippi, a few rods below.

You are in doubt when you think of ascending, but with the conviction that what *has* been done can be done, you start, and somewhat after the manner of the "frog in the well," you ascend. We linger while I tell you of its winter beauties, when the congealing spray has clad each tree and shrub in a "coat of mail," and rehearse some pleasing reminiscences of each previous visit.

The beautiful and graphic poem of Rev. Dr. Phelps is most appropriate here:

>When o'er the prairie first
>   The Indian trod,
>And on his vision burst
>   This work of God,
>No wonder he should claim it
>   A lovely sight,
>   A laughing sprite,
>And shouting forth should name it,
>   With wrapt delight,
>   Minnehaha!
>
>Long ages past, I ween,
>   And none came near
>To view this charming scene—
>   This music hear.
>Before the forest ranger
>   Heard its sweet clang,
>   It rushed and rang;
>To human eye a stranger,
>   It smiled and sang,
>   Minnehaha!

To summer blooming flowers
  That fringe the brook,
To clustering leafy bowers
  That on it look,
To the deep vale, extending
  Far on below,
  Where echoes go,
'Twas ever sweetly sending
  Its tuneful flow,
    Minnehaha!

When winter's mantling snow
  Lay by its side,
When bright flowers ceased to grow
  Along its tide;
Amid the frost-harps builded
  By the ice-king,
  Each silver string
With golden sun-light gilded;
  It still did sing
    Minnehaha!

Stars in the silent night
  Might be enchained,
Birds in their passing flight
  Be long detained,
And by this scene entrancing,
  Angels might roam,
  Or make their home,
Hearing, in waters dancing
  'Mid spray and foam,
    Minnehaha!

Methinks there is a strain,
  A saddened sound,
A half-concealed refrain,
  A requiem found,
A tear drop softly falling
  Along the steep,

In the wild leap
Of sparkling waters, calling,
  For them that sleep,
    Minnehaha!

Thousands who erst have viewed
  This wild cascade—
Wild sons of solitude,
  Who hither strayed—
Have passed away for ever!
  Come they no more,
  Nor hear the roar
Of this bright, laughing river,
  Singing of yore,
    Minnehaha!

But hardy pioneers,
  A pale-faced throng,
Surmounting toils and fears—
  Stalwart and strong,
Their eastern homes forsaking
  For this Great West,
  Their chosen rest,
Blooms in the desert making—
  Are welcome, blest!
    Minnehaha!

Shout to the sons of peace
  A glad "what cheer,"
Whose pilgrim bands increase
  With every year;
Whose art and taste are giving,
  To lake and land,
  To prairie grand,
A glory bright and living,
  That long shall stand—
    Minnehaha!

Sing to the rising State,
  With cities fair,

> Whose power and honor great,
>   Her sons shall share:
> Bidding all foes defiance,
>   Their happy choice
>   Shall then rejoice,
> While Freedom, Truth, and Science
>   Blend with thy voice,
>   Minnehaha!
>
> Sing on—a hundred years,
>   And then how bright
> This glorious realm appears
>   To human sight!
> All good things here shall enter;
>   Blessings shall teem,
>   Religion beam,
> Our country's crown and center
>   This shall seem!—
>   Minnehaha!"

And so it will be the heart and center of America! Look upon this glorious land and doubt if you can.

From Minnehaha we have a fine drive of two miles to the Fort. The St. Louis House is on our way. Until recently it was a dilapidated mass of stone and mortar, having been commenced many years ago by one who had not "counted the cost." Enlarged, improved and completed, it is now a delightful summer resort for southerners and a great convenience to the excursionist.

We cannot pass the Garrison Cemetery without a passing notice. No marble slab marks the soldier's grave, but his memory is enshrined, no doubt, in fond and loving hearts. The oldest grave there is that of an infant of Col. Snelling, the first white child born in Minnesota, and the first over whose remains a grave-stone was placed.

Morgan's bluff, one mile to the right, is a sacred spot.

We can discern the rude slab which marks the resting place of two bright boys, of about the same age, son and grand-son of the Chaplain—each an only son, and one, of a widowed mother. It was a sad, sad day, when they were committed to their cold bed, and bleeding hearts "would not be comforted." Over them is written this inscription, in Latin: "Lovely and pleasant in their lives, and in death not divided."

On my first visit to the Fort, on the prairie which environs it, a tame buffalo was grazing, and the red man's teepee was pitched here and there in strange contrast with the elegance and refinement within the walls. Nature was arrayed in her mantle of green; rarely, if ever, had my eyes opened on a scene of such loveliness, and emotions new and wholly indescribable were awakened within my heart. I had found much to admire where I had anticipated nothing congenial, and refined companionship where I had expected to be isolated amid the rudest specimens of humanity. I drank deep from the fount of happiness, and from that day my path was one of flowers and sunshine.

Captain Eastman was then in command. His wife is a lady of considerable literary merit, and his own graphic pencil portrays scenes from nature like a true and faithful artist. "The Dakota," from *her* pen, exhibits the native life and character in a charming manner. The "Iris," illustrated by her husband, is a beautiful volume more recently published.

In Doctor Turner and his inestimable wife, I found firm and valuable friends, but they were long since removed to another station. She was the daughter of Robert Stewart, former partner of John Jacob Astor, and one of the founders of Astoria, in Oregon. His valuable and eventful life terminated very suddenly, in Chicago, in the winter of 1849. To Dr. T. I am indebted for much valuable information, as well as some of the most delightful drives and rides I have ever enjoyed. He was, emphatically, a gentleman and a Christian, every way worthy of the possession of so rich a treasure as she, who has no superiors, in all that makes the true woman, refined lady, and affectionate wife.

Now, turn your eye to the Minnesota river, turning, winding and smiling among the green foliage of grove and plain. I have somewhat to tell you of this river by and by; for the present, be content with gazing and listening to its own expressive language, as it winds onward to the Mississippi. Then look at those commanding bluffs on the opposite shore! Now a steamer is coming up the river and another coming down the Minnesota. Until 1853 this was Indian territory. Are we not a progressive people? But the lengthening shadow of the Fort admonishes us that we must not pause for a longer view.

Now we wind down this white sand-hill, the Fort buildings looking down imposingly upon us. You see that tree just beneath their walls? Once I climbed up that perpendicular sand-bank to enjoy the poetry of sitting beneath its shadow by moonlight. My descent was a part less poetical. It is always more dangerous in the physical, as well as the moral world, to go down hill than up. The company could render no assistance, but I managed, by holding to a twig here and there, and fastening my heel occasionally in the sand, to descend to a level with the rest of creation, with no bones broken.

Mendota, "mingling of waters," lies over there to the right. It has, for years, been the seat of the American Fur Company's operations—a pleasant spot; but with no prospect of a town. Pilot Knob, in the rear, gives one a more extended view than any other point in the country.

Crossing at the ferry, by means of rope and pulleys, we are again on the east side of the Mississippi, and have now a pleasant drive of six miles to St. Paul, over a level road, commanding an extensive and fine prospect. We must visit Fountain Cave, two miles from town, in a ravine some two or three hundred yards in depth. The entrance is a beautiful amphitheater of pure white sand stone, delightfully shaded, about three hundred feet in length, the height gradually diminishing until it is quite difficult to stand erect. Formerly, in a long narrow passage, leading from this room, by an ascent of some three or four feet, one emerged into the fountain room, the noise of its waterfall greeting the ear at the entrance. Beautiful as this room appears on illumination, one feels the chills and damps of the tomb, on having the lights extinguished.

The terminus of this cave has not been discovered. The long, low passage is now the bed of a perpetual stream, and the difficulty of proceeding has hitherto prevented extended explorations.

We have now made the drive of all visitors; another drive of twenty miles, with so much to admire and enjoy, can hardly be found. Come to Minnesota, kind friend, and I will be your guide through these Elysian fields.

CHAPTER XXXIII.

CITY OF ST. PAUL, ITS GROWTH AND PROSPERITY.

THE same act of Congress which organized the territory, made Saint Paul the capital. Then it contained not more than three hundred souls. At the close of 1856, very few of the original buildings are remaining; for they have given place to the neat and tasteful cottage, the modern, elegant mansion, the superb and substantial business block, and various public buildings, evincing the intelligence and enterprise of the ten thousand people now within the city limits.

"Saint Paul is a city of three elevations or plateaux, overlooking the Mississippi, and in the rear surrounded by a gracefully undulating and elevated ridge, already covered with cottages, and destined to afford sites for many more handsome suburban residences." The central plateau is about ninety feet above the water, with a good steamboat landing at each extremity.

The progress of this city is without a parallel. Its physical, mental, moral, religious, intellectual, and educational developments, are astonishing even to those who have participated in its wonder workings. The Yankee element, "enlarged and expanded, and having on a double pressure of steam," has diffused itself into every department of society. The latent principles of his nature are fully developed, and he is girded anew for action.

Society has its variety of shades and grades, every

class being found in our capital. The aristocrat and the plebeian—the rich and the poor, the learned and the ignorant, the virtuous and the vicious, the infidel and the Christian—all are here. Those who would toil for the good of their race, will here find a field commensurate to their desires, and no time to hang heavily upon their hands.

The soul-destroying rumseller has his licensed dram shops—the sources of pauperism, insanity, murder, and death, and his victims are numerous, though, as stated heretofore, there is a strong temperance "Maine Law" minority here, which *will* eventually triumph. The gambler, too, infests the town, and taints the moral atmosphere; his pestiferous influence insinuating itself into fashionable life, in the form of "card playing" and wine bibbing, mutiplying both drunkards and gamblers to curse our community.

The literary societies, schools, and churches, speak their own merits; and no town in America presents greater business inducements to the poor, the rich, or to him who would be rich. The rise of real estate is astonishing, and almost without a parallel. A correspondent of the "Chicago Press," spending a few days in this city, with a just appreciation of its merits, thus writes, under date of November 20, 1855:

"Here I am in St. Paul, the fastest and smartest city, of its size, in the world, by all odds. You see this striking characteristic in the place as soon you land—you see it in every man, woman, and child's countenance that you meet. They have the appearance of heroes, on whom the eyes of the world are cast, and who are determined to shine on history's page as neither laggards nor cowards. They seem to feel that they are the nucleus of a great city—the founders of a truly magnificent and beautiful country. If ever any city had reason to be called 'Young America,' in its character, that city is St. Paul. The property holders here are men who possess the elements of go-a-headitiveness in its highest forms. Bold, resolute, and determined, they have set out to make the city of St. Paul the greatest city in the north-western territory; and there is every probability that they will be successful."

The following computation, prepared and furnished me by Rev. A. M. Torbet, will be of value to those who desire particular information respecting our young city.

"The city of St. Paul is situated on the north side of the Mississippi River, and extends about three and one fourth miles from south-west to north-east. That portion of it which is surveyed into lots, contains 473 blocks; 427 of these are subdivided, and if the remaining 46 blocks were also subdivided, the entire number of city lots would be about 4,800. Allowing 800 of these for business purposes, and allowing 250 residents to occupy two lots each, for their dwellings, we find that there would remain 3,500 lots for dwellings, or about 3,500 resident buildings could be erected on the present surveyed plot of St. Paul, allowing eight persons to each dwelling, the population would amount to 28,000 inhabitants. Ten thousand of that number have already found a home in this city, and the balance will, doubtless, be found here at no very distant day. From these data, it can be seen, at a glance, that the value of real estate in this city must have a rapid advance over even present prices, though it has an amount of more beautiful, elevated, and attractive building sites surrounding it than is to be found around any other on this continent."

CITY OF ST. PAUL. 167

The citizens of St. Paul are resolved to keep up with the age in all improvements, and they have the wealth, energy, and perseverance, adequate to the accomplishment of whatever they undertake.

An elevated bridge is soon to span the Mississippi, connecting east and west St. Paul. Stock is fast taken for railroad connection with St. Anthony; and the several flouring mills and many saw mills are inadequate to the demands of the population.

The state-house, an imposing structure of brick, occupies a commanding position, and is an ornament to the city; the court-house is a substantial building of ample dimensions; the "Baldwin School" is a chaste edifice; the "College of St. Paul" is every way attractive; the "Pioneer School" is quite unpretending; though after ten years "paddling its own canoe," amid alternate "lights and shades," now rowing through shoals and quicksands, and then through threatening breakers; now through calm blue waters, and again on turbid billows, at last it has launched forth into the broad deep sea, attesting the principle that the strength of a vessel is known only by trial.

The most substantial, tasteful, and expensive erection for educational purposes (if we except the college, and indeed it is scarcely inferior to that), is a public school edifice, of stone, which would be an ornament to the old cities of the East, costing from $7,000 to $8,000.

St. Paul numbers eight churches, viz.: Baptist, Methodist, Old and New School Presbyterian, "House of Hope" (Presbyterian), Episcopalian, German Methodist, and Lutheran, besides the German and American Roman Catholic.

The frontier log tavern has given place to *first-class*

hotels, among which the "American," "Winslow," and "Fuller House," are most prominent. The latter has been built and furnished within the last year, at an expense of $150,000, and is capable of accomodating one thousand persons.

St. Paul *has* boasted of four well-patronized daily papers; but from a matrimonial alliance, the number is diminished *one;* the number of weeklies is the same, and there is one German paper. There are about twenty-five published in the territory; and the knowledge of its resources, thus diffused, has been a fruitful cause of its advance in population.

Gas works are constructed, which will contribute greatly to the convenience and comfort of our citizens; and the first perusal of this book will probably be by the aid of the improved light.

There are many good, substantial warehouses, which do a joint annual business of nearly one million dollars. Bankers and real estate dealers are daily *coining* money by the hundreds, and artizans of all kinds come in for their full share.

St. Paul has nearly one hundred "deep-read," thoroughly practical lawyers, and a score of doctors—all doing a good thriving business, though the latter are obliged to engage in pursuits distinct from their profession in order to make even a tolerable livelihood, the general healthfulness of the country rendering their professional services rarely necessary.

CHAPTER XXXIV.

THE STRANGER'S FUNERAL.

It was the first Sabbath in autumn, bright and golden as any of its predecessors, when the several bells of our city sent forth their peals of invitation to the sanctuary. The waiting congregation at the Baptist Church wondered at the pastor's delay, while the bell prolonged its usual measured toll. At length the sound of many footsteps is heard in the vestibule. With slow and measured tread they enter the audience room—the man of God, followed by eight young men, who bear the corpse of a comrade, and these again by some thirty others, who had come to pay their last tribute of regard to one *we knew not whom*. The only answer to the whispered inquiry was—"A STRANGER." But though a stranger in a strange land, it was evident that he had not been unloved in health, unattended in sickness, nor unlamented in death. The very presence of some forty fellow-boarders (and we have rarely looked upon a more interesting or manly group), seated as the only mourners of the occasion, with solemn face and tearful eye, spoke more than words their high respect for the deceased.

These had supplied the place of "loved ones at home;" had smoothed the pillow of sickness, and attended him to the dark stream; and they now, without inquiry, or knowledge of his means, had attended to every minutiæ of the last sacred rites which the most loving friends could have suggested. Noble hearted young men! may heaven as richly reward them as their own approving consciences!

As the speaker proceeded with the discourse, overflowing eyes attested the emotion of those who had never before heard of the deceased. Hearts deeply sympathized with friends in a distant city, who were yet strangers to the deep affliction that had fallen upon them.

A few months previous James S— had left his Philadelphia home, to try his fortune in this youthful territory. Fired with youthful aspirations, he had entered on a course which promised to satisfy his ambitious mind; but in an unexpected hour the hand of disease was fastened upon him; partial aberration of mind succeeded, and the "last enemy" claimed his victim. A long line of our citizens on foot and in private carriages followed the stranger to "Oakland Cemetery," and dropped a tear upon the green sod as they left him with the sleepers there, while the wood-birds caroled their anthems amid the fading boughs above his head.

A few days later, the pastor who officiated in these obsequies received a valuable token of regard from these same young men, who so nobly incurred the burial expenses; thus further testifying their high estimate of their deceased friend. Such instances are not rare. We have cited this to illustrate the kindness which characterizes the citizens of St. Paul in particular, and the territory in general. There *have* been and still may be exceptions, but circumstances demanding relief, or sympathy, need only to be known, and willing hearts and ready hands are sure to move.

The "Young Men's Christian Association," fostered into a healthful existence in the autumn of 1856, by the persevering efforts of Rev. A. M. Torbet and Mr. D. D.

Morrill, already has a fund of several hundreds, and a well-supplied and a nicely-arranged reading room, open to all. The association is fast gaining friends, popularity, and influence, and invites the stranger and the world-weary to share its benefits.

The Minnesota Historical Society, which owes its existence to Rev. E. D. Neill, is a valuable institution, founded in the infancy of the territory. It has secured many valuable historical antiquities and scientific specimens. The corner-stone of the Historical building was laid in June, 1856, with enthusiastic speeches, and much pomp of civic and military parade. Never before had there been so grand a "turn out" on any public occasion in St. Paul.

The corner-stone has also been laid of the Masonic building, which is to cost forty thousand dollars, and will outvie in elegance any public building of its size in the northwest.

"Whitney's Daguerrian Gallery" has a well-earned reputation, which will not suffer so long as its business is conducted by the accomplished artist, Mr. M. C. Tuttle, to whose skill we are specially indebted for the illustrations of this work.

Connected with the above is the studio of an artist, whose skillful designs from fancy, and the delicate touches of whose pencil, are only surpassed by his unobtrusive modest merit. Whoever visits St. Paul should not fail to call at these rooms on Third street, and add his own to the fine collection of pictures which adorn the walls.

CHAPTER XXXV.

A STRANGER'S OPINION OF ST. PAUL.

THE language of the interested citizens of St. Paul, respecting their young and thriving city, is universally the same, and might be regarded as a "one-sided view." We therefore choose, as far as possible, to allow *disinterested* persons to speak, that in the "mouth of two or three witnesses" the truth may be established in the mind of the reader. We subjoin a letter from a gentleman, making a second visit here, bearing date—

"*June* 28, 1856.

"St. Paul has advanced very considerably for twelve months past, more so, perhaps, than any place I have visited. Not that its population has increased very materially or in a greater ratio than many other cities of the West. Its advance has been one more of wealth, enterprise and energy, than of population. The question, 'Will St. Paul be a large city?' appears to have been solved, and that in the affirmative, since my last visit; and there is little or no croaking regarding the 'crash' that people all around had predicted would overwhelm it sooner or later. The fact is, its position as a great commercial center of Minnesota—as a grand center for the territory, North and West—is now fairly and irrevocably established, and St. Paul cannot fail to become a large and populous city. Those whose fortunes are locked up in her 'corner lots,' now feel safe; they talk, act and walk with a firm, don't-care-gait, and rattle the loose change in their pockets as if they 'dined on ducats.' Her merchants also feel satisfied; ask prices with a 'stiff upper lip;' despatch a customer without worshiping him, and drive fast horses after business hours, that will vie with any city in the Union. St. Paul is comparatively an infant city, with a population of probably ten thousand souls; but here, 'every man counts.' Here men are picked, not from the fossilized haunts of old fogyism, but from the swiftest blood of the nation. Every man here, to use a western expression, 'is a steamboat,' and is determined to make his mark in the history of Minnesota.

"One thing is sure to attract the attention of eastern men on their first visit to St. Paul. They come expecting to find a new, unshaped city, with a rude, rough and unrefined people; but they find a much higher degree of elegance, fashion and display, than in any other city of its size in the world. It is decidedly fast in its character. The ladies revel in finest silks and satins; the gents carry gold-headed canes, keep splendid driving establishments, and there is a much larger display of finery and jewelry than is consistent with a modest taste. All this, however, is indicative of success. It requires prosperity to keep up such luxuries; and although extravagance may be indulged in to an extent not commendable, still, as the city settles down, these matters will regulate themselves.

"There are a large number of new buildings in course of erection all over the city; some of a most permanent and costly character. Several large warehouses are building; some of stone, others of brick, on a scale of magnitude known only in the West.

"The new hotel, one of the largest out of New York, to be kept by Messrs. Long & Brother, well known as the first landlords in the Territory, will be equal to the best in the United States.

"The progress of St. Paul has not been only material. In all that pertains to intellectual and spiritual advancement, there is a healthy action kept up by the people. Schools and churches are well and willingly supported, and societies, both literary and benevolent, are kept up with spirit and zeal.

"A bridge is about to be built across the Mississippi at this point.

"The bluffs all around the city are now being thickly dotted with splendid residences; and if things progress as they have, during the past year, it will not be many years before St. Paul casts in the shade some of the older eastern cities of wealth and importance."

Another writer from the "Great West," thus discourses with an eastern editor:

"It is a strange medley, indeed, that which you meet aboard a Mississippi steamer. An Australian gold-hunter, just returned by way of England, from Melbourne; a merchant on a trip of pleasure; a professor in an eastern University, going out to invest in Minnesota; a St. Croix raftsman, returning from a trip down river, with a small fortune of logs; a New York doctor, with a pocket full of land warrants; an eastern man, who administers electro-chemical baths; a South Carolina boy, with one thousand dollars and a knowledge of double-entry; a sturdy frontier man, with a saw mill for the interior; an engineer, who escaped the Panama fever on the Isthmus railroad; a Yankee schoolmaster, who has become a small speculator

A STRANGER'S OPINION OF ST. PAUL. 175

in oats; and scores of others of doubtful character, who sport heavy moustaches, and keep their mouths shut. Verily, a strange medley do you find aboard a Mississippi steamer!

"Now, half wearied by observation, you sit listlessly in the front gallery of the great steamer, watching the golden clouds piling themselves high towards the zenith, in preparation for a regal sunset. Presently the crowd thickens about you, the knowing ones are on the alert, and all catch the spirit. You turn to your next neighbor and ask him the cause of excitement. He glances at the shore and replies, 'St. Paul's just round the next curve.' The boat presses nobly against the current, and you feel yourself swinging around towards the west. The ladies have come from their cabin to the forward deck, books are laid aside, Fremont and Buchanan are forgotten, conversation flags, and all eyes are strained towards one point. Another turn of the wheel, we shoot from behind the forest, and the miraculous city bursts into view. First, an amphitheater-like basin, benched with ephemeral houses, and a huge steam-mill puffing in the mid arena. Then the high bluff, crowded with more substantial tenements of brick or stone, from among which spires and cupolas of churches and public buildings rise with sharp outlines against the orange clouds. Coaches from the different hotels, warned by our whistle, already cluster around the plank. Runners from different establishments show a commendable zeal in skimming the cards of their respective establishments. 'Winslow House!' 'Snelling House!' 'Merchant's!' 'American!' 'Fuller House!' are shouted from the coaches. One by one the vehicles are filled and rolled away; the freight of stoves, groceries, grain and machinery, is being carried ashore, when we press our way through the crowd, and seek a private boarding-house high up the bluff.

"St. Paul, the diadem city, because standing at the head of navigation, glows really a bright jewel on the brow of the Father of Waters. It is situated in lat. 44 deg. 52 min. 46 sec., long. 93 deg. 4 min. 54 sec., 2,070 miles from the mouth of the Mississippi,* and about 350 above Dunleith, the western terminus of the Galena and Chicago Railroad connection with the East. During its long winding route to the Gulf, the great river falls some eight hundred feet. St. Paul, situated on a bluff, may be considered about nine hundred feet above the ocean.

"The history of the town is brief, and no where out of the Great West can we find an analogous instance of prosperity. Eight years ago, had we come up the river as we have done to-day, and swept in against the unimproved levee, quite a different scene would have been spread before us. Then high on the bluff a half dozen huts environed the diminutive Catholic Chapel, and had the whole town turned out to meet us we would not have seen over one hundred and fifty people. Even at that time a small irregular town plot had been staked out, but no one, not even the projectors of the village, had yet, in imagination or judgment, penetrated the teeming future of their infant settlement. Indians were then abundant, and daily visited the town, exercising their pilfering propensities, greatly to the annoyance of the pioneers.

"When on the 3d of March, 1849, Congress organized the territory, and by an organic act constituted St. Paul the capital of the inchoate state, then were the people's eyes

* The writer probably means in a straight line, for with its windings it is nearly 4,000 miles.

anointed, then they saw a second Chicago springing up on the forest-covered bluff, and property at a single leap went up two hundred per cent. Addition followed addition, quarter section after quarter section was cut into building lots, until the city plan reached its present limits. Each addition was laid off according to the caprice of the owner, and such was the variety of tastes that the finished plot of St. Paul has much of the irregularity of a European metropolis.

"From the date of the organic act immigrants flocked into the new capital in great numbers. They came chiefly from the Northern States. Maine has a great many hardy men, reared among the pineries of the Penobscot and Kennebec, and perhaps is the most numerously represented of any of the States."

The first Legislative Assembly convened in the Central House, on the 2nd of September, 1849 ; now a brick capitol of imposing proportions, furnishes more commodious quarters.

The number of steamboat arrivals during the early period of the town's history, was as follows:

In	1846	there were	24
"	1847	"	47
"	1848	"	63
"	1849	"	85
"	1850	"	104
"	1851	"	119
"	1852	"	171
"	1853	"	235
"	1854	"	301
"	1855	"	563
"	1856	"	759

In 1850 only seven boats were engaged in the trade,

in 1856 there were seventy-nine. The average date of the opening of steamboat navigation is the 10th of April, and the average close the 18th of November, making the period of navigation about 219 days. The average annual increase of the number of boats for the last 12 years, is thirty-six per cent. An increase for the next four years of only twenty per cent. will make the number of arrivals in 1860 nearly 1,600. Think of this, you, who have doubts as to what St. Paul is, and what it will be!

The arrival of the *first* steamer, is invariably retarded from one to three weeks, after the river is clear above and below, by ice in Lake Pepin. This, too, is the case at the close of navigation. If by any process we could induce this lake to conform to the habits of the river we should have annually four weeks, at least, added to the season of navigation.

The arrival of the first steamer of the season is a great day for St. Paul. Anxiety has long run high; eyes are strained in anxious expectation, and when finally it rounds the bend, hundreds of citizens gathered at the river, send forth a prolonged shout of welcome, and the bluffs echo the general joy.

Such is the ambition to be the first boat through the lake, that on one occasion, when several had long waited for the ice to yield, and some had returned in despair, both passengers and crew of the "Highland Mary," volunteered their services, and actually chopped the ice till there was no further impediment to progress, and received, as they well merited, hearty shouts of congratulation from the people of St. Paul.

CHAPTER XXXVI.

ST. CROIX VALLEY.

STILLWATER, on the St. Croix, was the first town in the territory to attain to any importance. A saw-mill was built there in 1844. This formed the nucleus of a village, and as for a long time the supply of lumber was little more than sufficient for home use, the other points remained unsupplied. So in 1847, when St. Paul could boast but three white families, Stillwater had a score, and nestling sweetly beneath towering bluffs, was the "*self-styled metropolis.*" Soon, however, the tables were turned, and the former outstripped the latter.

For several successive years, Stillwater made a slow and steady increase; the lumbering interests giving it its chief importance. In 1856 it has a population of about 3,000, and with every element of business life at work, the town is fast spreading itself on and above the bluff which overlooks the placid waters of Lake St. Croix. It is the seat of Washington county, contains the Court-house and Penitentiary, has several excellent hotels, but in church building, has not kept pace with other towns. The original portion of the town has frequently suffered severely from inundations, and persons have been obliged to go to and from their dwellings and places of business in boats, which constantly plied through Main Street. During an unprecedented rise in 1850, the "Lamartine," a large craft steamer, passed up this street, and fastened her cable to the pillars of the "Minnesota House."

The St. Croix derives its name from a Frenchman,

who was drowned near its mouth at an early period in the history of the territory. It enters the Mississippi about fifty miles below St. Anthony, by a frith or lake, is twenty-five miles long, and from one to five wide. The first steamer that undertook to navigate its waters was the "Palmyra," on July 17th, 1838. Then its valley was regarded as valuable only for its lumbering facilities, but now rich thriving farms skirt its banks, and several fine little towns are mirrored in its waters.

Prescott and Point Douglass, at the mouth of the St. Croix, the former on the Wisconsin, and the latter on the Minnesota side, have equal geographical advantages, but the former the greater real importance. Point Douglass, unlike other western towns, has been for a long time *in statu quo*.

Hudson in Wisconsin, is a quiet thriving town, reposing on the verdant hill side, and smiling amid graceful foliage. It is surrounded by majestic bluffs, the highest of which claims a passing notice. By toiling over a circuitous route, I had ascended that bluff, and stood upon the brow of the abrupt summit that overlooks the town; white cottages appeared in pleasing contrast with the verdure of spring ; the lake stretched far away with bold broken shores, and the mellow evening sunlight threw a halo upon the scene. From more distant objects I drew my attention to those nearer, and there, upon the very pinnacle, was a grave! In surprise and wonder I sat down to meditate. The lines of the immortal Gray seemed strikingly appropriate—

> " Perhaps in this neglected spot is laid
> Some heart once pregnant with celestial fire,
> Hands that the rod of empire might have swayed,
> Or woke to ecstacy the living lyre."

"Here rests his head upon the lap of earth,
A youth to fortune and to fame unknown,
Fair science frowned not on his humble birth,
And Melancholy marked him for her own."

Friends in a far-off land might long have wept over the unknown fate of him who slept beneath the flower-grown mound, and never perhaps would they learn his untimely or early death! It was a sweet resting place, almost up among the clouds; indeed, sunshine often settled upon that grave when the frowning clouds were beneath. I plucked a flower, and pensively started on my return to town, where I sought of an "old settler," the solving of the mystery of the lone grave. Years before a town was contemplated at that or any other point on the lake, a young adventurer admiring the gorgeous sunset scene, and with his eye upon this bluff, desired his companion to *bury him there*, should his grave be made in this country; a promise was made, and one week from that day was fulfilled. While flowers were blooming over his resting place, my mind instinctively sought that land "where they never fade," and where the weary traveler shall never say "I am sick." In that new earth, which shall be the home of the blessed, the flowers shall bloom in perpetual beauty, but they will never adorn *the grave*.

CHAPTER XXXVII.

A VISIT TO THE FALLS OF ST. CROIX.

IN 1847 I made my first visit to the valley of the St. Croix, which extends as far as the falls, some thirty miles above Stillwater. At this place I was passing the holidays with a friend of recent date, as all western ones then were, when an invitation was received from the family of Judge Perkins, to make them a visit. We needed no arguments to induce compliance, and a pleasant party, whose hearts were gushing with delight, were coursing the only thoroughfare along the river. Naught broke upon the silence save the merry jingle of sleigh bells, and the spirit's overflow of the happy company. The blood-stained snow upon the ice, told of the fatal encounter of the wolf and deer; and the wondering gaze of the wandering Chippewa gave evidence that such companies as ours were not frequent in those wilds.

Amid scenery where nature had displayed her wildest freaks, and where art had seemed to copy from her example, we rode until we reached the mansion, and drew around the cheerful fireside and well-filled board of our refined and intelligent friends. That, like a subsequent visit, is an oasis in life's retrospect. The appointments of the house were in keeping with the dignified affability of our host, and the lady-like, graceful demeanor of our hostess.

In the then limited state of society, the distance of

thirty or forty miles was little barrier to social intercourse. No envy or jealousy crept in to mar and destroy the mutual confidence and well-appreciated congeniality of friends, who, separated from all the rest of the world, were all the dearer to each other.

So enraptured had I been with my winter visit to the Falls, that I could not refrain from compliance with the oft-repeated request, to repeat my visit in the bloom of summer. During the June rise of 1850, when the streams were all swollen to an unprecedented height, the steamer "Lamartine," having on board a pleasant party, undertook the trip.

The wild, romantic, beauty of the river banks was heightened by the richness of their verdure. The numerous wooded islands were so many Edens reposing on the bosom of the stream, and the dark shadows from shore, sent a thrill through every fiber of the soul. The scenery tasks my powers of description; sublime and magnificent are meager terms with which to describe the approach to the Falls. For two miles the river has forced its way through rocks, which might seem, by some frightful convulsion of nature, to have been thrown asunder, forming an almost perpendicular wall of an hundred feet or more on each side. Surmounting these majestic battlements, is a wild chaos of rocks and trees in grand confusion, mocking at our diminutive appearance so far below.

Dangers began to threaten the boat as it neared this point, and prudence forbade further attempts at ascending the rapid current. But I had resolved "not to give it up so," and as a skiff was to make the *trial*, I gave myself to the care of a ministerial friend, with the assurance that trusty and skillful oarsmen were to manage the frail craft. There were several gentlemen, myself the only lady, and the skiff was loaded nearly to overflowing.

The swift current would sometimes send us dizzily backwards, with the rapidity of a rail car, and threaten to dash us against the rocks, from which there could have been no escape; with lightning speed the oars would be thrust into a crevice in the rock, and arrest our downward progress; vigorous efforts would bring us forward again, and again we were whirling back. Once as we were on the point of being dashed on the rocks, the man in the prow sprang to a foothold, held on to the line until the eddy was passed, and thus saved us from inevitable destruction.

The impressive grandeur of the scene, was not unnoticed, nothwithstanding our imminent peril; and stoic-like I sat, with folded arms, gazing on the sublime spectacle before me; every nerve strained to its utmost tension. 'Twas well the eyes were thus riveted, for a dizzy head like mine, would, by a moment's gaze at the whirling water, have been quite sure to capsize the boat.

Suddenly my eye caught sight of a delicately hued flower, modestly bowing a welcome, and a "never fear." It had performed its mission, for my soul was inspired with new courage, and confidence in the governing and providential care of its Creator, and I said to myself, "If God so clothes and protects the flowers of the forest, which to-morrow fade and die, how much more will he care for thee, child of immortality!" In contrast with the delicate flower, and yet the product of the same Almighty hand, appeared the notable chimney, which, detached from the main land, rises sixty feet above the water. Huge oblong rocks seem to have been thrown together by some freak of the elements, and thus in *ir*-regular order, or regular disorder, bid defiance to all who desire to scale their summits.

The dangers to which we were exposed, are not always attendant upon the voyage up this stream. In low water it can be ascended with comparative ease, and small boats have even gone up the rapids to the foot of the falls. The stream here is so narrow, and such is the position of the warehouse, seen nearly a mile below, that it seems to occupy the entire width, and impresses one as being the terminus of navigation, if not of land conveyance.

One mile accomplished, and the most desperate of all efforts must be made, for here was a bend in the river, around which the waters raged with madness. A few quick words passed between the men, and "*Now mind your oars—we are in it*," was followed by the determined stroke of the oars; when "Danger is over" enabled us for the first to breathe freely; and swift as an arrow we shot across the river, and heartily rejoiced to stand on *terra firma*.

From this point the rapids proper commence, so that all merchandize must be discharged at the warehouse; and so narrow is the stream, that boats coming here must *back out* for half a mile. A circumstance was related to me by Captain Smith, whose boat was among the first to arrive at this point, when there were few others than lumbermen in the vicinity. These gathered to the number of sixty or seventy, and came on board clamorous in demand for liquor. The captain was not then, as he has been since that time, running a Temperance Sabbath-keeping boat; still he refused. Continuing peremptory in their demand, in order to bring him to terms, they went on shore, ascended the bank far above, and commenced rolling rocks upon the boat. As the only alternative for safety, he promised to "treat round," if they would desist. Forming a circle, the "flowing bowl" went round and round, while in reply to remonstrances, they insisted that they " had not drunk *round*," nor had they until the whole company were intoxicated.

A windlass raises freight from the deck of the boat to the floor of the warehouse, and thence on an inclined plain it is raised to the plain above. This is the nearest approachable point to the town, one mile distant.

A sequestered walk, after we had slaked our thirst at a spring, and a warm greeting, awaited our arrival at "Wildwood Cottage," the fairy-like mansion of our excellent friends. Here the wild and romantic admirably contrasted with the elegant and refined. The chaste dwelling, of Gothic style, looked as if it had alighted from another planet, and chanced to find a lodgment there. In front we had a fine view of the Falls, and the boiling rapids; and their music quite forbade our attempts at conversation.

We were not satisfied with treading the rich carpets within, while there were such inviting prospects without. A spacious enclosure surrounded the house, containing also the rustic arbor, and majestic forest trees, where birds had built their nests, and cheered the inmates of the mansion with their morning, noon-day, and evening songs. Here the witch hazel, and brier bush grew, and the gray old rocks contrasted with the many-colored wild flowers. The out-buildings are arranged for ornament as well as convenience, all denoting the taste of the proprietor, and comfort of the occupants. Here was an enclosed pond, with the tame and wild goose swimming upon its waters; a poultry yard, containing the usual varieties of domestic fowls; and a house for Juno, a beautiful spotted fawn, which at a call would come and eat from our hand. We rambled at the Falls, got into all the dangerous places we could find, galloped over the country amid the picturesque scenery, and were filled with *ecstacy*. During one of these excursions in the wilderness, we called at the house of a lady, whose neighbors were the rude Chippewas, who, aside from her husband and little daughter, were her chief society. The notes of a sweet-toned piano vibrated on the air, amid the green old trees, attuning our spirits to the harmony. We were regaled with rich fruit cake, and the purest and coldest water, and left with the full conviction, that happiness is not the growth of any particular soil or circumstances.

Within the mansion at "Wildwood" were abundant sources of amusement and profitable entertainment, and if a rainy day intervened, a resort to the well-filled library furnished us all delightful occupation.

Sabbath morning came, and in an unfinished dwelling an attentive people listened, for the first time in many weeks, to the earnest words of Life, from the lips of Rev. Mr. Whitney, who had made one of our company in coming hither.

Quiet as this rural hamlet seemed, it had but recently been the theater of tragic scenes and bloodshed. Two young men, after a dispute of small importance, parted in anger, and met the following morning, each armed with a revolver. Several shots passed, when one fell dead, and the other severely wounded.

Captain Wilkins, who had figured largely in the Mexican campaign, delegated by authority, had come hither at the same time with ourselves, with an armed force, in pursuit of a Chippewa who shot a white trader for refusing him more whiskey, when his brain was already crazed by the distilled pestilence. The attempted arrest was a failure.

A young lawyer, admitted to the bar at the spring term of Ramsey county Court, in a fit of *delirium tremens*, jumped from a rock eighty feet high, giving it the name of DRUNKARD'S ROCK, into the foaming rapids; and his body was picked up several days afterwards at Oseola, six miles below. May a doating father and fond mother never know of his untimely end!

One man, under the influence of liquor, stabbed himself; and another, who went raving through town, knife in hand, determined to kill all he met, was secured and placed in confinement. At this juncture, the better part of the community banded together and passed rigid resolutions for the suppression of the nefarious traffic. These scenes, except the first, had transpired within the week previous to our visit; but all was quiet while we were there.

In the summer of 1848, a Chippewa, infuriated by whiskey, shot the man of whom he obtained it, was arrested; and in want of other power, was tried by the citizens, and a deputation was sent to Stillwater, to obtain concurrence in his death sentence. A steamer was chartered, conveying most of the male citizens to witness the execution. There could be no legal trial; but it was a fair and impartial one, and seemed the only alternative. The criminal acknowledged his sentence just; it was concurred in by his wife and aged father,

A VISIT TO THE FALLS OF ST. CROIX.

who witnessed his death; and he employed his last breath in earnest warning against the intoxicating cup.

The water power at St. Croix Falls is immense, and the inexhaustable pineries above keep the dozen saws in active operation; but its improvement has been sadly retarded by long litigation. The property is in the hands of a Boston company. Since the boundaries were set to Wisconsin, the village on the east of the river comes within its jurisdiction. Little importance is now attached to this, since one, denominated Taylor's Falls, is hastening to maturity on the Minnesota side.

We reluctantly bade adieu to friends, whose hospitality we had *so* much enjoyed, and with our gentlemanly host and others, embarked in the "Queen of the Lake," a fine large skiff, for Stillwater, thirty miles distant, where we arrived in nine hours. The day was delightful—the ride charming. A basket of refreshments had been provided; and, with a tin cup, we caught the cold spring water which came trickling down the rocky banks.

Arrived in Stillwater, a strange scene greeted us. A rough box stood by the roadside, into which a lifeless human form, taken from a wagon, was placed, and the lid being carelessly nailed down, it was replaced in the wagon and sent off for interment, the chief actors of the scene returning to the grog shop and gambling saloon. On inquiry, we learned that the Sabbath previous, two drunken raftsmen were on the lake in a small boat, which was overturned, and both were hurried into eternity; and this was the last of the two just recovered from the water. Alas! for the tempter's power!

A recent calamity has brought overwhelming grief to the hearts of loved ones—sorrow and mourning, and finally, desertion to "Wildwood Cottage." The accomplished wife is a stricken widow. The fair daughters and promising son are fatherless. In their dwelling, domestic bliss had "sate a queen and knew no sorrow," until its light was suddenly extinguished. Judge Perkins was aiding his workmen at the mill, in the arrangement of some machinery, when his foot slipped, and he fell into the water, and sunk to rise no more. No timely aid could reach him, and the following day he was found, erect, where he went down.

In the dense old forest, tree after tree may fall, and yet the vacancy be imperceptible; bouquet after bouquet be gathered from the prairie flowers, and still there seem none the less. But cut down one of the pleasant shade trees from around the dwelling—remove the mainstay of the household, and the loss is *felt*. One after another may fall, in the crowded city, and the ranks be unthinned. The old country "burial ground" may be full of dead, while the number of the living is seemingly undiminished. But in the *new* and sparsely populated portions, where prominence is given to each individual of moral worth, the *death of one is felt*. There are none to spare! "What THOU doest we know not now, but shall know hereafter." "How unsearchable are Thy judgments, and Thy ways past finding out!"

CHAPTER XXXVIII.

ST. ANTHONY'S FALLS.

FROM my earliest recollection, St. Anthony's Falls had been a theme of wondering admiration to my childhood's fancy. A *knowledge* of their remote existence seemed shrouded in mystery; but now I trod the soil which environed them, and my romantic interest increased rather than diminished.

As I caught the first distant view of the foaming cataract, my entire being was imbued with a new enthusiasm. The very atmosphere seemed to emanate from the Creator's immediate presence—and the flowers seemed to have sprung along our pathway, for the gladdening of angelic spirits, and to breathe the poetry of Heaven. Silence was more expressive than words. We felt not the overwhelming awe of Niagara; but calm, delighted, pleasurable admiration! I was recalled to the fact, that the spirit was still confined to its earthly tenement, by measuring with the feet the long space that intervened between us and the cataract.

Thorns and thistles had not defiled the land, for the white man had not commenced its tillage! No sound of noisy mill made discord with the music of waters; but Nature reigned the acknowledged queen—her loveliness confessed by all.

A small log cabin, built in 1837, by Franklin Steele, the first claim-cabin between the St. Croix and Mississippi, stood where now, enlarged and improved, it stands, overlooking the fall, at the most convenient distance. This was our hotel, and here our home being prepared, tempting viands were spread. Our table was an old bedstead, with rough boards laid across, concealed by our own snowy table cloth. Never was a meal eaten with sweeter relish than this, my first one at St. Anthony. It was, too, my first great intellectual feast in this flowery land. I had quaffed the overflowing bowl pressed to my lips. I had clambered among the crags, and sat down to reflection upon the rocks, amid the surging rapids, and then climbed up a perpendicular steep of sixty feet, because I had rushed into a danger from which this was the only escape. I had been in the cataract's mist, and delight inexpressible thrilled my heart. Nor was it all excited by what the eye saw in the scene before me, but the prospect of the moral world, and the thought that here I was privileged to labor, and realize the dreams and yearnings of childhood were overpowering.

> " I had been lonely, even from a child,
> Though bound with sweet ties to a happy home,
> With all life's sacred charities around me;
> I had been lonely—for my soul had thirsts
> The waters of this world could not assuage.
> *   *   *   *   *   *
> I had high dreams
> And strange imaginations—yea, I lived
> Amid my own creations; and a world
> Of many hopes and raptures was within me,
> Such as I could not tell of; for I knew
> Such feelings could not bear a sympathy;
> They were too sacred to admit communion,
> Too blessed to need it; to the fields and woods
> Did my heart's fullness pour them; solitude
> Was the expansion of my secret visions,

When I could ask my soul to tell me all;
And many a bright and blissful reverie
Hath cheered my wanderings—I have heard sweet music
In my own thoughts, mysterious harmonies
Felt, but not understood—vague, happy musings
And shadowy sketches of my future fate,
In bright and glowing colors."

The fall is divided by Hennapin Island, and on the west side of the island there is much the largest volume of water, as well as the most imposing view. Spirit Island, once within, but now below the falls, has connected with it a legend of woman's wrongs and woes. The superstitious Dakota sees the spirit of the abused wife, with her child clinging to her neck, darting in a canoe through the spray, and "the sound of her death-song is heard moaning in the winds in the war of the waters." The story has been graphically portrayed in verse by Rev. S. W. Pond, formerly a missionary among the Dakotas, which we copy. I saw an old canoe wedged in the rocks and playing amid the waters; and as I abstractedly gazed, I half imagined it the one in which the deserted wife seated herself with her beautiful boy, to avenge the father's neglect, while the wild death-song was heard from beneath the boiling flood.

When winter's icy reign is o'er,
  And spring has set the waters free,
I love to listen to the roar
  Of thy wild waves, Saint Anthony.

For, gathered here from lake and glen,
  The turbid waters, deep and black,
With foaming rush and thundering din
  Pour down the mighty cataract.

I love to watch the rapid course
   Of the mad surges at my feet,
And listen to the tumult hoarse
   That shakes me in my rocky seat.

Entranced with visions strange and new,
   The 'wild'ring scene amazed I scan,
As with a wild delight I view
   Nature unmarred by hand of man.

But go through all this earth so broad,
   Go search through mountain, vale, and plain—
Each spot where human foot has trod
   Is linked with memory of pain.

A sight these rugged rocks have seen,
   Which scarce a rock unmoved might see;
On the hard hearts of savage men
   That scene was graved indelibly.

And though, since then, long years have fled,
   And generations passed away,
Its memory dies not with the dead,
   Its record yields not to decay.

No theme of love inspires my song,
   Such as might please a maiden's ear;
I sing of hate, and woe, and wrong,
   Of vengeance strange, and wild despair.

Unskilled to sing in polished lays,
   I tell no tale of mirth and glee;
A tale of grief in homely phrase
   I tell you, as 'twas told to me.

Long ere the white man's eye had seen
   These flower-decked prairies, fair and wide;
Long ere the white man's bark had been
   Borne on the Mississippi's tide

ST. ANTHONY'S FALLS.

So long ago, Dakotas say,
    An-pe-tu-sa-pa-win was born;
An Indian maiden, blithe and gay,
    Rejoicing in life's rosy morn,

I of her childhood nothing know,
    And nothing will presume to tell;
Or of extraction high or low,
    Or whether she fared ill or well.

I know she was an Indian maid,
    And fared as Indian maidens do;
From morning's light till evening's shade
    Hardship and danger ever knew.

The flowing river she could swim,
    She learned the light canoe to guide;
In it could cross the broadest stream,
    Or o'er the lake securely glide.

She learned to tan the deer's tough hide,
    The parchment tent could well prepare;
The bison's shaggy skin she dyed,
    With art grotesque, in colors fair.

With knife of bone she carved her food,
    Fuel with ax of stone procured,
Could fire extract from flint or wood;
    To roughest savage life inured.

In kettles frail of birchen bark
    She boiled her food with heated stones;
The slippery fish from covert dark
    She drew with hook of jointed bones.

The prickly porcupine's sharp quills
    In many a quaint device she wove:
Fair gifts for those she highest prized,
    Tokens of friendship, or of love.

Oft on the flower-enameled green,
  With troops of youthful maidens gay,
With bounding footsteps was she seen,
  Striving to bear the prize away.

The Chippewa she learned to fear,
  And round his scalp she danced with glee;
From his keen shaft, or cruel spear,
  She oft was fain to hide, or flee.

Thus she, with heart now sad, now gay,
  Did many a wild adventure prove;
Till laughing childhood passed away,
  Succeeded by the time of love.

Now wedded to the man she loved,
  Clasping her first-born infant boy,
Her swelling heart the fullness proved
  Of nuptial and maternal joy.

Thus did her heart with love o'erflow,
  And beat with highest joy elate;
But higher joy brings deeper woe,
  And love deceived may turn to hate.

But he whose smile as life she prized
  Sought newer love, and fresher charms;
And she, forsaken and despised,
  Beheld him in a rival's arms.

Whate'er she thought, she little said;
  No tear bedimmed her flashing eye;
Her faithful tongue no thought betrayed;
  Her bosom heaved no tell-tale sigh.

Long had she hid her anguish keen,
  When on yon green and sloping shore
The wild Dakotas' tents are seen,
  With strange devices painted o'er.

ST. ANTHONY'S FALLS 197

An-pe-tu-sa-pa-win was there,
    Painting her face with colors gay;
And her loved boy wore in his hair
    Feathers, as 't were a gala day.

Why braids she her neglected hair,
    As though it was her bridal day?
Why has she proudly decked her boy
    With shining paint and feathers gay?

See, she has seized her light canoe,
    And grasps with haste the slender oar,
Places her baby in the bow,
    And thus, in silence, leaves the shore.

With steady hand and tearless eye,
    She urges on that frail canoe;
Right onward to those falls so high—
    Right onward to the gulf below!

Her frantic friends in vain besought,
    She still held on her fearful way;
Nor turned her head, nor heeded aught
    Of all that friend or foe might say.

All quake with horror—she alone
    Betrays no sign of grief or fear;
With gentle words and soothing tone
    She strives the trembling babe to cheer.

The faithless husband trembling stood;
    A father's feelings check his breath;
His son is on that raging flood
    So full of life—so near to death.

The quivering bark like lightning flies,
    Urged by the waves and bending oar;
No swifter could she seek the prize,
    Were death behind, and life before.

The fearful brink is just at hand,
   And thitherward she holds the bow!
See eager Death exulting stand!
   No power on earth can save her now!

And now she raises her death-song
   Above the tumult shrill and clear;
Yet may she not the strains prolong—
   The fatal verge is all too near!

The song has ceased—the dark abyss
   Swallows with haste its willing prey:
The bubbling waters round them hiss:
   Mother and child have passed away!

The fragments of a shattered bark
   The boiling waves restored to view;
But she and hers in caverns dark
   Found rest—though where, none ever knew!

Yet that DEATH-SONG, they say, is heard
   Above the gloomy waters' roar,
When trees are by the night-wind stirred,
   And darkness broods o'er wave and shore!

In haste, and with averted eye,
   Benighted travelers pass near;
And when that song of death is heard,
   Stout-hearted warriors quake with fear.

CHAPTER XXXIX.

IMPROVEMENTS AT ST. ANTHONY

At the period when our history of Minnesota commences, Canada was in the hands of the French, who then displayed far more enterprise in pushing their discoveries and military posts into the wilderness than the English. They had indeed formed the design of taking possession of the whole Mississippi valley, which they claimed by right of discovery and occupancy. Their supremacy was not, however of long duration. In their subsequent contests with the English they met with a series of disasters which finally resulted in their relinquishing all claim to that vast territory watered by the Mississippi and its tributaries.

The small log cabin named in the last chapter was the first "improvement" at St. Anthony. Then "the whole country was a complete wilderness,* inhabited only by savages, principally Sioux and Chippewas, who watched with a jealous eye these first encroachments on their domains. But little did they then dream, that within fifteen years the 'westward march of empire' would extend far beyond the roar of the cataract, and the 'pale face' seize more than thirty millions of acres of their choice hunting grounds as his lawful prize."

In 1838 Mr. Steele broke up and cultivated some six or eight acres in the immediate vicinity of the Falls.

---

* The reader must not suppose it a forest, but a wilderness in the sense of being uninhabited by civilized men.

He bought the whole of the present site of the town, at three several purchases of as many individuals for the trifling sum of $500, including also Boom Island; the last purchase, however, was not made until 1846.

The land at this time had not been surveyed by government, and these of course were only "claims." It is quite safe to say that in ten years from this time this land was "entered" at the government price of $1 25, and now in 1857 the original purchase for $500 could not be made for as many thousands.

At the time of the government sale of lands at this point in 1848 there were but four houses, and in one of these was the store of R. P. Russel, esq., who established himself in mercantile business the same year. Great difficulties were encountered and overcome in the outset of these enterprises here, and various misfortunes befel the infant settlement. Many articles which could only be procured in the East were lost before reaching their destination: working utensils could hardly be procured at any price: provisions were scarce and of course very high: female help it was impossible to obtain, and men were employed to perform the duties of cook and laundress.

In September 1848, two saws commenced running, and two more the following year. From the year 1849 we may date the real commencement of the growth of St. Anthony. Several prominent and valuable citizens settled here, and the same year the "St. Charles" was built by Anson Northup. In this year also Mr. Steele sold one undivided half of his interest in the property of St. Anthony to Mr. A. W. Taylor of Boston, for $20,000; and in 1852 Mr. Taylor sold back his interest for the sum of $25,000, when Mr. Steele sold again one half of his interest to Messrs. Davis, Sanford and Gibhard of New York city. An eighth of what remained was sold to Messrs. Chute and Prince, the former of the two being the resident partner and managing the entire concern.

St. Anthony ranks the second city in the territory, and has many great advantages over other points. Its water power is immense, and the improvement of that power is astonishing. The magical developments of Yankee enterprise, in this wonder working country, are strikingly visible in this thriving young town. The citizens are characterized for intelligence, industry and enterprise, and their indomitable perseverance to *prove* themselves to be at the "head of navigation." Boats have been chartered by them at an enormous expense to test the fact, and *have* in several instances reached the town in high water. It is, however, with reluctance and much risk that the trip is undertaken, though St. Anthony, averse to yield, is experimenting still, dredging the stream, removing boulders, &c.

St. Anthony must ever be a place of importance; the lovely scenery and fertile country surrounding it, with its facilities for trade, giving it every advantage. No one can look upon it but with convictions of its future prosperity. Here the industrious farmer, the enterprising mechanic, the shrewd merchant and the intelligent professional man, find ample scope for effort, and a rich reward for their toil.

More decided action in favor of temperance has been taken by the citizens of St. Anthony than in any other town in the Territory. The conditions of sale of the first town lots were that no drinking or liquor establishment should be erected thereon for two years from sale, and thus the infant town was saved from the blighting demoralizing influence of earth's greatest curse. But the enemy has since crept in and "sown tares."

Here is also the seat of Minnesota University, a territorial institution, located by an act of the Legislature in 1851, within a plot of twenty acres of land, delightfully situated in view of the falls, yet sufficiently removed from the din of business. Two townships of land, donated by Congress, constitute a fund for the endowment of the University. This tract embraces some of the finest lands in the Territory, and is equivalent to forty-six thousand and eighty acres.

Two steamers, the Gov. Ramsey and the H. M. Rice, have been built here to ply above the Falls, at an outlay of twenty thousand dollars. The Suspension Bridge, built at an expense of seventy thousand dollars, has proved a profitable investment, the first annual dividend of tolls being twelve thousand five hundred dollars, equal to fifty dollars per day.

"No one can examine the river at this point," says the St. Anthony Express, "without being struck with the admirable facilities here afforded for bridging the Mississippi for railroads. The facilities, aside from this, are unsurpassed. Stone of excellent quality is at hand in abundance. Here, too, are all the facilities for procuring the requisite supplies of lumber. The banks seem as if formed by nature for this express purpose." Nor is the day far distant when St. Paul, St. Anthony and the whole calendar of Saints will have a direct railroad connection with the great Atlantic Cities.

Already the work of a century seems to have been accomplished as by a magician's wand. What would have been the emotions of Hennapin and Carver, when standing upon this soil where alone the "Indian lover wooed his dusky maid," could they have seen in prophetic glass what now the natural eye beholds! And yet to the eye of Nature's votaries art but detracts from its charms. How oft a sacred awe has stolen upon me in viewing these glorious displays of Almighty power!

The world is full of beauty! Winter and Summer have their charms! There are times when the soul is thrilled as with seraphic harmonies, inspiring a love for HIM who created all these glorious objects.

A view of the falls from the west shore is the most desirable. And here a town has sprung up in three years that rivals many at the East of half a century's growth. In 1849 there was but one family residing on this shore. A thrilling adventure of a young lady in this family has entitled her at least to the character of a heroine, and to notice in our book.

Miss Bean had come to the river on her way to school, and the boatman being absent she determined to "paddle her own canoe." She managed the oars dexterously for a time and arrived at the middle of the stream, when the rapid channel hastened her onward to the Falls. A rope had been extended across the river to provide for such an emergency, and was now about three feet above water. As the skiff passed underneath she caught and firmly clung to this rope, and here she remained swayed by the current for half an hour, when she was rescued from her perilous situation by her father.

In company with a friend I encountered similar and even greater peril, as there was no rope which might render us aid. In haste to cross, our call for the boatman from the other shore met no response. My friend objected to my proposition to try our own skill in rowing, he being a novice in the business; but his gallantry forbade obstinacy, and when he saw me seated in a canoe, paddle in hand, he took a reluctant seat, thinking probably, *he'd not let me drown alone.* We pushed from shore making the absurdity of our circumstances a theme of merriment. My back was towards the shore and I had begun to feel that we were making fine headway, when my attention was directed to the starting point. Surely, *we were* under headway, unless providentially arrested, to inevitable death! With dexterous hand each plied the paddle, and with all the energy arising from the conviction that *our life depended upon it;* each, however, in the excitement, counteracting the efforts of the other. By accident my paddle in a deep dip *struck bottom*, and *we were saved!* by a providence which our own coolness would not have devised. We very wisely concluded that rowing a skiff on Lake Champlain was quite another affair from paddling a canoe on the rapid Mississippi; especially in proximity with its foaming cataract; and that henceforth we had better leave the paddle to those who understand its use.

CHAPTER XL.

MINNEAPOLIS.

MINNEAPOLIS, the name of the town alluded to in the last chapter, as having sprung up mushroom-like on the west of the falls, is compounded from the Sioux and Greek language. "Minne," the Sioux term for water, and "polis," the Greek for city; hence, the "city of waters," or Minneapolis. It is finely located, the bank of the river above the falls rising from five to twenty-five feet, and extending back in a beautifully rolling plateau.

The old Government mill of ancient date, and the mill-house, were the first and only buildings here until 1850. My valued friend, Col. John H. Stephens, has a just claim to be considered "the first settler." Having served in the Mexican war with distinction, acting a conspicuous part in several battles, under command of Gen. Scott, when his services were no longer required on the tented field he sought the "Elysian fields" of Minnesota. For the sharer of his joys and the divider of his sorrows, he chose an intelligent and accomplished wife from the Empire State, and built his rural cottage on the West bank of St. Anthony's Falls. The floral adornments of his ground soon betokened the taste and refinement, the quiet and domestic bliss which dwelt within doors. In a lecture before the Minneapolis Lyceum, in speaking of his first arrival here, Col. Stephens says:

"In the month of April, 1849, a colony of some ten persons might have been seen wending their way from

St. Paul, looking for a settlement—a permanent home. In that colony were a Doctor, just entering manhood, who has since arrived at the highest pinnacle of distinction in his profession, and a school-master; the rest were farmers. Leaving St. Paul, with no favorable impressions of the territory, we were divided in opinion which part of the country to examine. Directing our attention to Fort Snelling, we, for the first time, found that the land west of the Mississippi was not opened to settlers; hence we left the fort and pursued our way to the Falls of St. Anthony, in order to get back again on to Government lands. As we journeyed from the fort the character of the country was beautiful beyond description. Not a solitary house, except the old mill property, was to be seen; an unbroken wilderness surrounded the site of Minneapolis. We saw a number of wolves start from their lair; and eagles, even, seemed disposed to dispute our right to visit the crags below the falls.

"The smoke from the chimneys of only two houses could be seen from St. Anthony. They stood solitary and alone. Money could hardly buy a meal; pork and beans and coffee were all that we expected, if indeed we were thus favored.

"Little did I then think that St. Anthony would in 1855 contain a population of three thousand, and Minneapolis one thousand. At that time there was not a newspaper in the territory, although the Pioneer was brought into life by the late lamented Goodhue the same month. There was not a church and the whole Territory only contained one school-house.* When I speak of a church, I mean a Protestant church. These remarks are neces-

---

* In this the Colonel mistakes; besides the one at St. Paul, to which he alludes, there was one at Stillwater.

sary, for my intention is not only to show the rapidity of the growth of the territory, but of Minneapolis.

"We go back again to the colony I was connected with. It might perhaps be well to say, that J. P. Miller, formerly of lower Minneapolis, and myself, are all of them that remain in the territory. There were no sick—the doctor left in disgust; we had no children, and the school-master went to another part. The farmers of the company did not like the east side of the river, and being adventurers like myself, they all went to California. Two of us determined to remain, and I pitched my tent on the west side of the Falls of St. Anthony, there to live, perhaps to die. We struggled long for a permit to occupy the reserve, and that object was in time accomplished. My present dwelling was erected in the winter of 1849-50, being the first house *built in Minneapolis by a private citizen.* As soon as the house was completed I moved into it, and for the first year our only neighbors, (with the exception of the family of C. A. Tuttle, esq., who left his home on the east side of the river in a few months after our residence in our present home,) were the Indians. We have often retired at night and opened our eyes in the morning upon the wigwams of either the Sioux, Chippewas, or Winnebagoes, which had gone up while we slept.

"My oldest little girl is the first white child born in Minneapolis, and her age is only four years. 'Little Willie Tuttle,' the only son of my ancient neighbors, is the second child born here. My family and Mr. Tuttle's had remained alone for some time, when Mr. Miller was fortunate enough to get a permit."

Another and another followed until they numbered nine families, when, says Colonel Stephens, "We now thought ourselves representing quite a city, the nearest distance between our residences being half a mile. We had good times—peace and harmony reigned in our midst. Occasionally the Rev. G. H. Pond, who is one of the very best men in our territory, would give us a sermon. On such occasions we all gathered into my house and listened to his useful and instructive teachings.

"Thus we remained for some two years, when others obtained permits and our village started schools. One of the first objects of the early settlers was accomplished in securing the services of Rev. J. C. Whitney, who was the first settled pastor in Minneapolis. The Rev. C. G. Ames, the worthy and excellent pastor of the Freewill Baptist Church, was the second minister of the Gospel that settled with us. Then followed Rev. A. A. Russel, of the Baptist Home Mission Society. They could not have made a better selection, for he is truly 'the salt of the earth.'

"One of our early and most perplexing difficulties, was the selection of a name for our embryo city. Col. James M. Goodhue thought 'All Saints' to be a good name. Miss Mary A. Scofield wrote many letters for publication east, and she always wrote from 'All Saints.' At our first claim meeting in 1851, 'Lowell' was adopted. At an accidental meeting in November of that year, the whole of Minneapolis was present, and we hit upon 'Albion.' This name the citizens soon got tired of, and at last, as a compromise, it was left to George D. Bowman, editor of the St. Anthony Express. He selected 'Minneapolis,' which met some opposition at first, but Mr. Bowman would come out every week with an article on 'Minneapolis;' and all finally swallowed it. It is allowed on all hands to be a beautiful combination of the native Sioux and classic Greek,

"One year ago the village had only twelve houses; now you can count over a hundred, some of which would do credit, both in structure and durability, to the city of New York.

"Hennapin County, of which Minneapolis is the shire town, is bounded by the Mississippi on the east, the Minnesota on the south, Crow River on the north, with the beautiful Minnetonka in the center, all navigable for steamboats; together with rich prairies and fertile woodlands, copious small pebbly lakes, filled with fish, besides brooks and gushing springs in abundance, and all conspire to make it, at large, a favorite location for the immigrant, who is in search of a home in the great northwest. The highest hopes may be here realized. Bilious attacks are seldom known; consumption is rare; fever and ague are banished from our midst. All the facilities necessary for a poor, worthy and industrious man, either with or without a family, can be found here. More than twenty school districts have been established in the county, and the spires of different churches can be seen pointing towards Heaven. Every part of Hennapin appears to be combined to help agriculturists.

"Minneapolis and Milwaukee brick are known in the West, and *are hard to beat.*

"We have but one doctor. He has little to do, and is certainly worthy of patronage would he go to other countries, but not here. I refer to Dr. A. E. Ames, whose familiar face is known to all as a citizen and an upright man, but not as a doctor. Few ever require his services."

The first death which occurred in this town was an infant child of Mr. Bean, in 1850; the second was Mrs. Case, in 1853. She was the first woman who went the land route to California, and with no female associate.

She was a young bride, buoyant in hopes and spirits, and relished every hour, as she said, of the long and untrod path. After spending two or three years in the land of gold, she and her husband returned rich in its avails, and with a cabinet of rich and rare specimens gathered there and on the route. No spot presented so delightful a location to their minds as their beautiful claim on the western border of Minneapolis, where, in their snowy dwelling, amid the adornments of taste and comfort, life's golden days sped on. But the "pale horse and his rider" came with a summons, which could not be unheeded. The young wife was removed to her last earthly abode—the narrow charnel-house. Thus, the fairest and brightest of earth's prospects fade away.

The editor of the Saint Anthony Express says: "It may not be amiss here to state, that Minneapolis is located on what was formerly the Military Reserve of Fort Snelling—a reservation of nine miles square around the fort for the purpose of forage. By an act of Congress passed in 1852, the reserve was, for the most part, thrown open to actual settlers, and the following year began to be rapidly settled. Probably the first building erected in Minneapolis (he should have said west of the river), is the old stone mill built by Government, for the purpose of grinding grain for the use of the fort, and which is still standing. A saw-mill was also erected by Government near the same place; but this, we believe, has been almost, if not entirely, rebuilt within two or three years.

"It was in this old mill that the first United States District Court for the Territory of Minnesota, west of the Mississippi, was held by Judge Meeker.

"A ferry was maintained for several years across the Mississippi, opposite Col. Stephens's, for the use of the fort. This has been superseded by the elegant wire suspension bridge.

"On the 5th of March, 1855, an act of Congress was passed, granting the right of preëmption to settlers on the reserve. The title to the lands had previously rested in Government. As soon as the proper arrangements could be made at the Land Office, settlers commenced proving up; and soon all entitled to preëmpt had obtained their titles, the same being true of nearly all the reserve within two miles of the city of St. Paul. For the passage of this act the people are much indebted to the faithful, persevering and efficient labors of Hon. H. M. Rice, their delegate to Congress. Thus was happily ended a difficulty, and a source of most harassing anxiety and suspense to hundreds of settlers, who had been trembling lest their beautiful, hard-earned homesteads should fall into the hands of the relentless speculator.

CHAPTER XLI.

THE WEST.

"THE WEST," says an eastern writer, who, in the summer of 1855, traveled through the Mississippi Valley, "where is it? In New England we talk of the West—of its beauties and deformities, and of removing thither; but seldom define its locality. In New York, Michigan, Illinois, and Wisconsin, they talk of the West and its future promise, and of the advantages of going thither to become identified with its high hopes and future greatness. Still, our ideas of the real genuine grandeur and future prospects of the West (the valley drained by the Mississippi and its tributaries), are exceedingly limited, until we traverse some of its prairies, wander among the magnificent timber there growing, falling and wasting as though no part of the family of man would be glad of a winter's supply therefrom; or take a trip of a few hundred miles on board of some one of the great number of steamers plying on the rivers, freighted to their utmost capacity with people from every state of the Union and nation of Europe—all going west! Sit upon the deck, and gaze for hours on the high and overhanging rocks and unsurpassed scenery; visit the cities of the West, that have been planted, laid out, and built, within the memory of nearly every inhabitant thereof who has seen half a score of winters; ride a day on their railways; and then the absolute greatness of the West will begin to be realized. Colleges are being built, and richly endowed. The common school-house is often seen, to remind the New England wanderer that he is still with those that have, in other days, been inmates of eastern homes. New churches of rich architectural beauty already rest on the soil of the West; and, indeed, all you there behold serves only to make you love it more, and long to say '*It is my home.*'

"It is hard to select a home in the West; there is so much in every state to attract the emigrant. Wisconsin alone has the resources of an empire. The people are enterprising, and are fast developing the resources of the state.

"Minnesota, too, with rapid strides, is developing herself, and will soon knock at headquarters, demanding her freedom suit, and to be ushered into the constellation of states; and before her representatives shall have been long enough at the national capitol to form the acquaintance of all their brethren, will be head and shoulders above some of her older sisters. Indeed, Minnesota is far-famed, but no more so than fair-valed. Perhaps no lovelier scene was ever presented to the gaze of mortals than may be seen in going from St. Paul to St. Anthony. As the traveler approaches St. Anthony, looking forward and a little to the left, his eye rests upon the promising village of Minneapolis, and its back grounds. It is one of nature's best efforts to make a beautiful landscape, and the effort was crowned with complete success.

"Many have asked me, since my return, what part of the West is best for a home. This depends much upon what the person going thither requires. For New England people, I think Wisconsin and Minnesota best adapted. There is less ague than further south, and the climate is more like the East. Minnesota, with a clear bracing atmosphere, with cold but uniform winters, cannot fail to be attractive, and the western parts of Wisconsin none the less so. The soil is *rich enough* in almost any part of the West. Wisconsin, in some respects, is already the first state in the Union. With its inexhaustible resources it is making rapid strides to wealth and influence. At the present time it is ahead of Minnesota; but wait ten years, and possibly, perhaps probably, I shall be constrained to give a different opinion."

Such is the disinterested testimony of one whose knowledge of the *extent* of the beauties and resources of Minnesota was comparatively limited. What shall be said, then, of those whose eyes are daily opening on its new and rare excellences, and who regard with astonishment its newly-discovered beauties! We do say, without fear of contradiction, that the natural scenery of Minnesota is unsurpassed in loveliness by any other on the globe; and in this we have the concurring testimony of several who have visited every quarter of the world, and nearly every island of the sea.

A bird's-eye view, such as we get from the high bluffs of the Upper Mississippi, of broad, undulating prairies, carpeted with green, and richly set with flowers of purple, crimson, and scarlet; woodlands and lakes intermingling, and the streamlet gliding

"Like a line of silver, 'mid a fringe of green,"

enwraps the soul in enchantment, and we cannot imagine the loveliness of Eden to have been more perfect.

Strolls and drives amid scenery like the above, have made indelibly their impressions upon my mind. My soul oft wanders in blissful dreams, and reposes upon some green isle of the crystal lakes, where myriads of shining water-fowls are gracefully sporting, and the finny tribe leap from their transparent element, to impart life and gladness to the scene; and the tiny wild flower lifts her head with her own sweet smile, to kiss the island sprite as it passes by! All these scenes of loveliness are fronted by the towering grandeur which skirts the mighty river. The Mississippi is sublimity itself. It is the central thoroughfare of our mighty nation—bearing on its bosom hundreds of richly-freighted steamers, traversing in its windings a distance of more than four thousand miles; and by its tributaries having access to more than half the states in the great confederacy. But here, its mountain shores give a peculiar character to that sublimity; the towering rocky summits requiring little play of the imagination to form them into the remains of ancient castles and ruins of monuments and towers. And its bluffs, from one to six hundred feet in height, have a more grand, extended, and picturesque scenery than is to be found on any other river in the world, stretching back into beautiful table lands. The trees on their slopes present to the traveler the singular appearance of an orchard in an old settled country, and prompt a desire to start in quest of fruit; but the absence of human habitations dispels the illusion.

It is a singular fact that the bed of the river is here free from rocks and snags, notwithstanding the boldness of its rocky, wooded shores; the only obstruction to navigation being sand-bars, which in low water cause slight detention.

An occasional trading-house, and a few "*paper towns*," staked upon the river bank, denoted by a claimant's cabin and log-warehouse, were the only evidences of civilization above the old French town of Prairie du Chien, on my first ascent of the river in 1847. The Winnebagoes and Sioux were the principal patrons of these trading houses, where they disposed of their annuity money for trinkets, blankets, and whiskey. But Yankee enterprise has been at work, as may be seen in the fair young towns of La Crosse in Wisconsin, Lansing in Iowa, Winona, Red Wing, and Hastings in Minnesota, and innumerable others of less note.

CHAPTER XLII.

MAIDEN'S ROCK.

As we have intimated, nothing in nature can be more magnificent than the scenery of the Upper Mississippi. To see and not admire, to contemplate and not love, one must be deaf to the voice of nature, and callous to the finer feelings of the soul! How oft, in the few years gone by, have I gazed enraptured from those lofty banks, or from the "guards" of a steamer, upon the waters of the swiftly-coursing stream, wherein the fairy moonbeams danced; the towering shores, or graceful elm of the "bottom lands," mirrored therein, while the sound of the Frenchmen's oars, the boisterous shout of the uncouth raftsmen, the mournful dirge of the forest child, chanting her sorrow at the grave of the departed, and unuttered music, sweeter than the Eolian harp, were wafted upon the breeze!

The lovers of natural scenery are seized with an almost irrepressible desire to enjoy the extended view from the summit of these bluffs; and whenever the boat stops "to wood," they are to be seen toiling up the height, where, ravished by the sight, they remain until the bell summons to a hurried descent. On an occasion like this, by frequent pausing for breath, my feet had attained the acme of my desires. In the foreground, like a speck on the water, lay the "Dr. Franklin," her busy men appearing of Lilliputian stature; near by was the cabin of the woodman, his half-breed wife, and tawny, untutored children at the door; beyond was the extended plain, the densely-timbered "bottom land," with silvery lakes reflecting the sky, and small streams winding around until they reached the large one at our feet. "Why, O why," I exclaimed, "such a rare profusion of beauty, where there is no eye to enjoy, no heart to relish it?" My traveling companion had passed months in the wilderness, had roamed where the foot of no other white man had trod, had made his bed of the bear skin in the Indian's wigwam, or on the cold earth, with heaven's canopy for a covering, and the stars keeping faithful vigils over him. "And there," he replied, "have I seen such glorious displays of the beautiful, that I could not divest my soul of the belief that unseen spirits were enjoying what no mortal eye had seen!" This was to me a new and beautiful idea (let it be understood that this was some two or three years before spirit-rappings had begun to craze the world). Perhaps the spirits of our departed friends are silently gazing upon the enrapturing scene! I will cherish the idea; or, rather, that the wise Creator has evinced his matchless taste and skill for his own glory, and to furnish theme for the admiration of those whom he hath "given to his Son," and who are now "heirs of an inheritance that fadeth not away."

Lake Pepin, one hundred miles below the falls, is an expansion of the Mississippi, thirty miles long, and from two to five miles wide. Its rendering, literally, is "Lake of Tears." The first voyagers who made the explorations of this lake, were accompanied by a flotilla of canoes of the Sioux Indians, some of whom were disposed to destroy their companions in charge. These cried all night over those who opposed them, hoping thereby to gain their consent. Hence Lake of Tears, or Lake Pepin.

"Maiden Rock," or "Lover's Leap," about midway on this lake, an object of interest to all travelers, is about five hundred feet high. Connected with it is a sad legend, a tale of the heart, which lives in Indian story. Winona was the pride and joy of her chieftain father, who in his fondness had pledged her to a favorite brave of his band. She loved another, and promised to be his, or die. The father was incorrigible! No more her laugh rang in the joyous sport; no more she sang in strains of native melody; no more her elastic feet out-stripped her companions in the race; no more she braids her hair beside the mirroring water: but all night long her soul chimed with the mournful notes of the whippoorwill, as she gazed upon the pale star ere it sank to rest. The cruel father had placed the cankerworm at the heart of his dearest idol, as thousands in civilized lands have done, with less excuse.

Winona, goaded to the quick, at last feigns a compliance with her father's importunities. Seeking an interview with her heart's chosen one, mutual vows of constancy were renewed; and with affected indifference she watched her father's arrangements for her nuptials with the object of her supreme aversion. With assumed cheerfulness, she wandered forth with her dark-browed companions for the delicious berry to grace the feast. They knew not the bitterness of her crushed heart, nor the determined spirit with which her sorrows were disguised. She wandered a little way from her attendants, who knew it not until a wild death note struck their ear. As they moved toward her she waved them back, and, as if awe-struck, they obeyed, while with the fleetness of a fawn she bounds towards the forbidding precipice. Wild flowers and feathers of gayest plumage adorn her raven hair, and a snow white blanket enwraps her queenly form. One moment she pauses, upon the brink—raises her arms, as if in supplication to the Great Spirit, and the next she is lying motionless in the depth below. The forest sends forth a wail of sorrow, and the obdurate, but relenting father, grieves for the loss of his darling, and survives her but a few weeks. The faithful lover plants flowers by her untimely grave, and till the midnight hour watches the moonbeams play thereon. He fancies the zephyr's voice her spirit whispers, and longs to go to the Spirit Land. He wanders, he knows not and cares not whither; cold and hungry, he seeks shelter and food in a wigwam, unlike any he had seen before, far away on the shores of the Great Lake. There the missionary is teaching his red brethren the story of the Cross. He listens and believes, and in simplicity and sincerity of heart, exclaims, "Lord, take poor Indian just as he is, poor and suffering, heart-sick and wicked, and make my heart happy."

The abode of the missionary was joyful with the praise of a new born soul, and the "poor Indian" went forth to tell the wonderful story of Calvary to others of his tribe.

CHAPTER XLIII.

UPPER MISSISSIPPI SCENERY.

THE most striking features of the Upper Mississippi are the boldness of its shores and the beauty of its island scenery, mirrored on its unruffled bosom. A gifted writer in Putnam's Monthly—one of the two thousand five hundred excursionists to the Falls of St. Anthony, in June, 1854, in commemoration of the union by rail of the Atlantic and Mississippi, says:

"The celebrated bluffs, which continue in ever varying forms, for some hundreds of miles, do not resemble the romantic highlands of our Hudson; they bear small resemblance to the cliffs on the Rhine, and yet they remind one of the Rhine more than the Hudson. They are unique—they have no likeness—they daguerreotype new pictures on the mind; they call forth new sensations. Their images cannot be conveyed by description, they must be seen; and now that the chain of railroads is completed to the Mississippi, the fashionable tour will be in the track of our happy 'excursion party, to the Falls of St. Anthony.' The foreign traveler must go there, and the song of the bridegroom to many a 'Lizzie Lee' will be, 'Ho! for the Falls of St. Anthony!'

"There is a curious diversity in the form of the bluffs Some have monotonous, heavy outlines, like the horizon line, to which an eastern eye is accustomed; others run up to a sharp point, like the 'Aiguilles' of the Alps; and some stand apart, regular cones; but all are covered with rich prairie turf, gentle declivities, or sharp precipices; and the long grass, absolutely shining with the verdure of June, and brilliantly embroidered with flowers, waves over them. The bluffs at some points make the shore of the river, then they recede, leaving a broad foreground of level prairie. They are planted quite to their summits, with oaks mainly, and trees of other species, as Downing, with his study of nature and love of art, might have planted them: now in long serpentine walks and now in copses, and then so as to cover, with regular intervening clear spaces, the whole front of the declivity, producing the effect of a gigantic orchard. Midway up the bluffs you sometimes see a belt of rocks, reminding one of the fragments of walls on the Rhine; but still above and below it, the same bright green turf. 'If we were to put it in there, and statue it down,' said a practical observer from our rocky New England, 'it wouldn't stay!' But the surpassingly beautiful marvels of all, are the mimic castles, or rather foundations of ruined castles, that surmount the pinnacles. These mere rocks of lime and sandstone so mock and haunt you with their resemblance to the feudal fortresses of the Old World, that you unconsciously wonder what has become of the Titan race that built them; and go on wondering, where are the people that planted these magnificent terraces; where the lordly race that has so kept in garden beauty, free from brush and brake, these 'grounds,' stretching in ever-varying loveliness for hundreds of miles, and tempting you to apply the magnificent insolence of a celebrated phrase, and call the vaunted parks of England a 'mere patch' in comparison. But no! no human hand has planted them—no human imagination embellished them—no human industry dressed and kept them. They have the fresh impress of the Creator's hand:

"'His love, a smile of Heaven impressed
In beauty on their ample breast.'

"We glided along past this enchanting scenery, for four days and nights of our blessed week, amidst sunshine, moonlight and clouds, each variation of the atmosphere serving to add a new charm or reveal a new beauty. Our light boats skimmed the surface of the water like birds; and with the ease and grace of birds they dipped down to the shore and took up their food, their fiery throats devouring it with marvelous rapidity.

"No racing was permitted. The sailing was so ordered, that what we saw by the exciting moonlight going up, was resplendent, in the full light of day, coming down; and, for it seemed as if the clouds coöperated with the benignant commodore, that what was draped and softened by mist, in our ascension, was unveiled and defined in our descent. The boats, at the approach of evening, were lashed together, to allow an extension of social intercourse, and visits were interchanged, and the general voice was of satisfaction and enjoyments without number. The lights of four paralleled boats streamed, with charming effect, upon the shores of Lake Pepin, where the river, unbroken by islands, is five miles wide.

"Ah! you should have seen that beautiful tower of St. Paul, sitting on its fresh hill-side, like a young queen just emerging from her minority. You should have seen the gay scrambling at our landing there, for carriages and wagons, and every species of locomotive, to take us to our terminus at St. Anthony's Falls. You should have seen how, disdaining luxury or superfluity, we—some among us accustomed to cushioned coaches at home—could drive merrily over the prairie in lumber wagons, seated on rough boards. You should have seen the troops and groups scattered over St. Anthony's Rocks, (what a picturesque domain the saint possesses!) and you should have witnessed the ceremony performed with dignity by Colonel Johnson, of mingling the water taken from the Atlantic at Sandy Hook *one week before*, with the waters of the Mississippi; and there and then have remembered, that but three hundred years ago, De Soto, after three months of wandering in trackless forests, was the first European discoverer of this river. What startling facts! What confounding contrasts!"

And the writer, too, should have remembered, that within the memory of the veriest child, all the "improvements" which surrounded her there, had been made; and had she known, she perhaps would have added, that but seventeen years before Franklin Steele built the first cabin there and made the first advances towards the settlement of the territory, as we have before stated.

The "excursion party" was anticipated, and the generous citizens of St. Paul had made ample arrangements for their reception, and chartered all the carriages of the livery stables to take them to the falls. But a day sooner than expected the fleet of steamers rounded the point and received a salute of welcome from the shore. Much to the regret of all, the majority of the best carriages were out of town, hence the necessity of resorting " to every species of locomotive." It was a day, however, replete with interest and long to be remembered by Minnesotians, and doubtless by all who partook in the rare enjoyment of the excursion.

The writer goes on to say: "In returning from St. Anthony to St. Paul, we all left our vehicles to follow the wheel-plow, as drawn by six noble yoke of oxen; it cleared the tough turf, and upheaved it for the first time, for the sun and hand of man to do their joint fructifying work upon it. The oxen (not the men) looked like the natural lords of the soil. It was the sublime of plowing. When will our poets write their bucolics?

"Our next sight, and hard by the plowing, was one of nature's perfect works—the falls of a creek, poetically called by the Indians, 'Minnehaha'—*laughing waters.* Miss Bremer says they deserve their picture, song, and tales. So perfect is this fall in color, in form so graceful, so finished, that by some mysterious accident of association, it brought to my mind at once, the Venus de Medici. The last incident of this day's most pleasant circuit, was an unlooked-for visit at the old border fortress of Fort Snelling. We were received with great kindness; courtesy and gallantry are twin virtues in military life.

"The inhabitants of St. Paul, with the unstinted western hospitality that had everywhere awaited us, gave a ball in the evening to the thousand excursionists. Unhappily, long prefatory speeches, and the punctual departure of the boats at 11 P. M., cut short the hilarity."

CHAPTER XLIV.

NEW TOWNS ON THE UPPER MISSISSIPPI.

On Wabashaw Prairie, in the summer of 1848, were assembled the feeble remnant of the once powerful Winnebagoes, preparatory to their final departure from the beautiful lands in Northern Iowa and Southern Minnesota, which they had ceded to the United States. The treaty had been conducted by a few chiefs, and many of the "*common people*" evinced their attachment to home and native scenes by an obstinate refusal to leave. To the judicious management of H. M. Rice, who was delegated by Government for their removal, we are indebted for an amicable reconciliation and their tacit consent to abide by the treaty.

Difficulties having subsided, a steamer, chartered for the purpose, weekly and semi-weekly, discharged its *living* freight in St. Paul, amounting to from two to four hundred, each trip. These lawlessly pitched their "*tee-pees*" wherever it best suited their convenience, to the no small annoyance of the few citizens, before taking up their line of march to their new homes at the North.

On Wabashaw Prairie, in 1856, like a young Miss just blushing into her "teens," stands the fair young town of Winona; PROGRESS is "*written upon the very bells of the horses*," and ENERGY upon the brow of every citizen.

In the month of June, 1852, there was but one habitable house on the prairie; and a visitor there, at that time, says, "I was obliged to occupy, as a lodging place, the floor of a shanty, which was the only part of a building then completed, save its two sides. Ends and roof were minus." How great the change! Stores and shops, warehouses and offices, schools and churches, commodious residences, elegantly furnished; and men and women of intelligence are here, who *firmly believe that their* town is destined to *surpass all others in the territory, not even excepting the capital.*

Winona *must* be one of the largest towns below St. Paul. It is admirably adapted by Nature for this purpose. The prairie is some ten miles in length, and three in width, and so level, as not to require the grading of a single street, and the country in the rear, like that "backing" all other towns, "*is unsurpassed in agricultural facilities.*"

On the authority of its "*oldest inhabitant,*" one thousand acres have been laid off in town lots, making between three and four thousand lots. At first they were donated, to a limited extent, to those who would build upon them. After the erection of a few houses, lots began to sell at from $10 to $150. Farmers, by thousands, came in to the back country—tradesmen, mechanics, and artizans of all kinds came into town, in such numbers, that ninety houses had been built in as many days, and still the cry, "more room!"

Town property went up rapidly. Lots that found no purchasers at $150, sold, one year later, for $2,000, and an acre of land offered for $50, rose in that time to $900. Men of money and experience have been added to the population, and new projects of improvement engross the public mind.

Hastings, three miles above the mouth of the St.

Croix, on the opposite side of the Mississippi, had no existence as a town until 1853. The rush of immigration to this point has known no parallel out of our young territory. Property has gone up here with a rapidity that astonishes men of the greatest sagacity, and the inabitants are numbered by hundreds; churches and schools have been organized, and every department of business has its representatives. In short, Hastings is one of the "smart" "fast" towns, where no money is lost by investment.

Since writing the above, I have made a visit to this precocious young town, for the avowed purpose of obtaining a sketch of it, to embellish the pages of this book, but failed, with the jocose assurance, that "the business activity and bustle have been such that they have not kept still a sufficient time to obtain a daguerreotype impression." But as *divided pleasures* are always doubled to the participators, I cannot refrain from imparting a little of the spice of this winter ride to my readers. Thoroughly "hooded and cloaked"—for it was one of the sturdy days near the close of 1856, with the thermometer at fifteen degrees below zero—we left our own comfortable sitting room with an exhilaration of spirits, which such weather always here imparts, for a seat in the sleigh of a clerical friend, who was going to attend a "ministerial conference."

The woodmen, all intuitively understanding the necessity for an increase of fuel, with mammoth loads, were hastening to town. We crossed the river and pursued the narrow road winding among the bluffs, now in the ravine and now on the summit, risking the danger of being precipitated far down the declivity as we passed. Load after load claimed the "highway." Nothing more serious occurred, however, than the depredations of a load of wood on the outer garment of my friend, leaving it in a condition more fit for the rag weaver than clerical wear. Again, to prevent a *break-neck ride*, the horse was headed *upward*, until the son of Erin had passed with his load, and in returning to the thoroughfare, there was no alternative but a grand *overturn*—a half-somerset, while he who had occasioned our bad and *good luck* (good in that we got no broken bones), very *kindly* remarked, "it was too bad," and hastened on with his wood, leaving us to pick up ourselves, our sleigh, and its contents, and mend the broken "thill," which was done with a strap from the harness. Finally, after some eight or ten miles' ride, we emerged into a fair landscape scene, where there was nothing to break off the keenly biting prairie wind.

Well nigh frozen, I was questioning if we had not left Hastings to the left, and were now some distance below, when, with *grateful* satisfaction, we learned that it was yet "*six miles there*," so, resolved to endure a little longer, and leave the freezing process until another time, we summoned all our latent *will* to accomplish the ride. Glad, indeed, were we to draw around the cheerful cabin fire of a friend just without the precincts of town, having never more fully appreciated the *comforts* of a home. That evening we listened to an appropriate and excellent sermon before the "conference." The following morning we looked over the surprising town—only three years old—with its neat and tasteful residences, its substantial business blocks, and fifty-six stores, all doing above a *living* business! The world affords no finer farming country than stretches back from Hastings, for fifty or sixty miles, supporting it greatly by its products.

We were especially gratified in a long-desired drive to Vermillion Falls, one mile from the Mississippi, and included within the limits of the town. The utilitarian spirit of the people has destroyed much of their original interest, but cannot rob them of all their native wildness and grandeur. A creek of the same name winds through the fair prairie, with gently sloping banks, and plunges at once into a wild chaos, such as we have rarely, if ever, seen. The fall is created by terraced rocks, some sixty feet in height, and thence the stream rushes madly on through a deep gorge, where rocks and trees, in mingled confusion, give a peculiar wildness to the scene.

Hastings numbers four Protestant churches, and the Roman Catholics have one. With their usual foresight, they have laid the foundation for immense wealth, having early secured a large amount of real estate in the heart of the town. What a blessing to the world would Protestants manifest the same commendable zeal!

The Baptist church, gathered by the persevering efforts of Rev. E. W. Cressey, have called to their pastorate, Rev. John Hyde, a native of Vermont, and recently from Philadelphia; a young man of fine ability, high attainments, and a correct appreciation of the wants and labors of the West.

The mercury had risen two degrees ere our horse's head was homeward turned. We drove to Douglass, in order to take the "Cottage Grove" route home, and found it a great improvement over the other. We, on the whole, concluded that this is a very, *very* beautiful world, and winter not devoid of charms, though the cold *does* bite intensely. Go where one will, in Minnesota, there is always something new to admire—some new

NEW TOWNS ON THE UPPER MISSISSIPPI. 231

phase of beauty. Were it not for SIN, we would want no brighter or better world than this!

At Red Rock we took the river; night soon closed upon it; the horse refused to keep the path, and the dim *snow-light* was our only guide. To increase the variety, "sleigh-sickness" seized me with a firm and unrelenting grasp. Half our time was consumed in hunting the track, and all the while we were in fear of the many air holes; but a kind Providence guided us safely, and we hailed the light of home with delight, feeling that few had experienced more rich social enjoyment and rural variety, in a fifty miles' tour, than we did, in our trip to Hastings.

The editor of the St. Anthony Express gives an incident in his experience, while passing this town, of which we are reminded, and which we quote:

"While sitting upon the deck," he says, "enjoying the delightful breeze and the flavor of a mild Havana, we were accosted by a young man of most genteel address, and faultless moustache, in blandest terms, requesting the favor of lighting his cigar by our own. Assuring him that it afforded us great pleasure to grant him the favor, he drew up a vacant chair on our left—conversation once opened, was not difficult of a continuance, under such circumstances, with so well-informed a person our as new aquaintance seemed to be; especially in regard to Minnesota affairs; for, to believe his own account, he had traveled over nearly every part of the territory, from Iowa to Pembina, from Superior to the Rocky Mountains. He had slain buffalo on the plains, elk on the Red River of the North; dug ores on Superior, trapped with Kit Carson, and sold peltries to the Fur Company in St. Paul, while in the full flush of his power. He seemed to know every house and landing on the river, and by whom and when it was erected.

"'Do you observe that light a few rods from the bank,' asked he, pointing in a direction to our right, and (as we subsequently recollected) accidently grazing with his arm or hand, our left side. '*There*, a desperate encounter took place ten years ago this month, between the Sioux and Chippewas—the latter took some twenty scalps of their enemy, and—hallo! here we are at Hastings. I expect a friend on board here, and will go down to meet him.'

"Upon entering the saloon as the boat pushed off from Hastings, our 'better half' inquired, 'How on earth we had torn our coat so?' Torn our coat! ha! ha! The side pocket was slit about four inches, as neatly as any finger-ring knife could do it, and of course our *wallet gone*. Fortunately, however, it contained only some fifteen dollars, reserved for passage money, so the rogue did not make his fortune by the operation. We made some search for our newly formed traveling acquaintance; but as we saw no more of him on board, presumed he had gone ashore to find 'his friend.' We were half inclined to forgive the rascal for the theft, on account of the scientific manner in which he performed the job, he being evidently no bungler in the profession he has adopted."

On the entire length of the river, where but a few years ago was heard naught but the howl of the wolf, and the "whoop" of the Indian, embryo towns, and farming communities, and Yankee improvements, greet the eye of the wandering traveler, and he can scarcely credit his senses. Everything wears a new, *fresh* appearance; but time will bring the impress of maturity, and that at no very distant period.

The last bark lodge is destroyed, the last skin teepee removed from the village of "Little Crow." The mission house has new occupants, and the missionaries have gone with the band towards the setting sun. The nucleus of another village is there, and Koposia smiles under the hand of the industrious Anglo-Saxon. Cultivated farms stretch far back above the bluffs so recently surmounted with scaffoldings for the Indian dead, and the whole region smiles with plenty. The car of human progress has passed over the land, bearing the motto, "Enterprise!"

CHAPTER XLV.

THE UPPER MISSISSIPPI.

THE scenery above the Falls of St. Anthony, undergoes a pleasing change. Its sublimity is lost in sweet fields, pleasant groves, undulating plains and meandering streamlets, with low, verdant banks.

The agricultural resources of Minnesota, all things considered, are unsurpassed; hence we find all lands subject to private entry already entered, and to a great extent improved. The march of civilization has advanced with the upward windings of the river, and for a hundred and fifty miles above the falls, farms have been opened and are yielding in rich abundance. Captain Pope, whose authority is before quoted, says, " he has traveled this territory from north to south, the distance of five hundred miles, and with the exception of a few swamps, has seen not one acre of unproductive land." This vast region is not only capable of sustaining an immense population, but in climate and otherwise presents great inducements to immigrants.

The timber most abundant in this region is the ash, and birch of small growth, while higher up and on the tributaries, grow the white and yellow pine and other large forest trees. These are cut and floated down the river and at various points converted into lumber for the use of the embryo towns, both above and below the falls.

The towns here as elsewhere are making efforts to rise

in the world's esteem and hold a distinguished rank. Manomin, seven miles above the falls, is first in this direction. John Banfill was the original settler and proprietor of the town, having made his 'claim' here in 1847. His was the only cabin *grown to a respectable size* when first I visited the spot, but long since

> " City lots were staked for sale
> Above old Indian graves."

It is located at the mouth of Rice Creek, which has its origin in a lake of the same name, and its name from the abundance of wild rice growing therein.

Skirting the river are the increasingly important towns of Itasca, Monticello, St. Cloud, Sauk Rapids, &c., &c. The last mentioned is noted as including among its " first settlers," Minnesota's most gifted daughter, " Minnie Mary Lee." Her charming letters and tales of the "goodlie land," bright with her own poetic fancy, bring the living reality to the mind's eye. Long may she live, singing in melodious strain the echoes of her own heart. But I fancy I catch a plaintive note; for the fiat has gone forth, and her pet-darling, the cherished rose-bud of their domestic circle is withered, and the gentle spirit seems to nestle among the prairie flowers inviting her to plaintiveness.

St. Cloud, three miles below Sauk Rapids, on the opposite side of the river, is destined to outstrip that older town. It is located on a beautiful plain elevated above the river some thirty or forty feet, with an easy and natural road from the steamboat landing at the lower extremity of the town. On this elevation stands a large and beautiful hotel in the modern style of architecture, which does honor to the enterprise and forethought of the citizens. In the rear of the present surveyed town-plot, is Lake George, and the extensive rich valley lands of the Sauk River, through which the Red River teams pass in their semi-annual visits to St. Paul. This place is now attracting the attention of men of wealth, and capital and energy are being employed to make it the most important town above the Falls. It has one of the best saw-mills in the Territory; several dry goods and provision stores, a charter for a University, and is the county seat of Stearnes County, and has a weekly mail over a government road to Lake Superior. The entire region of country is destined to share largely in the commerce of the northwest.

At the mouth of Crow Wing River, about twenty miles above the Falls, is Waterville, a young town, of which Lyman Dayton, of St. Paul, is proprietor. The location is a fine one, and the elements at work will not leave it long behind its more advanced sisters.

On the north branch of the Crow Wing River, is Forest City, which sprang suddenly into existence in the early spring of 1856. A few months previous, a young man from the East had surveyed a claim, and thinking it too remote to be interfered with, without '*proving up*,' left for the winter. He returned to find a town site occupying his claim, and some thirty dwellings already erected. Such is the rapidity with which towns are started in this progressive land and age.

On the south branch of the Crow Wing River is Hutchinson, founded by the celebrated vocalists, the Hutchinson brothers. The inhabitants here are of the choicest character, and all business matters relative to the advance of the town, are transacted under the strictest temperance regulations. The conditions of sale of town lots are such, that if in after years any liquor trafficking establishment is erected thereon, the land reverts to the original owner. A noble example, and in exact keeping with the principles of these noble brothers and their associates.

Thirty miles from the mouth and on the Crow Wing river, is Fort Ripley, built in 1849 and 1850, a defence of the frontier against the encroachments and depredations of the Chippewas and Winnebagoes. A stage route and mail line connects this and intermediate points with St. Paul. The citizens in this region have no feeling that they are cut off from the busy world. Many portions of New England and of the Empire State are vastly more isolated than the most obscure parts of Minnesota, while the glowing, natural beauties of the latter, afford unalloyed companionship—an ample compensation for any lack of society.

One hundred and fifty miles above the falls, we come to Long Prairie. Formerly, the seat of the Winnebago Agency was here. At Bell Prairie is the mission boarding-school, established by Rev. Mr. Ayer and his excellent wife. Great good has been effected through their unwearied efforts, with the Chippewas, to whose improvement their lives seem especially devoted. Buoyant with hope they toil on, amid discouragements calculated to appal the stoutest hearts, while even the Christian world has no just appreciation of their valuable labors. Eternity will alone develope their full results.

Still further up, and extending to the British lines, is Pembina, the most northern county, where one finds a busy, scattered population, of English, French and half-breeds. The latter are mostly living in the manner of their red ancestors, without fixed habitations, abiding for a time in lodges, and in character and habits evincing little of their Anglo-Saxon extraction.

CHAPTER XLVI.

INHABITANTS OF PEMBINA.

THE majority of the half-breeds of this region subsist chiefly by the avails of the hunt. A company of hunters are usually absent from their homes from one to three months, and three or four days are consumed in reaching the heart of their hunting grounds. Their women always accompany them to take charge of the spoils, prepare the food, and perform any other service required by their husbands.

The white traders have mostly married in the Indian country, and their children have few of the benefits of civilization; hence the mixed, uncultivated race that flood the land. Some of these men, however, to their honor be it said, are devoting great care to the education and improvement of their offspring, thus supplying, as far as possible, the want of cultivation and intelligence in their Indian mothers.

They are, as a race, brave and hardy; fine horsemen and skillful marksmen, and might be valuable citizens did they not, as a whole, repudiate civilization. In religion they are Romanists, and strongly attached to its forms and ceremonies.

Efforts have been made to introduce evangelical religion amongst them, and not wholly without success. The Baptist Home Mission Board appointed Rev. James Tanner, a half-breed Chippewa, as their missionary, who made long and fatiguing journeys, ostensibly for the good of his people. He accomplished several trips to St. Paul, seven hundred miles, with a dog-sledge and snow shoes, and was baptized here in the winter of 1852. For reasons well understood by the denomination, the patronage of the Board is withdrawn, and he has been deposed from the ministry.

During his first visit to this place, he so graphically depicted the miseries and spiritual wants of his degraded countrymen, that Elijah Terry, a valuable young member of the Baptist Church, was induced to offer himself a sacrifice upon the missionary altar, and return with him to instruct them in the Gospel. It was a season of thrilling interest, when the dangers, trials and difficulties, involved in that decision, were publicly set before him. Extending to him the "hand of fellowship," Mr. Tanner bade him welcome to the hardships and toils of his own path, and portrayed most vividly the scenes through which he would be called to pass. Sufferings from cold, hunger and fatigue—a bed of snow, with heaven's canopy for a covering, the wolves keeping night watch near by, were trifles in comparison to the conflicts that awaited him. "The arrow or the tomahawk," says Mr. Tanner, "may lay yon low, and the scalping knife finish the work. You may be required to take up *my* lifeless remains and lay them in their last resting place, and move on in your perilous journey alone; or it may be *my* duty to cover *your* mortal remains; or we may both fall a prey to the jaws of a hungry wolf, or worse, the blood-thirsty spirit of the savage. In view of all these things, and even more, can you still trust in God and move forward? *Do you still say you will go?*" Every breath was suspended for the moment. Distinctly and *decidedly* came the answer, "I WILL GO."

On foot, with occasional restings upon the "train," they alone passed over the trackless wild; but news of their safety reached St. Paul, and the young volunteer had entered upon his labors with alacrity and delight. The sacrifice was not laid upon the altar to be withdrawn, though there were foes on every hand and threatening dangers all around. Again there were tidings from this remote spot. The Indians had done their worst; for cause unknown, and never yet understood, Mr. Terry had been surprised and murdered. He was found pinned to the ground by several arrows, his back in several places bearing the marks of the tomahawk; his scalp had been carried away by the murderous band.

With a half-breed, he had early in the morning started for the woods in search of timber to be used for the erection of a school-house. At the moment the arrow hit him he was chanting a favorite hymn. The first arrow brought him to his knees, and raising his eyes to Heaven he commenced an ejaculatory prayer, when the second, it is said, fastened him to the earth. Governor Ramsey took active and vigilant measures to bring the murderers to justice, but without success; he also issued a peremptory demand for the scalp, but it was never returned.

Some two years after this, Mr. and Mrs. Spencer were prosecuting the arduous labors of missionaries at the same point. While they were attending upon a sick child in the night-watches, having neglected the usual precaution to close the blinds, a company of drunken savages, guided by the light, sent a ball into the heart of Mrs. S. What an hour of trial was that to an affectionate husband! The lovely and accomplished wife of his bosom cut down so suddenly and by murderous hands, lay weltering in her own blood, while he could not leave her, and dared not leave the house for assistance! Thus for two long hours, waiting and wishing for the day, her life ebbing away with every breath, did he "watch and pray," while she remained perfectly conscious, calmly committing herself into her Redeemer's hands. When the sun looked through the casement upon that scene, the stricken husband and weeping children stood over the lifeless body of that devoted Christian woman, murdered by those she had sought to save. "Surely the dark places of the earth are full of the habitations of cruelty."

Yet, in face of dangers and violent deaths, the Indian must be sought and saved. His redemption has been purchased, and he must be instructed in the "way of salvation." A fatality has seemed to rest upon this station, and all its embarrassments may not here be enumerated. But there is wisdom in their design, and He who suffers them will "make the wrath of man to praise him"—will bring light out of darkness, good out of evil. His assurance is, "What I do thou knowest not now, but shalt know hereafter."

CHAPTER XLVII.

THE GREAT THOROUGHFARES, ETC.

WITHIN the limits of our territory, and within a few miles of each other, are the sources of earth's noblest streams, one flowing southward into the Gulf of Mexico, and the other northward into the Polar Sea—the two thus making one vast stretch through every clime, and furnishing great facilities for commerce to every part of this vast region. The Mississippi drains and fertilizes an extent of country unequaled by any in the world, and is, in fact, the great central thoroughfare of the continent. Bounding the territory on the east is the mighty inland sea, with the proudest craft navigating its waters. Until the summer of 1853, not a tree was felled at the head waters of Lake Superior. The birch canoes of the Chippewas were the only craft on those waters; and a trip thence to St. Paul was a daring adventure, which could only be performed with Indian guides through devious trails, and by enduring weeks of hardship.

J. A. Bullen, of St. Paul, was the first white man who hung his camp-kettle, filled from the waters of Lake Superior, over a fire of sticks gathered on its shore. Here he built his cabin, made his "claim," and resided for several months, with no society but his cook and the natives. But a city of surprising advantages and astonishing growth now stands on lands which were then taken by "squatters" at one dollar and twenty-five cents per acre, and within two years "sell at prices that indicate a value of over two million dollars for the whole." No vacant lands can be found within ten miles of the city of Superior, and lands in its immediate vicinity command fifty and one hundred dollars per acre. Two years later, and " fine steamers, as fine as any that float on Lake Erie, make weekly trips, with large cargoes and hosts of passengers, landing at the dock of Superior." The United States government has made a good wagon-road thence to St. Paul, at an expense of one hundred thousand dollars, " which mingles the commerce and travel of Lake Superior and the Upper Mississippi. The distance by this route is one hundred and seventy miles, and the trip is often performed in four days."

"A munificent grant of land has been made by Congress, for building a railroad from the city of Superior to Hudson, on the St. Croix," which will be completed in June, 1859. This will, of course, be extended to St. Paul; and thence to St. Anthony, which is already under consideration.

"A question whether it be not too cold for any great strides as a commercial city, is frequently propounded. To this one answers 'No. It is not so cold at Superior as Boston; and the climate is drier, more healthful, and every way more delightful. Can a city be built at Boston? The question is already answered. Then, a much greater and much pleasanter city can be built at Superior. It will grow with amazing rapidity, and reach one hundred thousand in less time from its beginning than Chicago did.'"

The mineral wealth of the contiguous region is unrivaled in the world, if we except California; its fisheries and lumber are unsurpassed in the Union; and besides, it is the mart of an immense agricultural country, such as no city of the East can boast. In the Minnesota Valley, coal has been discovered in limited quantities; building stone, of excellent quality, is found in nearly all parts, and abundance of clay, for the manufacture of brick.

Between latitude 47 and 49, and longitude west 97 and 99, is said to be an immense salt region. Its locality was ascertained and defined by an expedition sent out from Fort Snelling, by Major Long, in 1822-23. "Probably there is not a richer salt region on the face of the earth than the one in Minnesota. The territory is generally considered valuable alone for its agricultural and lumber resources. Nothing, however, can be more erroneous. True, its natural agricultural wealth is probably second to none in the Mississippi Valley, but its mineral wealth is not less extensive and valuable. Among the latter, salt stands preëminent." A soldier in the expedition says that they had been traveling for several days over a vast rolling prairie, with no trees or water, the troops and horses almost famishing with thirst, when they came suddenly upon the shores of a beautiful lake, about half a mile in diameter, sunk down in the deep plain. It resembled a vast sink-hole. From a height above the waters, a vast snow-bank appeared to line its shore; but on examination it proved to be an incrustation of salt, as pure and white as snow. The waters of the lake were like the strongest brine; so strong, that one bathing in it, upon coming out, in a few minutes would be covered with a white crystalization of salt. It is said that a short distance below the surface, the pure rock salt lies in strata, like coal or lime rock. Public attention being called to this fact, a "Salt Company" has been projected, and if the results are at all equal to expectation, Minnesota has more intrinsic wealth than any state in the Union; and, it is estimated by the St. Louis Union, is capable of yielding an annual income equal to the entire revenue of the country.

CHAPTER XLVIII.

A FRIGHT.

As before said, each spring and fall a caravan of a hundred ox teams, more or less, arrives in St. Paul. These oxen are driven *tandem* before a kind of cart peculiar to that region—not a particle of iron being used in their construction. These carts answer, perhaps, quite as good a purpose for the trackless prairie and openings as vehicles of a more *civilized* workmanship. The groaning of the rude wheel on the wooden axle is doleful to the ear; but the rich and valuable furs, the rare and delicately-executed specimens of needle-work, with which the rough cart-box is packed, are pleasing to the eye. These are exchanged for articles of domestic use, all of which must be taken back in the same way.

I wish to introduce my readers to a model garment, of curious and ingenious workmanship, and shall therefore be obliged to preface my description of it with an incident in my personal experience. Alone, one evening, in my room, wholly absorbed in reflection, I scarcely noticed a quick footstep in the adjoining hall. Soon there was a fumbling at the door, and as I turned my head in expectation of greeting a lady friend, a figure of preposterous dimensions stood in the half open door, with one arm elevated above the head. I remember no more than that I retreated a step or two, and fell to the floor. For a moment I was conscious of the tottering of reason, which seemed about to be dethroned, when a well-known voice, announcing a familiar name, the sudden divestment of the outer garment, and the appearance of the expected lady, who had kept back until "the surprise" was over, combined to rescue me from idiocy. Equipped "cap-à-pie," a friend had honored me with a call. "in a princely garb," and I, foolish girl that I was, had supposed him to be "the prince of darkness."

The coat was of Russian dog-skin, of a light tan color, and the thick massy hair, falling over the head within, had given the giant-like appearance to the wearer. The collar, cuffs, and entire margin, were of the curling hair. It fitted loosely, but smoothly, reaching nearly to the ground, and was covered with broad bands of red and green morocco, into which twenty pounds of gayest colored silk floss were wrought.

On the head was a blue cloth cap, with a broad cape, wrought with gay-colored beads, and from the peak waved a combination of various-colored ribbons; and so completely disguised by them was the wearer, that he could only have been recognized by his voice.

The thrilling tales and adventures of these hardy frontier men are full of interest. The rehearsal of his own experience, by a Scotch gentleman, was the first to arouse a spirit of inquiry relative to the vast region so rarely traversed by civilized man, and, until recently, almost unknown. He was connected with the Hudson Bay Company, and in prosecution of business had three times on foot crossed the Rocky Mountains between Fort Vancouver and Selkirk. In this high latitude, snows have accumulated for ages, and, incredible as it may seem, often cover trees which are two hundred feet high. Avalanches are frequent; and a providential delay, on one occasion, prevented his company from becoming victims to their resistless power. The entire and only pass was filled with crushed trees and ice, through which, with great difficulty, after many days, they effected their way, often wading, waist high, through melting snows.

Several voyages to Europe, with expeditions like the above, had not satisfied the adventurous spirit of this gentleman, and we last heard of him, with his wife and daughter, on the land route for California.

A romantic journey was performed by the Roman Catholic Bishop of Oregon, on foot and alone, in four months, from Astoria to St. Paul, where, after recruiting a few days, he left for Rome, Italy. Rich and varied were the displays of Almighty power, of chaste and delicate beauty, upon which his soul uninterruptedly feasted, when his ear would listen in vain for any sound save that of his own voice. Amid such scenes, the *skeptic soul* instinctively admits there is a God, and renders him unconscious homage. One's own self becomes a mere speck in the universe, while he *feels* the invisible presence of HIM whose hand hath formed it all.

Could a daguerreotype of natural scenery be made indelibly on the canvas of the soul, the justly celebrated Kit Carson's would present the most varied, rich, and unique, though his wanderings have not reached as far north as the limits of the field which we describe. One of his acquaintances, who was his frequent traveling companion, known in that region as Jim Goodale, was, with myself, a guest at the house of a mutual relative, and gave us a new insight into hunting, trapping, and voyaging life. Scarcely a mile between the Mississippi and the Rocky Mountains, from Mexico to Minnesota, but has been traversed by Mr. Goodale; and three times has he visited the Pacific coast. Possessing general intelligence of the foreign and commercial world, of gentlemanly and dignified deportment, and a devoted admirer of nature, he is peculiarly fitted to be the companion and guide of those who cross the plains. He relates many thrilling and hair-breadth escapes from the attacks of wild animals, and the no less ferocious Indians; he has been witness to many a tragic scene, and has himself been the subject of most astonishing preservations. Several hundred miles from human habitation, the small company, of which he was the head, once found, to their dismay, that their mules had left during the night, conveying away all their "outfit." Mr. Goodale immediately sent his men back to Fort Laramie, and himself, without food, and with no companion but a rifle, followed the track of the mules. In his first effort to obtain food his gun burst, and he soon lost all trace of the trail. He now shaped his course in the direction of an encampment; but that had broken up, and he could have no hope of overtaking it. After being four days without food, the cravings of hunger no longer haunted him. He now changed his course, and directed all his energies to reaching Fort Laramie, the nearest point of relief. Towards evening of the ninth day, having walked in all three hundred miles, he drew near the village of some friendly Indians, who saw his condition, recognized him as a friend, and aided him to a wigwam. To use his own language, "He had now become so weak, that he could not have held out an hour longer." Their care was like that of tender parents for a child. Giving him nourishment with the utmost caution and good judgment, they watched him through the night, resisting his uncontrollable entreaties for food, until it was prudent to satisfy his craving demands; and to their care and discretion he owed his double preservation from death.

11*

CHAPTER XLIX.

ADVENTURES OF EARLY TRADERS.

CAMERON was a trader of the early part of this century, whose grave is on the bank of the Minnesota. Volumes of rare interest might be written from the rehearsal of old Milnor, one of his employés, who is living at Mendota, still retaining strong muscular powers with a tenacity of life rarely met. The following is one incident in the ordeal of their endurance:

The winter was fast upon Milnor and his fellow-voyagers, and they had delayed so long collecting their packs of skin, that the ice formed one night too strong to permit their descending the stream in a canoe. There was, however, some hope of a thaw; and they kept waiting from day to day, until their provisions, of which they had but a slight supply, were exhausted. They had nothing left now, but to leave their packs of skins under the canoe, and take to the woods, in the hope that Cameron, who was at a distant trading post below, seeing the state of the weather, would send relief to them.

The snow was too deep to enable them to carry any burden; and with their last meal in their pockets, they commenced their journey. They met with no game of any kind on the way; and on the night of the second day, were reduced to the necessity of stripping the bark from a tree, which they tried to masticate. The next morning, the severity of the weather increased, and no alternative presented itself, but stopping to die on the way, or making the most desperate effort to extricate themselves. On the morning of the third day, two of the men became weak, and frequently urged Milnor to stop, but he always opposed these delays. The poor fellows knew that delay would be fatal to the whole party, yet the sense of present distress took away all ability to exercise.

Milnor, ahead of them all, came before night to a place somewhat sheltered from the piercing wind, and seeing some signs that the bushes had been disturbed, he stepped aside and found a dead Indian beside the remains of a small fire. He now shouted to the men to come on; and pointing to the Indian told them that would be their fate before morning if they stopped. Frightened at the sight, they kept up a good pace until a late hour; and Milnor being in a part of the country he was acquainted with, took one of the most active of the men with him and after great exertion had the good luck to catch two muskrats. With these they returned to the men who had built up a good fire; and having eaten one of the animals, they all lay down to sleep, and rested very well. In the morning they ate the other before starting; and as they were a little more cheerful, Milnor told them if they would walk like men, he would take them to a place where there were plenty of muskrats, and that as soon as they had laid in a supply, he would strike across the country to Traverse des Sioux, where they would be sure to hear of Cameron and get food. In several days they caught but one muskrat.

On the morning of the eighth day, they had not been marching an hour, when Milnor looking attentively to the southeast, declared that he saw a smoke in that direction and that there must be a fire. This, as he said, had the effect of a glass of *eau de vie* upon them, and they went briskly on for two or three hours. But this cheering sign disappeared, and the men were beginning to despond again, when the thought struck Milnor that if any party were coming for their relief they would naturally be keeping a lookout also. In less than an hour after, he had gained the bluff and saw a thick column of smoke, not more than three miles distant. He immediately waved his cap, shouted to his companions, and set off in the direction of the smoke, and found the relief he expected. Two men, each with a pack containing biscuit, had been despatched from Traverse des Sioux, and Cameron, with three others, was to leave in a canoe if the expected thaw should admit, and at any rate, he would start with an additional supply. Milnor, having rested himself, set out to meet his comrades with the reinforcement, and when they saw him the happy fellows began to dance.

This incident in the adventures of Milnor is very honorable to Cameron, who made so resolute an attempt to relieve his poor companions, when the chances were so much against his success.

CHAPTER L.

INDIAN TRIBES.

WE now come to speak more definitely of the several Indian tribes, found within th eprecincts of our territory. The Dakotas are a powerful tribe, numbering about thirty thousand. Their name signifies Allies ; the nation being composed of many clans united together. To the world, they are more generally known as Sioux—a name repudiated by themselves, as it was given them by their enemies, the Chippewas. Their country, above the Red Wood River, extends south from the Minnesota to the Platte River. Until recently it stretched several hundred miles on the Mississippi.

There is an impression prevailing at the East, that the Indians are cheated, wronged of their 'just and inalienable rights' by our government.

"Alas! *the poor Indian!*" said a worthy, honest-hearted, and (on other subjects) well-informed man. "How cruelly, how *unjustly*, they have been treated! There is not a nation on earth so guilty of gross injustice as our own."

"In what particular, sir, allow me to inquire, has our nation been so guilty?"

"Why, in a wholesale robbery in taking away their lands."

"But sir, does not our Government render them a full equivalent, and even more? So long as the Indian lives by the chase, the more remote he is from civilization the more fortunate for him. I do not vindicate the former policy pursued with them, while I do and must approve the more recent action of the government. He exchanges his lands———"

"But suppose a man comes and takes from me my home in this village (it was a quiet Eastern village) and gives me one out here among the mountains, which I do not want, would you call that justice?"

Certainly not, unless you fully concurred in the arrangement. But the Indians have no individual claims to the land, their lands are common; and our government no longer takes them without remuneration; and I have no doubt it is for the benefit of both parties. As civilization advances the game recedes, and while they will *not* till the land, to remove where game is plenty; is decidedly to their advantage, and the fifty thousand dollars annually distributed among a small portion of the tribe, ought to place them above want."

"But do they never want? Do we not hear frightful stories of suffering and starvation among them?"

"Certainly we do, but it is owing to their improvident use of money and time. *They are notoriously lazy.* They have far more sense than is attributed to them, and they *know* the benefit of civilization, but *will not profit* by it. My views in relation to them are greatly modified since coming in contact with them, and so will it be with any person's under like circumstances."

"Well, if the government is disposed to do right in relation to them, why does it not educate them?"

"So it would do. Two thousand dollars are annually expended on a single band in this way. There are also appropriations for their instruction in agriculture, and *stringent* laws against the introduction of liquor into their new territory."

"Ah! but it is all *injustice*," persisted my friend, "an injustice which our nation can never wipe from her escutcheons; and *must* suffer for, severely!"

I was conversing with a devoted veteran missionary on this same subject. "Such," he said, "were once his impressions, but," says he, "a twelve years' residence among them has entirely changed my views in reference to the injustice of both the traders and the Government. The imposition and fraud is on the other side, while the dealings of Government cannot but be considered as just and honorable. And so far from depressing him, the great defect in our whole system, as it is brought to bear upon the Red Man, is that of not bringing him under the restraints and protection of the law."

The moral as well as temporal condition of the Indian (to our shame be it said), is better in the main when he is far removed from intercourse with the whites. Where access is easy to the settlements, he has *all* the vices and few, if any, of the virtues of the white man. Away from the debasing influence of the whiskey seller, the efforts of the missionary are more potent for good, and in the remote stations churches have been gathered and the transforming power of the Gospel has wrought visible changes.

There are, in all, about twenty missionaries, devoted to the thirty thousand Dakotas, scattered over an immense territory, and, from their wandering habits, difficult of access. However, native schools have been established, into which the children and youth, as far as possible, have been gathered. Books have been translated, and, with the Bible, printed in their own tongue. The "Dakota Lexicon," prepared by Rev. Mr. Riggs, of Lac qui Parle, is a valuable work, and the result of great labor.

The first and probably only newspaper ever published for their benefit, was edited by Rev. G. H. Pond, and was really what it professed to be, "The Dakota Friend."

Said I to a devoted missionary lady, "Your labors are too arduous, your self-denials too great, with all your domestic cares, and a whole band of Indians making constant demands upon you."

"Oh no," she replied, "our sacrifices are very trifling in comparison to what the Savior has done for us. *We shall have to make greater sacrifices, and the Christian world greater*, before the poor Indian is redeemed as a nation from heathenism."

In my soul I wondered, what further sacrifices *they could* make; though I doubted if the Christian world was free from censure. They may repose on beds of down, beneath costly draperies, and be clothed in "purple and fine linen," while the anxious, toil-worn missionaries restrict themselves to a *prudent use* of even *the necessaries of life;* but the faithful servants of their Divine Master shall, by and by, receive their reward, and sweet to them will be the rest of Heaven.

Weary and sick, I was spending a few weeks at the Little Crow Mission house, during the time of their holy convocation—the "annual meeting." From three hundred miles distant the single ox-carts, covered with canvas, and laden with wives and children, cooking utensils, food, and beds, had come over trackless prairies, through forests and across streams, the company increasing as it advanced until it formed quite a caravan.

The full moon was riding high in the heavens, throwing its mellow light on wood and plain, on river and dale, as the procession drew up before our door; and I doubted, if in all her mighty round, she looked upon a scene more interesting. The greetings and rejoicings were melting to the soul. Some of the newly arrived company had scarcely seen a white face, save those of their own family, for a year. Could Christians at home have been there, it would have done them good and moved their hearts with sympathy for their self-denying brethren, who, far from all the refinements of civilized life, uncheered by the society of friends, are toiling on for the salvation of these children of the forest.

To Traverse des Sioux came Mrs. Hopkins, a fair bride of seventeen, when scarcely a settler had built his cabin on the Mississippi; and cheerfully she walked, hand in hand, with her faithful husband. A sweet smile played upon her features as she said, "The fairest home of her native state would not tempt an exchange for her home at Traverse." Both she and Mrs. Riggs would interest and grace the most intelligent and refined circles; but prefer the luxury of *doing good*, of laboring to save their red sisters, to treading in the courts of fashion or dwelling in homes of ease. They understand the true value and design of life.

The Dakotas little appreciate the value of education, and are, as a whole, opposed to the appropriation of Government annuities for schools. A harangue on this subject once greeted my morning slumbers before the sun had arisen. Old Shackopee, with his band, had pitched his teepee directly in front of my window, and thus early had he commenced an oration, the import of which was the injustice of the Government in insisting on an appropriation for schools. They "ought to have the disposal of their own money; schools were of no use;" and the "old man eloquent" labored long and hard to *awaken* a corresponding sentiment and a spirit of insubordination amongst his people. They remained on the ground for several days, and each morning about the same hour the same "eloquent" tones greeted my ear. Probably they expected a report of their dissatisfaction to be conveyed to Washington.

I occasionally strolled among their teepees, and never without seeing much to disgust me; and once I paused before the opening, to watch the women in their culinary operations. One was dressing ducks and another roasting the entrails, which were devoured with greediness; and a kettle of vegetables was suspended over a few burning sticks. Hearing a low moaning sound I entered the teepee, and there a poor woman in a raging fever, with throbbing temples, lay with her head to the fire, and no persuasion could induce a change of position. Passing on to another, I paused a moment at the open door, where several hale young men of the band were engaged at cards; all engrossed, they did not raise their eyes at first, and when at last I was discovered, they uttered words of insolence, and I passed on. Returning to the house, I encountered several little girls with huge packs of wood upon their backs, each of which would outweigh the bearer. A pappoose, perhaps a year old, was crying in the dirt, and at the sister's desire I placed it upon the burden she bore, and on they went staggering under their cruel load; and strange as it may seem, their merry laugh rung out full and free from their childish hearts. Poor children! born to misery and vice—doomed to ignoble toil! Other tribes have been Christianized, and these too will submit to the Gospel's benign influence. The precious seed is now sown—eventually the harvest time will come.

I now recall a most unpromising little girl, whom I

AUNT BETSEY.

frequently saw about the mission premises, almost "as wild as wild could be." She was finally adopted into the mission family, and underwent, in one year, a complete metamorphosis. She had in this time learned to sew and knit with surprising skill; had become tidy in person, could perform many domestic duties; had learned to read and write, and to sing with great sweetness, and spoke English with fluency. Grace, however, had not transformed her heart at this time, and when displeased, her only revenge was a threat to "*run Indian again.*" The Indian children are universally quick in perception, and when the mind is *thoroughly enlisted*, they make rapid advances in any course of improvement.

Labor is deemed an unpardonable disgrace by the men, and even the women think it degrading to their husbands and sons. One once said to Miss W., "Are you not ashamed that your brother makes the fire by which you warm yourself?"

Another complained of hard toil, lameness, &c., to whom Miss W. said, "Why does not your son chop the wood? he is strong." Highly indignant, she replied, "Do you think I would suffer my son thus to disgrace himself!" They deeply commiserate the case of the white man—*slave to the women, as he is!*

The Indians are incorrigible beggars. Give them once, and you may always give, or offend. So, too, must they be doubly rewarded for any service they render you. On the occasion that old Betsey gave me a couch in her canoe, being unable to attend to it myself, I saw Dr. Williamson amply reward her, and satisfaction lurked in every wrinkle of her face. A few days after she called at my boarding-house in St. Paul and demanded full pay, which was given, and she then called at the office of my physician, with her pitiful story of a "lame arm and no pay for it," and he, too, satisfied the demand, in order to get rid of her. No sooner had I returned in health, than with a doleful face, and the "arm lame so bad," she claimed a reward. Having learned the whole I determined to abide by advice, but, to credit her own statement, the arm was never well nor was the debt ever canceled. It is said that she can "steal more, lie more, work more, and withal has more character, than any woman of her tribe;" and I once heard it remarked, that she "had no redeeming quality but insolence."

As a nation, they are disgustingly filthy. Rarely is any article of their wardrobe subject to washing, and the greasy blanket which was originally white, answers various purposes besides that of a covering. The fruit, game and sugar are carried in it, slung over the back; and flour, bread or meat, which they may receive from the whites for their articles of sale; and perhaps just elevated above the shoulder is the head of the pappoose, whose extremities are dangling amid the condiments for the next meal. In their sugar camps, if the syrup is filtered at all it is through the blanket which has been worn all winter at least, and this sugar is offered for sale among the citizens; and not unfrequently the taste of the blanket is distinguishable. I need not say *that Indian sugar has become quite unpopular.*

They are fond of bathing in warm weather, practicing it to a great extent, and but for this and their active life they would doubtless suffer much from their filthy habits. It is not uncommon to see fifteen or twenty, at their village, bathing at a time. Indeed, there is scarcely an hour but the splashing water indicates the pleasurable excitement. Children of all ages can swim, and find genuine sport in diving, kicking and darting through the water with all the grace and fearless ease of young ducks, while their careless, hearty laugh, is echoed by the grove-covered shores. I have known Indian children not three years old leave their homes alone for a swim, exciting no alarm or anxiety.

CHAPTER LI.

THE WAKAN MAN.

The Sioux, like the Indians of most other tribes, have a strong belief in supernatural powers, and are filled with all manner of foolish fantastical notions; and great impositions are often practiced by the more subtile upon their weak and superstitious brethren.

A story is told, and believed, of a young Indian who was supposed to possess supernatural power, in a degree surpassing any who had before lived. He could eat fire, run himself through with a knife, live in the water like a fish, swallow poison, throw himself from heights, unharmed, and, in short, there was nothing that he could not do; and for years he had held his superstitious tribe aghast. At last, he announced that he would cut off the head of a man and restore it without injuring him. His father remonstrated; for he was a considerate man, and wished to prevent the rash act. As they, one day, were smoking their "kinnekricknick," he broached the subject, and the father repled:

"Son, it is not possible, that a man should live and act without a head!"

"Yes, father, a man can live with his head chopped off, until it can be replaced," replied the son.

"Son, I admit that you can do anything but what the gods can do; but when you talk of doing such an act, you go beyond all reason, and blaspheme the Good

Spirit, who will frown upon you. I say again, you cannot do it. The tribe have now confidence in your great powers—if your words come to their ears, there will be enough to believe you can do even this. In the experiment you will destroy the life of a friend, lose your reputation, and reduce yourself and family to shame. You know you cannot succeed."

"Father, it is not strange you should talk so, since you do not believe. I can do what I know I can do."

"Son, my hair is white, and in my day have heard wondrous sounds and seen wondrous sights, but have not heard of a man living without a head."

"Pshaw! you old men, who lived so long ago, whose hair has turned gray, and whose hearts and flesh have become wrinkled and soft like a potato that has been frozen and thawed again—who prayed to creeping reptiles—you could never do anything great, or understand great things; but I have a higher inspiration."

The young wakan man was incorrigible. He resolved to hazard the experiment, and his intentions were soon noised throughout the village, with the additional information, that whoever would submit to the experiment, was not only to escape uninjured, but be "wakan" like himself.

It was not long before a superstitious, credulous, and ambitious youth, unable to resist the influence of such a motive, and lose the opportunity of becoming great so easily, presented himself as a subject. The entire village convened to witness the novel performance. With much pomp and ceremony, uttering strange and hideous sounds, and assuming such postures as the inspiration suggested, the prophet proceeded to his work. The head was dexterously severed from the body, and thus far success was complete. But in spite of all his inspired efforts, the spirit had fled with the blow, and the young "wakan" retired in sullen, shameful despair, to hide himself from the curse of an enraged band, leaving the relations to the accustomed lamentations over the slain, instead of rejoicing that he was made "wakan."

A story of more recent date is told of a young girl, who, in altercation with an associate, and in a fit of passion, had dealt a deadly blow.

The deceased was a daughter of Black Whistle, a morose and cruel Indian, who, in accordance with their laws of honor, resolved on revenge. In anticipation of this, the girl, being an orphan, sought an asylum at the house of a trader, who kept her secreted from the enraged father, until an opportunity offered of effecting an escape to Wabashaw's village, where some of her relations resided. She reached Red Wing's village (where now is the pleasant civilized town of Red Wing), about a hundred miles from where the tragedy was enacted, and was still fifty miles from her destination.

While there, the father obtaining some clue to her, set out in pursuit, with the determination of full revenge. Succeeding in his plans, he was about to take her home to sacrifice her on the grave of his child; but was dissuaded by the interference of a white person, and he then resolved to take her home and make her his wife, or, in other words, his *slave*. Submitting to her fate, she was a long time acting in this double capacity, enduring all the misery of his ill-treatment, and constantly expecting that he would destroy her, when suddenly she disappeared from the band, and no trace of her could be found.

About this time there appeared at the village of Good Road, on the St. Peter's, a young Indian boy, stating that he had just arrived from the plains, and that on account of the disappearance of buffalo, which occasioned a great scarcity of provisions, he had come to their village. Their hospitable natures gave him a kind reception, and ere long he became a great favorite. One day, on a fishing excursion, he fell in with Black Whistle, who related his grievances; inquiring if he had seen the object of his pursuit, and expressing a determination to shoot her, whenever she should be found. The boy very coolly assented to the justice of this intention, and stimulated him to a renewed pursuit. He then again became the guest of the trader, who, in compliance with his request, was about to dress him in white men's apparel, when it was discovered that he was no other than the fugitive maid who had caused so much excitement. This discovery caused her to leave, and again join Little Crow's band, under the disguise of a Winnebago, making known her wants in broken Sioux, and seeking the protection of a noted brave, as some, she said, had suspected her to be a Chippewa, and threatened to kill her; and she begged he would defend her in case her fears were correct. He could not resist this strong appeal from a young and unprotected girl, and promised that no hand should be raised against her, and remain unrevenged.

The various disguises she had assumed, being well noised around, even this protection could not screen her; and some of the people arriving from her last home, she began to fear a discovery, and again disappeared, no one knew whither; and her retreat still remains a mystery. The determination and perseverance in so young a girl, and her well-devised plans of escape from her murderous pursuer, evince a spirit rarely found; and her history, if the sequel can be known, will be, indeed, a romance in *real life.*

The attachments of the Indian women are ardent, particularly when their object is a "pale face;" and wo to him who, taking advantage of her confidence, binds more firmly the fetters of sin, and wins her to desert her own people and the paths of virtue. Such instances are not rare; but the judgment of Heaven will sooner or later overtake him who incurs such guilt.

Virtue with them is not a dearly cherished principle, and yet noble and happy exceptions there are of those who will suffer death sooner than swerve from the instinctive dictates of woman's nature. An instance occurred at Little Crow's village, during the first winter I spent in the vicinity, which illustrates this truth.

The chief had pledged his sister to one whom *she did not love,* and with whom she refused all intercourse. Mortified and chagrined at being thwarted in plans which he had regarded certain, her lover planned and executed the base purpose of destroying her fair reputation. He willfully circulated insinuations against her chastity, beneath which her sensitive spirit withered. She could not endure the gaze of those who believed her degraded as themselves, when her soul was pure as the virgin snow. She was a forest child; but one of the few "who, without the law, are a law unto themselves." Stung to the quick by the consciousness of a base WRONG, her own purity was more sacred than ever. As the inmates of her lodge were one night sleeping around the center fire—all, save herself, who restlessly tossed on her uneasy couch—she slowly rose, emerged from the hut, and made her way through the trackless snow towards the forest trees, to which the whistling night winds seemed to woo her. The dim starlight guided her onward. One moment, she paused and looked upward, as if she heard a whisper from the spirit-world. But she understood it not, or it would have said, "SEE THOU DO IT NOT." Her eye singles a tree, and, heedless of the mournful winds which will soon cease to affect her, the fatal knot is adjusted. She ascends; ties the kerchief to a limb; commits herself to the Great Spirit; and a leap, a struggle, and she suffers no more. Swaying to and fro in the wind, on the following morning, her lifeless body was descried by the distant villagers. A self-accusing conscience forced a full confession from her accuser—her *murderer*.

CHAPTER LII.

INDIAN CHARACTER AND HOSTILITIES.

IN many respects the Indian is an object of admiration, but, as in many other cases, "distance lends enchantment to the view." As an equestrian, he is free, easy and graceful; his long hair floating in the breeze, and his blanket adjusted as no white man could do it. As a pedestrian, he is extremely dignified, strangely contrasting with his wife, who, being the "burden bearer" from childhood, has always a stooping, ungraceful, undignified gait.

Music has a wonderful power in taming the savages. This will oft attract them to school or worship, when all else fails: and they have clear, sweet, sonorous voices. Indian John, or as he is sometimes called, the "dandy" Indian, made frequent visits to my school, and often brought his hymn book, and sang in his own tongue, with some of the pupils aiding him. An interest was awakened, and he expressed a desire to become a pupil. Though he was reported to have been the murderer of his own father, and several other individuals, he was received, and his good behavior and studious habits fully justified my course. Wholly absorbed with his book, or some problem on the slate, the perspiration would pour like rain drops from underneath his massive and profusely ornamented turban, beneath which his long braided hair was falling over his shoulders. He was below the usual stature, slightly lame, and aping the whites sufficiently to wear a dress coat; his whole dress and demeanor fully entitling him to the cognomen of "dandy."

Old Hock-e-wash-ta, whom everybody knows, has had honorable mention in a former part of this work, yet at this point he claims still more attention. Never will the audience forget the smile that was throned upon the old man's features, as he burst into the room, on the occasion of a public recognition of the Baptist Church, St. Paul. His garb seemed composed of all the odds and ends of the cast off clothing of a century. He wore as usual, his tall crowned hat, bits of paper, ribbon and calico fastened to every point. In his hand was a long staff like the pilgrim's in the primer. The pastor had just concluded the ceremony of extending "the hand of fellowship," when this sudden vision appeared, and with the usual guttural salutation "how how!" claimed it his privilege also to *shake hands*. The place and occasion rendered the scene most inappropriately ludicrous, and though told to "puck a chee," (retire) he still kept on, and doubtless would have passed to all in the house, had not the pastor mildly directed him to a seat, where he remained until the close of the exercises, a puzzled spectator of the proceedings. But the old man has gone, with his tribe, to their new home, and perhaps ere this to the spirit-world.

It is only under the influence of strong drink that the Indians become dangerously troublesome; then there is no safety among them. I have known but few instances where sober, cold-blooded murder has been perpetrated upon the whites on their own ground. Soon after the last Sioux purchase, a small company were passing up the country to their new location, and were scarcely a day's drive from St. Paul. They had no apprehension of danger until Mrs. Keener, the only woman, suddenly fell with a mortal wound from an Indian's rifle. One man was severely, but not fatally, wounded in the face. The murderer, who was given up by his chief, assigned no other reason for the deed, than that the white husband was carrying the child, which the woman ought not to have permitted. He was taken to St. Paul, tried, and condemned. A second trial was granted, and finally after lying two years in jail, he suffered the penalty of the law.

Another, and a very sad instance, occurred in the spring of 1856, some ten miles above Fort Snelling. A family residing on the banks of the Minnesota, had adopted a little Chippewa girl, and their mutual attachment had become very strong. The child had forgotten its native tongue, and not only the tribe but the relatives had ceased to acknowledge her as belonging to the nation.

At length, for several days the mysterious lurking about of a company of Sioux, somewhat alarmed the few settlers whose claims were contiguous to each other, and for mutual safety the females were spending a day at the house of Mr. Ames, their husbands being at work but a little distance from them.

The little dark-browed girl was sitting on the lap of her foster-mother, when three ferocious looking Indians entered, shook hands with all, approached the child pleasantly, and offered to shake hands. She shrunk in affright, but encouraged by her foster-mother, who already trembled with fear, she extended her little hand, which was caught in a firm grasp, and in the twinkling of an eye she was hurled through the open door, and ere she struck the ground, several bullets from the rifles of those who remained without, had passed through her body. The women gave the alarm, but before their husbands could reach the house, the Sioux had disappeared with the reeking scalp of the innocent child, who had been guilty of no crime, but that of being born of Chippewa parents.

The Indians are great gormandizers; it is their invariable rule to eat all that is set before them, and when the make a feast, or when the hospitalities of the board are extended to another, it is an unpardonable offence for a guest to refuse whatever is offered, or leave any portion of food uneaten. Dog meat, in their estimation, is the greatest delicacy to set before a guest, and the greatest honor to bestow, is to slay the favorite dog for the feast. Well may the Indian be indignant, if such a luxury, prepared at *such* a sacrifice, is untasted. To illustrate the quantity of food their stomachs are capable of receiving, I barely cite one instance. In the early stage of settlement in St. Paul, a friend of mine permitted an Indian to sleep in her kitchen, and prepare his food by the fire. Two large kettles were suspended over the fire, one filled with potatoes, the other containing a quarter of venison. This, with a loaf of bread, which his kind hostess had furnished, was all devoured, and the liquor in which the meat was boiled, drunk at one meal. The Indians universally wear a girdle about the waist, which is lengthened and shortened at convenience. When very hungry, it is drawn very tight, which is said to afford a great relief to the gnawings of appetite; thus they go much longer without food than those who have not followed these teachings of nature.

CHAPTER LIII.

THE WINNEBAGOES.

The Winnebagoes were once a powerful tribe, owning some of the finest lands embraced in Iowa and Southern Minnesota; but war and the ravages of disease have reduced them to them to the mere remnant of three thousand. These, in 1848, were removed to their new homes on Crow-Wing River. Great dissatisfaction was soon apparent, and many returned to their former homes, with a determination to remain; and government having already expended twenty-five thousand dollars in their first removal, rather than compel them to return at the point of the bayonet, was at an additional expense of several thousands, in accomplishing amicably the desired result.

Some of this tribe are very well educated in the English language, and some there are who till the ground, and have comfortable cabin homes, with stoves, beds, chairs, and even carpets.

Baptiste, distinguished above most, and perhaps all, others of his tribe, is on many accounts a wonderful man. He is tall and majestic in person, with grace and dignity of mien, an eagle eye, a lofty, intellectual brow, and is, in short, a noble specimen of humanity. He converses in twelve languages, and reads five fluently; has all the virtues, and few of the vices, of the white man; is a Freemason and Odd Fellow. In his frequent visits to our capital, he stops at the best hotels, calls on our citizens and the governor, with whom he holds long "talks," walks

BAPTISTE.

the streets with a proud step, arm in arm with his white friends, sits in their parlors, drinks at their side boards, and deports himself as a gentleman. I first saw him in church, where he had accompanied the accomplished sister of Hon. H. M. Rice—a lady who has few equals and no superiors, who remarked, in pleasantry, "that she felt no little vanity in accepting such a distinguished escort." He wore a dark green blanket, and his keen eye rested intently on the speaker, his thoughts evidently digesting the subject. As he passed from church, he bestowed high encomiums upon the sermon, though he probably profited little by it.

He is noted for pleasantry, and politeness to the ladies. In short, he is one of nature's noblemen, capable of giant strides in intellect, of scanning abstruse sciences, and diving into nature's mysteries—a man who might be a blessing to his tribe and the world.

The spirit of insubordination continued long with this tribe; depredations, and even murders, were committed upon the whites residing in the vicinity, until troops and volunteers were demanded for protection. The exchange had not been a fortunate one; the climate was much colder than they had been accustomed to; and though game was more abundant, it was more difficult to obtain. Their grievances being properly represented to Congress, a more desirable home was offered them in the Southwest, and thither, satisfied, they took up the line of march.

CHAPTER LIV.

THE CHIPPEWAS.

The Chippewas are a powerful tribe of Indians occupying the northern portion of Minnesota, between Lake Superior on the east, and the Mississippi on the west. They are less numerous than their enemies, the Sioux, but better warriors. Their language, though sweet and musical, is more difficult of acquisition. They seem, in some particulars, less degraded than the neighboring tribes, but far from being civilized. Though the majority are blood-thirsty and revengeful, yet some have embraced the principles of Christianity, and are living meek, self-denying lives.

Their women are many of them noted for beauty, and the fame of "the Queen" is extended amongst the whites, as well as her own people. Her soft, raven hair falls upon the ground as she stands, which, with her nicely-chiseled features and sparkling black eye, renders her peculiarly attractive. She is subject to less hardship than the women of her tribe, having a home with a sister, whose husband is a white man; and it is said that the heart of many a white man has been led captive by her charms, to whom she shows no favor.

Hole-in-the-Day, or Bag-on-a-ke-shig, the head chief of the nation, is a brave warrior, with noble impulses of heart, beloved by his people, and respected by the whites. He is still a young man, and came into power at twenty-four years of age. His father, also a chief, was distinguished by great bravery and prowess, and at the

HOLE-IN-THE-DAY.

time of his death could boast of thirty-six eagle feathers, worn in his head-dress, each denoting an enemy killed and scalped with his own hand. His son possesses much of his father's daring; but a frail constitution, in which the seeds of consumption are sown, gives evidence that his career will be brief.

From time immemorial, with no tradition of its origin, a feud has existed between the contiguous tribes—the Sioux and Chippewas. The hatred has descended from father to son, with its practical fruits, and though mock treaties have been made, each party has only waited an opportunity to secure an enemy's scalp, ere it was broken.

Rumors of depredations and murders were constantly reaching the white settlements during their early history, exciting anxiety and alarm, and rousing the injured to revenge. The government forces at Fort Snelling were commissioned with power to quell the troubles, whenever amounting to an actual outbreak; but, unable to bring the Indians under restraint of law, they were wholly inefficient.

From the cruel and bloody massacre in the spring of 1850, on Apple River, when fourteen Chippewas fell victims to the scalping knife of the Sioux, who lost not a single man, it was evident there was no safety for either party. The citizens looked for a general outbreak, and expected that the scalps of the seventy who performed their last war-dance in the village of Stillwater, would soon grace a similar occasion among the Chippewas. A month later, and a Sioux was surprised near Mendota by five Chippewas, his scalp taken, and he left weltering in his gore, that his friends might know who had done the deed. The murdered man was a son of Old Betsey, of whom mention has already been made.

Now the spirit of the Sioux was more desperate than ever. The day succeeding this transaction was one of continued excitement. St. Paul was thronged with enraged Sioux, whose hearts panted for revenge. The "Dandy," quietly pursuing his studies in the school-room, understanding intuitively the movement of his people, dropped his book, and in the twinkling of an eye joined the war party in rapid pursuit of their enemies.

Soon after the company had passed, as many as fifty warriors, full dressed, or, in more proper words, *stripped* for battle, gathered round the school-room, their fifty heads darkening the windows. Fear was visible on the countenances of all; and as if to intimidate us still more, every gun was fired, though in a contrary direction.

Shrieks of alarm arose from the children, many of whom sought protection by burying their faces in the folds of my dress, while the Indians gazed with smiles of gratification and evident malice. Though myself much frightened, I feigned unusual courage, and even laughed at their boldness and presumption. I finally persuaded them to leave by telling them that children's hearts were *not strong like ours!* That night our streets were dark with the long line of enraged men returning from their unsuccessful pursuit for Chippewa scalps.

The evil had reached the height of endurance, and at this crisis Governor Ramsey wisely made an effort for a treaty, that, if possible, further grievances might be prevented. Some reluctance was manifested on both sides; but the Sioux were particularly averse to a treaty.

Hole-in-the-Day, though a mere boy in appearance, was a terror to the Dakotas, for he was a brave, undaunted warrior, who had never retreated before a foe, but generally borne off in triumph many of the scalps of his enemies.

In June, 1850, Hole-in-the-Day, with two hundred noble-looking braves and chiefs, a small detachment of United States troops, a few pieces of artillery, the governor, and many of the citizens of Minnesota, convened for council just in front of the gate of Fort Snelling. Here, in the scorching rays of the sun, they awaited the arrival of the other party. At last, when the day was far spent, and fears began to be entertained that evil was at work in "the camp of the enemy," a single horseman was descried in the distance. In breathless anxiety they await his approach. The brief announcement is made that the "Sioux would not be present until the morrow," and he quickly disappears.

Stimulated with the hope of a long-desired peace, the following morning all are again on the ground. The sun has approached the zenith, and still they wait. A dark cloud arises on the prairie; the sound of hoofs salute the ear; and a long line of horsemen dash furiously onward —their object, doubtless, to awe by their imposing appearance. Onward, with the fury of battle-horses, they dash, until fully past the lines, when they wheel, discharge a volley of musketry, and, rifles in hand, dismount. The Governor required the rifles to be stacked against the walls of the fort, and the council was opened.

After all were seated, and the pipe of peace smoked, there was an evident uneasiness on the part of the Dakotas, and the insolent expression followed that "They came to meet the Chippewas, not women, in council." Governor Ramsey, justly indignant, replied that "they were less fastidious at Apple River, where the presence of women, and even children, proved no objection to their cold-blooded massacre."

At this, Hole-in-the-Day, with the tact and forethought of his nature, and unaffected affability, arose and said that "He was glad to see so many sweet women there, and they were all welcome, with their bright faces, *on his side* of the council," at the same time shaking hands with Mrs. Ramsey and others. I need not say that from this time the ladies *were all Chippewas.*

Hole-in-the-Day now, in the presence of his enemies and the hundreds there convened, made the following speech to the Governor:

"My Father!—As you have sent for me, I have come. I came at once, for the reason I thought you would be here to enforce the treaty made by my father Hole-in-the-Day on this spot. I have always submitted to wrong for a long time; my father always did so.

"Since the day our agents arrived among us, we, your Ojibeway children, notwithstanding our many wrongs, have kept the peace. We consider it impossible for the Dakotas to lift the war-club, under the eyes of their Father, yourself, and the many whites that surround them, to strike our unguarded young men and women and children.

"Our Father, you know how we have been disappointed; and we hope that the blood of your Ojibeway children shall not smoke up to the Great Spirit for vengeance in vain.

"Since our Great Father has sent you to watch over your red children, a son of one of our oldest chiefs has been killed by the Dakotas; and fourteen old men, women, and children, while quietly making sugar on the lands of their Great Father, were butchered in cold blood.

"We have complained to our agent, asking for redress; but his answer to our complaints not being satisfactory, and considering that redress was in our own hands, we prepared for war. The war-club had gone the rounds of the villages, and we were on the point of marching into the enemy's country, when we received your message. We came to hear your words, depending on your protection, and placing our welfare and interest into the palm of your hand, knowing that you will accord justice to whom justice is due.

"We, your children, wish for peace; but have made up our minds to enter into no future treaty until our grievances have been atoned for, and the sore hearts of the relatives of our own murdered friends have been made whole."

Our limits will not allow us to enter into detail. Suffice it to say, that at the expiration of three days, the long-desired peace was ratified, whereby all past grievances were to be "sealed up," and future offences subjected to trial by the laws of the territory. The pipe of peace was again smoked, and they shook hands, each with his former hated enemy, and rejoiced in the prospect of the cessation of bloody hostilities and the horrid war-dance around the scalp of the murdered friend.

The council disbanded with evident satisfaction, though with a little distrust lurking in every countenance. .

The judicious and wise management of Governor Ramsey in effecting a treaty for the cessation of hostilities between these powerful nations, would alone have crowned him with unfading laurels; and long will he live in the affections of the tribes whose confidence he gained, and be enshrined in the hearts of Minnesotians.

But more recently, hostilities have again commenced. The treaty is buried: the tomahawk exhumed, and the unpunished murderer draws his reeking knife from the heart of his foe.

When these tribes shall abandon the chase, lay aside the blanket, and devote themselves to agriculture, then their hostility may abate. But not until letters and religion have exerted their transforming power, will they "learn war no more." The Indian in many particulars has high and noble instincts. He hears the voice of the Great Spirit in the rush of the waterfall, and the gentle murmuring of the brook; in the deep-toned thunder and the evening breeze. He sees him in the forked lightnings and the dancing moonbeams; in the wild tornado, and the nodding flower; and yet he grovels like the vilest reptile and cares for nought but sensual indulgence. The "leaven" is at work, and though many generations may pass ere these tribes shall rank among the civilized and redeemed nations of earth, they will *surely do so*, "for the mouth of the Lord hath spoken it"—"*all nations shall call Him blessed.*"

CHAPTER LV.

EXPLORATIONS OF THE MINNESOTA RIVER.

The knowledge of the valley of the River St. Peters, as it was called, until the summer of 1850, was derived only from missionaries, traders and voyagers. The duties of the former afforded no time for minute investigation of its resources—nor did the latter render such accounts as induced immigration, and therefore no just estimate of its real value could be formed.

The first exploration of the Minnesota River was made by a company of pleasure seekers from St. Paul, who chartered the "Anthony Wayne," and went up and returned on the same day, not ascending any considerable distance, but gaining the credit of being the first to supersede the canoe in those unexplored waters.

The glory of this achievement created a desire and spirited resolve on the part of citizens, to go "higher up," and consequently the steamer "Nominee" a temperance Sabbath-keeping boat, was chartered for the purpose. The state rooms were occupied entirely by the ladies, while the gentlemen found sleeping quarters on the floor of the spacious saloon. Hearts were beating high as our boat, after a short call at Mendota and Fort Snelling, for an addition to our numbers, and for "the Band," turned her prow into the dark waters of the Minnesota, where but once before had the finny tribe been disturbed by a like intrusion. A few miles up stream, we struck a sand bar, and remained for several hours, during which time we were visited by one of our sublime night showers, in which as Hennapin says, "the lightnings play upon the ground." A tree a short distance from us was rent by the lightning into a thousand fragments. This was the chief incident of the night. In the morning religious service was held in the ladies' cabin—in beautiful contrast to the savage whoop which resounded from the shore.

The Minnesota forms "the line of beauty," meandering through rich and varied scenery. Unlike the Mississippi, it has few islands; indeed we passed none for fifty miles, when in sounding a bend, a beautiful green isle appeared "like a verdant spot in memory." "*What shall we call that Island?*" resounded across the hurricane deck, where most of the party were congregated for a better view of the lovely scenery. "SMITH ISLAND!" cries one; and "Smith Island!" shouted a score of voices. Yeas and nays were called, and the honor was unanimously accorded to our gentlemanly commander.

A little beyond appeared its twin sister. Again, "What shall it be called?" "Nominee," was echoed and reëchoed, and a vote decided in the affirmative.

The night rain had cooled the breath of summer, and light fleecy clouds skimming the heavens, slightly obscured the sun's disc; if all had been arranged with special regard to our comfort, we could not have been more entirely gratified.

The tables were furnished in a manner to gratify the most fastidious taste, while mirth and humor, pleasant and dignified conversation made up the sum of enjoyment.

One hundred miles attained, it was deemed prudent to

return. Some time was allotted for rambling on shore, and seeking pleasures according to our tastes. Some gathered bouquets from soil which few white men and women had trod before, some examined the quality of the soil: many could only exult in gazing upon the wild scene which lay before them; while others crossed the prairie, and ascending the bluff in the rear, obtained a more extended view. One ascended the huge tree to which our boat was tied, nailing the inscription twenty feet from the ground,

"STEAMER NOMINEE
July 11, 1850.
HIGHEST POINT."

Long before we were satisfied, the bell called all on board, and our gallant and trustworthy steamer was wending her way down stream, almost with the swiftness of a bird in its flight. The novelty of a "pata watah," which many of them had never seen, had drawn the natives to the river *en masse*, on our upward course; when the shrill scream of the whistle would start them, and panic struck they would run over each other pell-mell, evidently terrified; then looking around, and discovering no cause of alarm, they would set up such a chorus of laughter as made these solitary places ring. Either to return our salute, or in mischievous retaliation, they prepared a warm reception for our return, and at every village, a whole volley of musketry was poured upon us, several balls penetrating the sides of the boat, and frequently passing very near individuals at whom they seemed to take deliberate aim, probably with "no intent to kill," but with little concern for the result.

Thirty miles up this river, at this time, is Shakopee's village, where is the mission station of Rev. G. H. Pond, who with his brother, twenty miles below, has long labored amongst the Indians. Here also was the trading post of Mr. Farribault, who occupied a comfortable white house of good size, attached to which was a fine garden of vegetables and fruit trees. We enjoyed the pleasure of a call at the mission house, and also a ramble through the village. I cannot say that my views of the filthy inmates of these lodges, for whom the man of God forsakes all the pleasures of civilized society, dooming himself and those God has given him to obscurity and privation of every kind, were materially changed. Every lineament of his countenance tells the sacrifice he makes! Again, in behalf of these toil-worn laborers would I say, let those who think the missionary's an easy life, spend one hour at his dwelling, and they will be convinced that he "labors not for the meat that perisheth."

The scenery here was devoid of boldness, the banks low, stretching back in the finest prairies or in gradual elevations, interspersed with the largest growth of timber in the territory, consisting of oak, elm, cotton-wood, basswood, butternut, ash, &c. The soil was pronounced by competent judges, of unsurpassed richness, and the finest farming country in the West. A gentleman well acquainted with the Miami valley, said the resemblance to it was striking. Occasionally a bold bluff with a rocky summit increased the variety, but there is very little, if any waste land.

I had feasted on many a rich scene in Minnesota, but this was unsurpassed. It was quite impossible to rid one's self of the belief, that we were gazing on an old country, deserted by its inhabitants, and its dwellings demolished.

A few hours previous to the termination of our delightful trip, the gentlemen organized in convention, and sent an invitation to the ladies, to a seat in the social hall. Resolutions were adopted expressing high satisfaction in the trip, and recommending as Government policy, a speedy treaty for the territory of the St. Peter's Valley. Said one, "These lands ought and must be ours." There was, however, no apparent wish to inveigle the Indian, but to render a full equivalent. Several spirited addresses were made; among the speakers was E. Rice, esq., a worthy and talented attorney from St. Paul, Col. Todd, late Minister Plenipotentiary to Russia, Rev. Dr. Williamson, of the Sioux Mission, and Judge Ewing, late member of Congress from Indiana.* The whole was happily conducted and met a very hearty approval.

The sun was just setting amidst clouds gold and purple, when we arrived at Mendota; and twilight was closing upon us, as we set foot on shore at St. Paul, better satisfied with this excursion, than any previous one of our lives.

We had been where no sign of human life appeared; yet earth teemed with beauty, as if lavished for the special enjoyment of mortals. I was forcibly reminded of the words of another, on a similar occasion, "that new adjectives must be coined before we could convey any adequate ideas of this land." "*Beautiful, charming, delightful, enchanting, enrapturing, overwhelmingly lovely*, yes, the whole vocabulary might be exhausted, and the half remain untold."

The "Anthony Wayne," determined not to be outdone, pushed her way in a second trip beyond the point reached by the "Nominee," and anticipating the "Yankee," raised an inscription, "COME ON YANKEE!" No less intrepid

* Since deceased.

than those whose name she bears, this enterprising little boat could not brook such defiance, and named her turning point "Yankee Bend," a few miles above the mouth of the Blue Earth river, and about one hundred and fifty above St. Paul, and triumphantly brought back the "shingle" of the Wayne, to which was appended "THE YANKEE DID COME IT."

At Traverse des Sioux, the missionaries and their families were invited on board, and the hospitalities of the boat accorded them, with an invitation to join in the voyage of exploration. High up the river is "Cotillion Prairie" so named by a party who left the boat to "trip the light fantastic toe" on the green sward—aping the customs of those whose soil they invaded. No sound of "merry viol" aided their "poetry of motion," but several bands of native musicians were present and quickened their movements by the tunes of "double quick steps," and as such music could not be gratuitous, it was followed by the presentation of *bills*. Thinking the demand quite too exacting, the pleasure seekers beat a retreat, but the brief acquaintance was all too impressive to admit of such speedy separation, and the musicians accompanied them to the boat.

The "Yankee" passed a few miles up "Blue Earth River," the first considerable branch of the St. Peters, and discovered some traces of coal. The Red Stone quarry, of which the Indian pipes are made, is located somewhere in this valley. It is the only one known in the world, and its location has been unknown to the whites until recently. A slab of it was sent as the Minnesota contribution to the Washington monument.

There yet appeared no obstacle to further progress, but the wood and coal were consumed, the weather excessively warm, the ice exhausted; and many of the ladies becoming sick, a vote of the passengers decided on returning. Wood must be procured, and both crew and passengers made alive the green old woods, with sound of ax, saw, and whatever instruments of power could be obtained. While some were thus engaged, an elderly gentleman from Michigan wandered off in quest of enjoyment, ascended a bluff a mile distant, and being much fatigued lay down to rest, and to use his own words "was just settling into an unconscious snooze," when the sound of the bell pealing through the woods, brought him to his feet, which were put in active requisition. For a while he quite despaired of reaching the boat, and found it no very enviable mental exercise, to resign himself to his fate; without ammunition or any means of procuring food, and not even in the vicinity of an Indian village. Redoubling his exertions, he gained the landing, just as the Yankee had shoved off, and was taken on board by the small boat.

The "Pioneer" remarks in reference to these explorations: "We have deemed the exploration of the Minnesota river an object of primary importance on several accounts. As citizens of St. Paul, lying but five or six miles below the junction of the Minnesota and Mississippi rivers, the natural and inevitable point of transhipment from the larger steamboats running below, to smaller boats of different construction adapted to the navigation of the rivers above us; we wished to know, and that the world should know, that the navigable waters above us, tributary to our trade, irrigate an extent of land as great, and at least as fertile, as the whole length of the Mississippi from St. Louis to St. Paul. All this has been demonstrated."

CHAPTER LVI.

PURCHASE OF THE SIOUX LANDS.

REPRESENTATIONS having been made to Congress, relative to the intrinsic value of the Minnesota Valley, negotiations were soon authorized; and in as little time as possible, to all of the Sioux lands bordering on the Mississippi, the Indian title became extinct.

There were ties to bind the red men to their old home— the graves of their fathers and the ashes of their council fires; still they were not long reluctant to a treaty, and in less than three years from the time the first steamer plowed the waters of the Minnesota, its whole beautiful valley was under Government survey, and the cabins of "squatters" were dotting the fertile soil.

The former occupants had passed on, and the eastern boundary of their present territory is the Red Wood River. When again the Indian shall take up his line of march, his wigwam will be built beneath the shadow of the Rocky Mountains, and he will start at the sound of the snorting fire-horse as it passes on its route to the Pacific.

The preparations of Government for removing the Sioux to their new home, and the attendant arrangements for military defense of the frontier, combined profit with convenience and pleasure, and accomplished at public expense what private enterprise had not done. The people, since the "Yankee's" ascent in 1850, had greatly desired further explorations of the Minnesota valley, "but the region being unknown to boatmen, and the risk of running so high amid serpentine windings, labyrinthine dells, entanglements of heavy timber and undergrowth, being considered very great," as no business called in that direction, mere pleasure would not justify so great an expense.

The steamer West Newton, one hundred and fifty feet in length, Captain D. S. Harris, was chartered by Captain Dana, of the Quartermaster's department, to make a pioneer voyage, for the establishment of a new Fort on the frontier. She left St. Paul on one of the last days in April, 1853. Never was a more hopeful, joyous group, than was convened in the ladies' cabin. In relation to this, Mr. Owen, of the Minnesotian, who was one of the passengers, says:

"Our number is small, and those composing it of the most agreeable and intelligent character. With us journey the veteran pioneer of the American penny newspaper press, Moses Y. Beach, and his agreeable lady, accompanied by their traveling companion, Miss Hobbs, an English lady of education and brilliant accomplishments, and withal one apparently specially sent to enliven and add to the charms of a journey in the wilderness. Then we have the lady of Captain Harris, a proficient in, and an enthusiastic admirer of, the natural sciences, which is of great advantage to us in our researches among the soil, rocks and plants of the Upper Minnesota. She has as her guest, a well known St. Paul lady, whose enthusiasm for pioneering, and being the first white woman to set foot upon this and that remote out-of-the-way place, is proverbial. Captain Dana, to whose energy and determination we are indebted for having so commodious a boat for the trip, with several other of the United States Army, and six or eight other gentlemen, complete the list. A very excellent and desirable company, neither too large nor too small."

At Fort Snelling, two companies of infantry, with their effects, were taken on board, which were to form a part of the garrison at the new post. "Soldiers and soldiers' wives, and soldiers' children—soldiers' stores and soldiers' equipments—soldiers' cattle and soldiers' dogs, were huddled together and strewn about the boat from engine-room to 'Texas.'"

The river is at this time high, some thirty or forty feet above low-water mark, the bottom lands all under water. The prospect is fine, the air bracing from the hills, and no one can stay pent up in the cabin. Every eye is open, every heart beating rapidly in rich expectancy.

Our noble steamer plows "like a thing of life" the turbid waters. We pass Bloomington, a clean, tidy looking place, with farms opening all around, and evincing that the rich soil has passed from savage to civilized hands. The mark of the pioneer is apparent all along the shores.

The boat first rings her bell at Shakopee, a town six months old, thronged with busy life. "Quite a difference this," says Mr. Owen, "since 1850, when boats used to land in front of the Indian village just below, and all were compelled to pay tribute to the old beggar chief, from whom the town is named, who rigidly enforced his 'custom house' regulations, backed by his young men as tide waiters and executors of the requirements of a revenue police generally." We now find here the proper elements for a go-ahead town. This is some twenty miles from the mouth of the river.

A few hours, winding among the stately trees of the verdant banks of the stream; and a broken shaft gave all the privilege of a long stroll on shore. Hard by our landing was a "claimant's cabin," framed and of respectable size. Thinking the "lady of the house," in such an isolated situation, would not be averse to a call, even from strangers, we rapped at the half-open door, where with mutual surprise on meeting some old St. Paul friends, we salute each other; but the "*lady*" was not there. Three young men were keeping house, or rather the house was keeping *them*, and they assured us that we were the *first white* women that ever trod that soil. We found no little theme for pleasantry, in their manners of life, their household arrangements, &c. The one spacious room was the apartment for all domestic operations, and served as shop for various trades, if we could judge by "the workman's chips." The declaration, "It is not good for man to be alone," was forcibly impressed on our minds as we surveyed their premises, and saw the need of the renovating hand of woman in their cheerless looking abode.

Thence we strolled to the table lands above the bluff, and sat down on the shores of a miniature nameless lake, which, in honor to the afore-mentioned English lady, we named Lake Frances. To my lady readers it will not be an uninteresting fact, that the "*brilliant accomplishments*" of this lady so wrought upon the heart of our editor, that he deemed the *one week* all too short, and felt that one who could so cheer and enliven the wilderness could bring sunshine to the domestic circle. Hence she became the sunbeam of his home—the companion and solace of his heart.

"Paper towns" are numerous on the river banks, but make very little show on land. Henderson claims some notoriety, and well it may, for its complete inundation at that time deserves special attention. All we could see was an immense wood-pile, on which a lonely looking man, conspicuously clothed in red flannel, had sought protection from wet feet; and a miserable hut, the roof and chimney being barely above water. It must, however, have some advantages, for it now claims to be a "right smart town," and a very well conducted paper is published there.

Le Seur impressed us as a very eligible site, and some improvements by way of *town making* were evident, from the skeletons of buildings which were then to be seen.

At Traverse des Sioux, the whole population, white and red, turned out to welcome the Newton. The Indian village was broken up, but an encampment was there, and about twenty neat white dwellings contrasted smilingly with the verdant prairie, and energetic citizens were astir in every department of business. What a change had two years wrought! Then many hundred Indians were assembled in Council with the Governor and Commissioners, for the disposal and purchase of this beautiful valley. It was during the pending of this treaty, on the bright morn of the glorious FOURTH, that Rev. Mr. Hopkins found, while bathing in the river, a watery grave. In his death the world sustained a severe loss, for he was a *good man*, and wholly consecrated to the work of missions.

Mankato, one hundred and fifty miles up the river, claims to be recognized as a town, and a long call to wood gave us an ample opportunity to see how the "land lay." We found here our old friends, P. H. Johnson and wife, in their spacious log-house, "alone in their glory," and never relished a meal more than the one to which we were here invited. The nice ham and eggs, the beautiful biscuit, the duck-stew pie, the golden sponge cake, and pure spring water, were all such as might tempt the most fastidious palate.

Our progress was slow, owing to the heavy load and time lost in turning the numerous bends. Above the mouth of the Blue Earth the river becomes narrower, and its windings increase.

We were now upon waters new to all our party, the "Tiger" preceding us only a few hours, and felt in reality that we were without the bounds of civilization. But we were in an ecstacy of admiration. The men declared the soil to be the richest they had ever seen, the trees larger and more numerous, and the river more "snakishly twisted about and contracted."

There were occasionally strong indications of iron ore, and some slight signs of coal. Snags and sawyers, the accumulation of ages, filled the stream, and as we tied up for the night the Indians fired a "salute of welcome." Early the third morning we are again under way, pass the Tiger, which was "lying to" to wood, all hands making the woods resound with the sound of ax and saw. This point was very appropriately named "Tiger Bend."

We now exulted in being the first explorers of this meandering stream, and every mile of progress into the wilderness of silence increased our admiration. The perfection of beauty was over all!

Once we saw some Indians in the distance, and once we spoke with a trapper with his pack of furs by his side, more than fifty miles from human habitation. With these exceptions we saw not a vestige of human life for more than one hundred miles.

No language can paint the emotions, when, so remote from settlements, an ample sized and comfortable abode appeared in the distance; or our surprise when, going ashore, we accosted a company of Indian women and half-breed children, and were answered in English; nor was our surprise diminished when we reached the house and found it comfortably furnished.

"The site of Little Rock is a bold point, forming the extreme inner angle of one of the great bends of the river, which is skirted on either side with level and rich prairie land, extending back a half a mile to the bluffs. The point is covered with huge granite rocks, some the size of medium dwelling houses."

It was the trader and his family, with others, who had come down to welcome our arrival—his long cherished wish to see a steamer at his door now realized. He chose this position, so beautiful and commanding, in 1838. The land about is of the best quality, as the well cultivated fields and the springing grain gave evidence. Thrift and comfort marked all we saw at and around the trading post of Joseph La Frambeau, and "Little Rock" has since been plotted by the surveyor and the foundation of a town laid.

We proceeded to our destined point, some six or eight miles beyond, and here Nature had been lavish of beauty. On these uninhabited shores, where the dying embers of the council fire still smoked, and where but a few days since the war-whoop resounded, some two hundred United States troops were landed to erect a defence against the encroachment of the Indian. A strange confusion of bales and boxes, and every kind of "plunder," mingled in the scene.

A solitary Indian approached, and with folded arms and speechless tongue watched the operations of the soldiers, and with inquisitive glance looked at the many barrels as they were rolled on shore. When the soldiers' tents were pitched, their camp-fire built and camp-kettle hung thereon, our visitor slowly and sadly ascended the bluff and disappeared in the distance. One suggested that he was doubtless reflecting on the probability or improbability of obtaining something to eat; another thought he was wondering whether or not the barrels contained whiskey, and in what possible way he could obtain some. But *we* thought of his tribe, once dwelling on those pleasant lands—of his loved ones' graves, and all the tender associations of home and country, and we doubted not his thoughts were like our own, and hence originated the following effusion :

THE LONE INDIAN.

Not a word he spake, not a gesture made,
    As he gazed on the passing scene ;
But he folded his arms across his breast,
    With proud and majestic mien.
The warrior's plume is adorning his head,
    The fire of the brave in his eye,
His pallid lips are together pressed,
    Nor kindred, nor friend is nigh.

Closely with grace his blanket he drew
    As he thought of the white man's skill ;
But he mastered each muscle of face and form
    With an Indian's iron will :
For surely no good was tokened to him
    In the scene that was passing around ;
For the strong defence of the white man's walls,
    Would rest on his hunting ground.

He looked on the graves where his fathers slept,
    On the spot where his teepee had stood—
On the stream where glided his light canoe,
    And the wild deer coursed in the wood ;

And never again to his vision would seem
    The sky so bright and fair,
Or earth be dressed in such beauty and green,
    Or so pure and serene the air.

The pale faces come, so potent in skill!
    His own race were dwindling away;
The remnant doomed, how brief the hour,
    They might on their hunting-ground stay.
And sadly, oh sadly, his spirit was stirred,
    For life was bereft of its charms—
Since these flower-clad plains and crested bluffs
    Were marked for the white man's farms.

And closely, more closely, his blanket he drew,
    More firmly his lips compressed;
And stronger he folded his brawny arms
    O'er his painfully heaving breast.
His eagle eye had divined the scene—
    The river and plain he has crossed;
And he climbs the bluff, and, westward away,
    He is soon in the distance lost.

The following morning we roamed through natural parks and flower gardens, and snuffed the pure air of the prairie, until our being seemed possessed with a new inspiration, and our spirit scarce communed with earth.

High upon a bluff overlooking the scene of the busy soldiers and boatmen, so high that the distant hum of a hundred voices scarce reached my ear; with tall trees gracefully waving their long arms above my head, and flowers nodding all around, I sat down alone to meditate. There is, kind reader, a spell, a charm, an indescribable, unanalyzed something about this fair land, unknown in the seats of classic lore; in fashion's halls; in cities' crowded marts; and which is peculiar to Minnesota. 'Tis not the *name*, but it is a spirit emanating from the Creator's presence. Under such influences I sat down to meditate.

"What a country is ours! How vast and inexhaustible in resources; yet, comparatively few know anything of its intrinsic value; its innate, undeveloped wealth, its glorious scenery, and unparalleled beauty!" Then my mind ran off towards the rising sun; for memory still lingers around the scenes of my early home, and the loved ones there! The heart clings to its rooted loves. The sacred ties of home are always hard to sever; but when transferred to a home on this noble soil, there is scarcely anything of sufficient potency to weaken them. Trials but rivet the chain; and time imparts strength to the principle.

I have never so forcibly felt the magnitude of our national glory, the extent of her resources, or the vastness of the field for the development of her energies, as when giving free scope to contemplation amid scenes like those described above. I have never so felt my soul glow with enthusiasm, with the fact that I am an American woman, as in scanning the vast field which the West presents for the exercise of our best faculties, for effort and expansion.

My spirit's sweet communion was broken by the growl of the Tiger, which, panting and puffing, was nearing the bend below. Half doubting my own identity, or the fact of having any connection with humanity, and with one long earnest gaze upon the rare scene, I descended to the river. Here I found my friends surrounded by a troop of Indians, to whom our proceedings were as novel, as was their appearance to the ladies, who, for the first time stood amid such a company.

13*

Several valuable trinkets of their own manufacture, and worn by them, were purchased from the natives, and generous presents bestowed by our company, made bright with gladness the countenances of those who received them, the less fortunate ones looking sad and displeased. And we, who had no jealous husbands in the way, were half inclined to fall desperately in love with a handsome, noble looking young brave, who excited the envy of his comrades by the numerous presents he received.

But the bell calls "all aboard," and the few who return, make their regretful adieus to white friends and Indians, and are soon hurrying down the rapid current. The abrupt bends, and now the strong wind, send us hither and thither, now dashing into the woods, now smashing down trees, till at last we are fast, not to the land, but in a mass of trees, where we remain twenty-four hours, the wind blowing a perfect hurricane. At last there is a calm, the boat "fires up," and at twilight we are tied up, *woodless*, at the point known as Cameron's Grave. It was "holy time," but after being pent up in the cabin all night, so long without exercise, we could not resist the temptation to a stroll on shore the next morning. It was a beautiful wildwood that adorned that high bluff, and we ascended to its summit watching the shaded waters, and the golden-edged clouds until the night dews admonished us to descend. The woods were gleaming with torch lights, and the echoes of many axes were ringing through them.

The following day excitement ran high; so large a boat in so narrow, rapid, and serpentine a stream, might have encountered serious difficulties with any other than Captain Harris at the helm. His careful, quick, discerning eye, saw everything at a glance, and made all his calculations with a lightning velocity of thought; so that we struck no snags, collapsed no flue, and burst no boiler; though we did tear off the guards, throw down the pipes, and leave the cabin maid's-washing of linen "high and dry" on a tree, which bent down to receive the line. This trip alone, would entitle Captain Harris to a wreath of fame.

We tied up next a few miles above Traverse, and learned on our arrival there the following morning, that the little community on the previous evening, was thrown into a state of great excitement and confusion. A young man, named Starr, had several months before made a claim in the immediate vicinity, improved it, and left on business. Three brothers, named Kingsley, arrived in his absence, and though warned by the people to desist, they tore down his cabin, built their own, and made all their arrangements as if they had a right so to do. Starr returned, and knowing that both law and justice would sustain him, adhered to his right. The Kingsleys determined to drive him off, and not effecting it otherwise, this evening had shot him; though then alive he died in a few days.

The citizens were unanimous for hanging or shooting the murderers forthwith. They had not been organized into a county; no magistrate was yet appointed, and to wait the tardy movements of law, the guilty men might escape from justice. The missionaries remonstrated against putting them to death, and therefore the people burned their cabins, shaved their heads, and with the savage "cat-o'-nine-tails" whipped them at the post, until they begged for death, and the last man of the thirty engaged in whipping them was exhausted.

They were then sent adrift in a canoe, to live if they could, and under penalty of death if they should return. How plainly government is an ordinance of God the present improved condition of our territory, in contrast with its then unorganized, lawless state, attests. May we duly prize our blessings and be grateful.

The achievement of the "Newton" was hailed with acclamations of joy, by the people of St. Paul, and the territory generally; and never will any who were on board, recount the events of that week, but with feelings of inexpressible satisfaction, and a conviction that the half of what their eye had seen had not been told.

CHAPTER LVII.

LAND TRIP THROUGH THE MINNESOTA VALLEY.

During the summer of 1856, our territory was visited by Rev. B. M. Hill, D.D., Corresponding Secretary of the Baptist Home Mission Board, for the purpose of ascertaining its religious aspects, and investigating its spiritual wants. For this he traveled nearly six hundred miles in various directions, and mostly by land, following the routes of the principal thoroughfares; thus having more ample field for observation and study.

It was my good fortune to be one of the carriage party, in his tour through the Minnesota Valley, together with Rev. A. M. Torbet and Mrs. Lyman Dayton; and to the courtesy of the latter, we were all indebted for the rich and rare feast of enjoyment. Her elegant carriage would have vied with many of Broadway; but was not at all unsuitable to the smooth, hard-beaten roads of the level prairies.

It was an oppressively warm afternoon, in midsummer, that the spirited western steeds were headed "*up country,*" promising us an opportunity of "sight-seeing" on land, in a direction we had only traveled by the river. After crossing the river, at Fort Snelling, the prairie presented no striking variations, and nothing *new* greeted the eye, until we approached the timber, about seven miles above, when a church spire loomed up in the distance. This we subsequently learned was erected by Rev. S. W. Pond, formerly a missionary to the red man; and here a few scattered sheep weekly gather, and the *word of life* is dispensed.

The scenery is now varied with rich woodlands, through which a small winding stream is coursing its way. The golden tints of closing day are reflected from prairie, river, and woods, as we cross to the south side of the Minnesota, at that delicious hour when Nature, hushed to rest, sheds a subduing influence upon the heart. So smooth and shorn did the distant bluffs appear, with the dark shadows in the deep ravines, that Mr. T. suggested that "some Indian maiden must have passed over them with her broom."

We were not prepared to see the tokens of improvement, the opened farms, fields of ripening grain, and neat farm houses scattered all along our route, on soil where but three years previous, the red man's teepee had stood, and the "Indian lover wooed his dusky maid."

Dark clouds gathered in the heavens, big rain drops come pattering upon our carriage, and night closed around us; but we were not far from Shakopee, as the lights from its numerous casements indicated; where we found comfortable quarters at the "Wasson House"—a far better house in all its appointments than would be expected in so new a town. Only six years before we stood on the ground of this embryo city, walked through the Indian village, visited the house of the missionary, and placed its present advance in civilization at least half a century in the future.

A refreshing sleep, an early breakfast, and we were again on our way; a bright sun and smiling earth imparted buoyancy to the spirits, and we determined to proceed. A group of Indians, seated in a circle on the ground, with white eagles' feathers weaving from every head, was a novel sight to the Doctor. They were *en route* for Washington, being delegated by their band.

The country, as we advanced, became much diversified, and some portions really picturesque, which, with the magical workings of improvement, elicited constant ejaculations of surprise and admiration. Living streams of purest water, ever and anon, crossed our way, inviting the thirsty beasts *to drink*, and *we* (the ladies), on such occasions, became pedestrians, and greatly did we relish the exercise, often distancing the carriage so far as to have ample time to gather boquets and wild fruit which grew along our way.

Once we rested at the door of the "Jordon House;" politely entertained by its loquacious owner, who gratuitously imparted to us, from his vast fund, much information respecting this beautiful and fertile region. The "house" is a small cabin, of two rooms (at least we saw no more), on the confines of the most beautiful prospects ever spread before the eye of man. Riding along, we passed over a high prairie, descending on either side. On the one hand was the Minnesota, with its wooded bluffs of varying forms, on the other, woodlands of richly varying green. For ten miles the view was one of extreme loveliness. On the margin of a heavy belt of timber we halted at the door of a cabin, and the rap was responded to by a hale frontier man, who was taking his noon repast.

"Can you tell us, sir, where we are?" was the first inquiry of our party.

"In the territory of Minnesota, sure," was the prompt response, "and on the road to most any place beyond here."

"But what means the bad road over which we last came; we feared that we were on the wrong track?"

"Only changed its course, by fencing a field. You may be sure you are right."

"Right for La Seur?"

"Yes, or any other place."

"Any chance for dinner on the route?"

"Your best chance will be at the Frenchman's, as you enter the big woods."

"How far is it, there, pray?" for our appetites were becoming somewhat whetted by the bracing air.

"Well, about six miles."

A consolation, this, to hungry men and women; but we had all, before this, learned to make "a virtue of necessity," and now rejoiced in the fact, that it was *no further*. Our horses, too, seemed to smell the dinner afar off, and pushed past the emigrant wagons, cabins, and farm houses, with renewed ambition. We admired "Bell Plain," notwithstanding our eagerness for dinner. Again we call to inquire the distance; and some tempting melons, by the proffer of still more tempting lucre, find their way into our carriage, and are very refreshing as we journey on.

The "Big Woods" in the distance! At length "*the Frenchman's*" cabin is indistinctly visible through the foliage. We hailed it as the harbinger of *refreshment*, and sat down amid the dirt, "with sweet delight;" but there was a well-filled table, with a good French cook. Three immense beds and a cradle composed the furniture of the sitting-room; and wearied as we were, we would sooner have thought of an hour's repose beneath those mammoth trees, than on such a mountain of feathers. Our gentlemen rested upon the "*soft side*" of the floor, with shawls for their pillows, while *we* strolled in the dark shade of the green woods.

"Twelve miles through the woods," declared one of our party, as we were again seated in our carriage. I have always loved the woods—the warbling of its songsters, the hum of its many insects, and the mournful cadence of the breeze in its deep recesses. And so absorbed was I in this rich feast, that I scarcely noticed the many windings and twistings of the road, or the numerous stumps, of an undesirable height, standing in close neighborhood to each other, and occasionally in no desirable proximity to the carriage.

Tiny lakes smiled amid the foliage, and the smoke of the emigrant's camp fire, and the white canvas of his wagon, enlivened the way.

The sun was casting his golden rays horizontally through the dense foliage, when deep-muttered thunders gave warning of the approach of one of our sublime summer showers. Strong trees were soon bending beneath the blast, and interlacing their long branches overhead, and in strong contrast with the black clouds, the lightning flashed vividly. Approaching a stream, a fallen tree intercepted the way; and as this was no uncommon occurrence, where the course of the road had been changed, we concluded, without investigation, to turn into the slight wagon track to the right. We proceeded about two miles without a sign of human habitation; and finally we hail with joy, the sight of the rudest specimen of a cabin. Our Reverend Doctor raps at the door; no answer is returned; a slight push and it flies open, but reveals no inmates, though signs of its having been occupied are visible. The rain is now dripping from every part of his garments as he enters the carriage, and proclaims this the terminus of the road. It may have rained *as* hard—it may have rained *harder*, in Minnesota, but never "within the memory of the oldest inhabitant;" and those old woods never echoed the gushings of more cheerful spirits than now, while we retrace our winding way.

The deceptive tree which drove us from the track, had been prostrated by the wind but a few moments previous to our reaching it, as we subsequently learned from a wagoner who was a little in advance of us. A few moments sooner and we might have been crushed by the fall! A fine road across the fordable stream, soon took us out of the woods, and La Seur appeared to our anxious view.

The horses were reined up to the door of the "hotel," but neither landlord, hostler, or any other useful appendage to a frontier tavern, was "at home;" and being informed that there was a comfortable house at "Upper La Seur," one mile beyond, we soon found ourselves around the well-filled, wholesome board of an old *St. Paulite*. The cabin in the woods, on which we had unceremoniously intruded, proved to be the property of our La Seur landlord; so absolution was granted without severe penance.

We drove from La Seur with light hearts, refreshed in spirit and body. The atmosphere was cooled by the night rain, and there was no dust on the smooth prairie road. Our eyes were continually opening on the new beauties and rare excellencies of the country, which had been already well appreciated, and hundreds of acres·were smiling with the golden harvest. Surely the Minnesota valley *is the* great agricultural region of the north-west.

There is no language which can convey an adequate

impression of its vast resources. The possession and improvement of all this rich valley, resulted, in a great measure, from so trifling a cause as the chartering of the "Nominee" for a pleasure trip, by St. Paul citizens.

The progress of Traverse has been slow in comparison to that of some of its younger sisters; but it smiles still, amid enchanting scenery, and is an inviting spot for quiet rural homes.

The young city of St. Peter is distant one mile from Traverse, a school section intervening, and is making rapid strides in settlement and honorable distinction among the cities of the north-west. A more definite notice of this unrivaled young city seems to be here demanded.

The original site of the town was "claimed" by Captain Dodd, in 1852. The sagacity of George Hezlup, esq. determined it as a most desirable point for a town, and by him the original plot of St. Peter was surveyed in 1854. The first frame dwelling was erected the same year, by Mr. Johnson, whose wife was the *first* white woman resident there. Let my reader remember, that our visit was in less than two years from the time of the erection of the first house, and now neat and tasteful cottages, stores, and business blocks, warehouses, mills, and a fine, substantial hotel, of stone, three stories high, were scattered in admirable irregularity over that fair site, in delightful connection with the verdant, rolling, ascending plain. The "St. Peter's Courier" is a well-conducted paper, published here. The citizens are of the most desirable character—not the refuse of other towns, but men and women of standing and influence, who are bending all their energies to place the stamp of maturity upon the youthful city, whose population, with the close of 1856, numbers little less than one thousand.

The St. Peter's post-office is in the receipt of a daily mail, and has five stage routes leading from it. Every one acquainted with the geography of the country cannot but be impressed with the advantage of this over every other point in the entire valley, as the great railroad center of the territory. In less time than is required by the cautious New Englander to deliberate on its feasibility, the *westernized* Yankee, with his *double pressure of steam power*, will have built a road from Dubuque to St. Peter, and the steam horse will have left the slow emigrant wagon far in *the rear*. And before the telegraph wires will have conveyed the intelligence of its completion to the Atlantic coast, another, and yet another, will be completed, and stock taken for connecting it with St. Paul, St. Cloud, and various other points. This is no visionary speculation, but the sober calculation of reason, as deduced from observation and experience, and an *actual knowledge* of the elements at work. St. Peter must and *will* be *the* grand center for the Minnesota Valley trade—*the St. Paul* of the Minnesota River; *not a rival, but one of the two important towns of Minnesota.*

Having seen all the sights of town, and become confident of all above stated, we took a regretful leave, after having secured a site for a Baptist Church, donated by the landholders. It should have been before stated, that a liberal policy has been pursued in relation to churches, and a site is designated for each of the four leading denominations, Baptists, Presbyterians, Methodists, and Episcopalians.

Our horses now felt the inspiration of being "homeward-bound," and we resolved to reach the five-mile house, the most inviting in appearance of any in the woods, though *every* house is open for the entertainment of travelers.

In immediate proximity to the dwelling, the underbrush had been removed, and majestic trees threw their long shadows aslant the clean-swept yard, where flowers grew and children sported; and a fine field of wheat, and another of corn, at the right and left, testified to the quality of the soil. A crystal spring issued from the base of a giant tree in the rear of the house, and this, made to pass underneath a trough, hewn from the trunk of a tree, subserved the purposes of cellar, milk-room, and pantry.

All the blithesomeness of childhood returned, and we quite coveted a race with the squirrels, or to take wings with the birdlings and soar to the topmost branches of the tallest trees. At supper *we* announced the fact that we *had* been to the top of a tall tree—though, in fact, it had fallen from its former estate, and we took a horizontal direction amid its boughs. Having played with the children, sported with the house dog, searched out all the mysteries and beauties of the environs, till wearied nature *begged* repose, we crawled beneath musketo bars, into one of three beds, which, in a spacious room, furnished accommodation for ourselves, with the mother and five children, and sunk away to the refreshing shades of dream-land, with nought to disturb our slumbers save the *snore* of the many sleepers above, and an occasional *out-cry* among the juvenile inmates of our room.

We learned that the family (and certainly one of which Minnesota need not be ashamed) had been induced to emigrate from Indiana, by representations, as they said, "from the pen of Miss ———," nor were they a *little* surprised on learning that she had been the guest of the previous night—one whom they had particularly desired to see, and to thank, for presenting the inducements that brought them to their lovely woodland home.

The dew drops glitter in the sun, like so many diamonds; and we are early out for a refreshing draught of pure air. Seated on a huge stump, abstracted in reflection, we were recalled to consciousness by a well-known voice from the back door exclaiming—

"Patience on a monument!"

"Thank you, Doctor! but it would have been vastly more poetic to have descried a 'wood nymph.'"

"Yes; but wood nymphs would have no necessity for breakfast, which I have come to announce, and lest you are actually changed to one I have ordered the horses that as soon as it is despatched we may be under way."

We could hardly decide on a preference between the limited foot rambles or the more extended sight-seeing from the carriage. The woods rang with native melody, every leaf glittered with its sparkling dew in the early sun, and our spirits seemed to hold communion with the good and beautiful. All too soon we emerge into an open country, and in the midst of interesting and animated conversation we are admonished of the fact that we are off the track. All, save our reverend driver, tried to solve the mystery when and where we left the main road: a close observer might have seen a twinkle in *his* eye, and yet an air of uncertainty which left us no room for query. We occasionally passed, or were in sight of, a claim cabin, but no token of human life was any where visible.

After miles over this cart-road, we steer for a habitable cabin, which appears in the distance. The inmates are "not at home," but a slight insight is obtained into their domestic arrangements, revealing some of the characteristics of frontier life to the uninitiated of our party. Several months later we are assured that this dereliction from the right path was all a *ruse* on the part of ——, acting upon a desire to see that portion of the country which we would not otherwise accomplish. We concluded we might safely recommend him for a topographical engineer. We had no further incidents worthy of record, save that our horses undertook to explore the depth of the mud beneath a corduroy bridge, and one became so alarmingly lame that we feared his ability to reach home. This was rather increased than diminished when we left Shakopee the following morning, but nothing worthy of note transpired until we were within a few miles of the Fort, and passed the last stopping place. As if to add to our dilemma, the patent wheels became *fast*, and no coaxing would induce them to turn. There was no alternative but to return two miles to the nearest house. But in view of our lame horse, and the immovable wheels, *we*, with the obstinacy of most ladies, preferred to "go ahead!" There was not a shrub to afford a shade, nor even a stone on which to rest, while the burning heat of the sun was scarcely relieved by a breeze; but we walked on between three and four miles, and hailed with delight the sight of a fenced field. We took a rail from the fence and *sat down* to *real enjoyment*, spiced with not a little *fun*. While we were vigorously fanning ourselves with our bonnets, two carriages drew near, in which we recognized the faces of friends, and finally we yielded to their solicitations to ride. Having crossed the ferry at the Fort we await our party, forget our fatigue in the pleasing rehearsal of various incidents, and arrive home, feeling that the retrospect of the romantic trip would have been incomplete without this last incident.

CHAPTER LVIII.

SOUTHERN MINNESOTA.

SOUTHERN MINNESOTA is attracting much attention, and thousands are annually finding homes—desirable homes—on its fertile plains, the unentered lands of to-day being occupied to-morrow.

This portion of our territory is said to be "rich in every variety of soil and varied with every phase of surface—forest, opening, and prairie. It is watered generally with purer streams than we have seen elsewhere. These streams, rising from and fed by springs which gush out from almost every high locality, supply an abundance of water-power, which the capital and energy of that section are fast turning to account. On every hand saw and flouring mills are erected or are in progress. Villages, which in the East would be the growth of a quarter of a century, have sprung into existence within two years, and that without exceeding the wants of the adjacent country. The whole section, when the recent extinguishment of the Indian title is considered, seems to the traveler a panoramic illusion, rather than the product of sober, delving labor."

In 1854, Rev. J. R. Cressey commenced the labors of an itinerant missionary in this section, when on his field from Iowa line to the head of Lake Pepin, there were not one thousand souls; six months later and the population is eight thousand, and two years later it numbers more than twenty thousand.

The amount of lands entered at the Winona Land Office is almost incredible. Two hundred thousand dollars have been received in thirty days, at the rate of one dollar and twenty-five cents per acre, and most of it preëmpted by actual settlers.

The soil is of the first quality, all ready for the plow, with sufficient timber for fencing and fuel. A squash raised near Winona, weighed two hundred and twenty-one pounds, and measured seven feet ten inches in circumference. A watermelon also weighed sixty-four pounds.

Several inland towns have sprung up in the Cannon River Valley, which are rapidly increasing in wealth and population. Cannon City, Cannon Falls, Northfield, Lakeville and Farribault, are claiming most attention. The latter is the county seat of Rice County, about fifty miles from St. Paul, forty from Hastings, and fifty from Red Wing. "The town site is on a point of one of the most beautiful and rich prairies of Minnesota. It is surrounded on three sides with a belt of the best timbered land in the territory. There is a daily line of stages established between this point and Hastings, and also from Red Wing to this place. The roads between these places and Farribault are literally dotted with teams, conveying wares and merchandise to different points in that vast region; and the emigrant's wagon is to be met at frequent intervals, freighted with the utensils and furniture required by those who are destined to convert the public wilderness into a fruitful and remunerative private garden."

"The population of this place is about twelve hundred —a town built up without the powerful assistance of the press, or any superfluous abundance of 'gas.' A good school is in operation, a Baptist Church has been organised, and the Gospel proclaimed by ministers of several denominations. Several stores are doing a good business, and several saw-mills are in active operation. By the way, every pioneer of this new country regards the saw-mill with no ordinary interest, for on *it* he is dependent for home comforts and the general prosperity of the country."

We are often lost in enthusiastic (not visionary) admiration of this noble, unequaled land! We wonder if earth has a more perfect Eden! In its pure bracing atmosphere, the invalid will ever find a panacea, a temporary relief; and the languid frame will be invigorated by draughts from the pure fountains which gush from every hill side.

Stand with me, gentle reader, upon some of those high bluffs which skirt earth's mightiest stream, and you too will confess this the garden of America. Beautifully blended in one delightful panorama, are lake and prairie, grove and stream, farms and farm-houses, villages and cities! Or follow with me the windings of some ancient trail, along the margin of those crystal lakes and streams, there, where the dark shadows rest upon the waters, and no sound but the insect's hum and the wood-bird's note is heard, and *your* soul will instinctively feel the enchantment.

GOD *loves beauty;* so all HIS works declare. On mountain top and in darkest caverns, it shows forth his glory. In every land and clime it urges its votaries to come and adore him. But no where does it exist in such *perfection* as in the land of which I write!

Transplant New England institutions on our soil, and we could ask no more. But we are rapidly approaching a period when the WEST will no longer look towards the rising sun for her educational light, nor longer shine in borrowed rays, but will illumine the entire NATION with her own brightness.

CHAPTER LIX.

DARING OF THE WEST.

"It is no doubt a beautiful country," says one, "but then it is so distant, and your society is not what we of the East are accustomed to."

Distance, my friend, is annihilated; a week will convey you from St. Paul to any portion of New England: and as to your last objection the preference is in favor of the West—with all due deference to my native New England. I *love* the East, but I *glory in* the West. Opinions of western life, as drawn from books, present but one phase. True, there may be in them many pictures of *real life*. But where in this abused world can you go, without meeting much that is repugnant to a refined nature—many that are grossly ignorant, and even from preference? But Minnesota has less than I have found elsewhere, that is uncongenial and vulgar. True, every person can find just the society he desires; here are the low, the vicious and ignorant, as well as the intelligent, accomplished and refined.

The West, like all other regions, has its advantages and disadvantages to be set over against each other, but it is infinite in resources, and great already in its achievements. What other portion of earth has originated and built up great cities in so short a time? What other land has the facilities for the perfecting of steam power! for railroads and steamboats! We should not, however, forget our indebtedness to the East, for it has been, to a great extent, eastern capital that has built our roads, opened our inexhaustible lead and copper mines, and built our schools and churches. Our intrinsic wealth is more and more developed, and ere long the balance of power, in wealth and moral influence, as it is now in energy, will be in the West. The West regards the East as its Alma Mater. I have never seen half a dozen adult persons born west of Lake Erie, and only two men west of the Mississippi.

Say you, "There is more high-handed wickedness, more dark intrigue there."

I grant there is more bold and open defiance of law, among lawless men determined to carry out deep plans of wickedness in the face of all obstacles, but not more of intrigue, nor of pilfering, robbing and murder. In the one part of the country bad men are designing and subtle, and in the other presuming and bold. Everywhere there is a class of persons to be guarded against, or the inexperienced traveler may suffer imposition.

A circumstance was once related to me by a stage passenger, which will illustrate the nefarious system of counterfeiting practiced here, as well as in the East. He stopped at a hotel in the State of Illinois, when an acquaintance and traveling companion calling for a cigar, received change for a five-franc piece. My informant having had previous suspicions of the man, was doubtful of the coin, and to obtain it laid down a one dollar bill, took a cigar and the piece. Following the other man into an adjacent room, he pronounced the money he held in his hand to be counterfeit, and added, eyeing him intently, "*You are engaged in that business—you have become quickly rich, and no one knows how; to me, it is solved.*" The keen eye of the counterfeiter rested on him a moment with affected surprise, but suddenly changing his demeanor, he said, "Can you keep a secret?" Then followed a disclosure of facts and schemes, and names, among the first men of that and other states, engaged in the business of which he had now for the first time been accused. They had a thoroughly organized underground railroad system, so perfect that they scarcely feared detection. I inquired why he did not make a disclosure, and thus bring them all to justice. To which he replied, that "the counterfeiter had felt perfectly secure in making the disclosure: for the gang was so well organized, and so connected by a telegraphic chain, that any attempt at disclosure would be perfectly useless, nor could he be in any portion of their domain but a dozen balls would be ready to enter his heart."

Another friend, emigrating to Minnesota, had with him a large sum of money, which he wisely deposited at Galena. A young man made himself agreeable on the boat and desired to occupy the same state-room. My friend was surprised on one occasion to find his trunk had been rummaged, but as he was sure no one but the occupant had entered the room, thought very little of it. His companion, under some pretext, returned on the same boat that brought him to St. Paul. He was soon after arrested for robbery, tried, and condemned, and confessed the sentence just. It appeared that he had gone to Minnesota with the express design of robbing a fellow passenger, who was known to start with a large amount of money, and his disappointment in not obtaining it hastened the commission of the act that led to his incarceration.

I have related these circumstances for the benefit of those who are inexperienced, though the caution involved is no less applicable in the East than the West.

CHAPTER LX.

THE SECRET OF HAPPINESS.

THE true secret of happiness is to live for the good of the world and the glory of God, making the best of whatever trials and privations betide. No where is there a more favorable field for the cultivation of a spirit to be useful, and to accommodate one's self to circumstances, than upon the frontier of a new and sparsely populated region, though this wonder-working age will soon scarcely leave room for enduring physical *privation*. We can scarcely realize the want of a blessing here, before we find a substitute. Minnesotians admit not the word " privation " in their vocabulary ; those residing in the larger towns, or their vicinity, have many more privileges than they formerly enjoyed in the East; and all are satisfied, all are happy, whether in town or country. True, the experience of the first settlers was somewhat different from that of those who now come here; but in all their rustic homes are found sweet contentment, and many sources of enjoyment peculiar to the West.

A man of affluence from an eastern city purchased two thousand acres of the finest land, embracing prairie, woodland, lake, and river, in the immediate vicinity of our capital, and set about plans for extensive operations. This was in the early organization of the territory, when limited quarters in a crowded hotel were the best accommodations. His wife, accustomed only to the refinements of the city, found enjoyment in long rides over the unfenced country, in devising plans for future comfort, and accompanying her husband amid the delightful scenery of their own possessions. Sometimes she would prepare the rural feast, and on one occasion, in her evening rehearsal of the day's delights, she declared, "the sweetest meal she ever ate" was the one she had that day cooked herself, amid the rocks and under the shady trees —coffee, steak, and potatoes, constituting the bill of fare. Smooth, flat stones were washed and used for plates, wooden forks were whittled with Yankee ingenuity, and a useful jack-knife performed several important duties on this occasion; and for the first time in many months she sat mistress of ceremonies at her own table.

At last, wearied with the process of tempering many irons in a slow but sure fire, she resolved to occupy their unfinished house, in spite of suggestions as to its unfitness; and there, without a plastered room, a door hung, or a window, they soon found themselves very comfortable, with the independence of home. Musketo nets were hung at the windows, a bed arranged upon the shavings, and she declared the happiest night she had yet seen in the territory was this first one in her own house.

No arrangement for culinary operations had been made, but two crotched sticks were driven into the ground out of doors, across which a pole was laid, "whence the kettle swung;" and thus, with such miserable help as could only be obtained there, cooking for two weeks was performed, and relished greatly. This experience prepared her to enjoy the happy contrast which followed. The elegantly-furnished mansion now stands amidst the verdant grove, commanding a view of almost the entire city of St. Paul. A full orchestra of nature's warblers join in concert to break the morning slumbers, and flowers are springing everywhere around. Everything now betokens thrift and comfort, and all the appliances of wealth abound.

This is not an isolated case, but only one of many, cited to prove that pure and elevated enjoyment is not the offspring of luxury; that the heart finds contentment, and even feasts, amid rural scenes and simple home delights. I have experienced more heart satisfaction amid the "brush and brake," and on the "banks and braes" of a crystal lake, than was ever knwon amid the gayest festive scenes. I have eaten food there prepared with a sweeter relish than at the most sumptuous table. I have "rowed" in a slender skiff over the blue waves of these transparent lakes with infinitely more satisfaction than I ever knew in the gilded boats of the Hudson and Lake Erie.

In short, I have known Minnesota from its infancy, and have loved it as a parent does a child, till my very being is entwined with her interests; and to me it is fit for a paradise. Come to Minnesota, but bring with you principles firm and unyielding. Come, but let your influence tell on its future weal; so shall your name be as a "sweet savor," and posterity shall bless it; so shall you aid in erecting a fabric which shall endure when suns and stars shall cease to shine, and monuments crumble to dust!

CHAPTER LXI.

AN INCIDENT IN THE EAST.

DURING the summer of 1855, I was traveling in a rail car in Eastern New York; and occupying seats near me were a well-informed gentleman and lady. Conversation, from commonplace topics, became interesting, and finally turned upon the West in general, and Minnesota in particular; the country, its merits and demerits, were pretty thoroughly discussed, and in an interval of silence the gentleman inquired if I "knew Miss B—, principal of a seminary at St. Paul?"

"O, very well, sir. Is she an acquaintance of yours?"

"More by reputation than personally. I have met her but once, and that on her way West. She was a pioneer in the cause of education in your territory, I believe."

"She was there at an early day, and has, I think, the reputation of establishing the first permanent citizen school, and that under the most unpromising and discouraging circumstances."

He replied, "I thought it at the time a very hazardous enterprise, and tried to dissuade her from it; but the reports of her success have happily justified her undertaking. She is still there, I suppose?"

"At present she is in the East."

"Not to remain?"

"Only a few months. Her health was slightly impaired, and her energies pretty thoroughly exhausted, by being overtaxed, and a suspension of effort was deemed advisable, which she is improving in visiting friends."

"It would afford me great pleasure to meet her, and I hope it may be my good fortune. I owe her an apology for skepticism, when she was so sanguine. You will please bear her my kind remembrances and hearty congratulations on her success, with the hope that she has *not forgotten,* but *forgiven.*"

"Receive now the assurance," said I. "I grant absolution, and we will shake hands as old friends!"

The surprise we leave the reader to imagine.

"And now," says he, "tell me, were there no disappointments—was there nothing to mar your your felicity? In short, have you never regretted going?"

"If there were no clouds, we would not appreciate the blessing of the sun; no dark nights, we would not so fully enjoy the full moon's influence. Shadows *have* fallen upon my pathway, but many genial rays of sunshine have gleamed upon my heart; and so far from regretting that I closed my ears to your advice, and willfully persevered, as some thought, against all counsel, it has been a constant theme of rejoicing that, at that early day, *I set the poles of my 'teepee'* in Minnesota."

"But you must have found much that was uncouth and uncongenial; must have experienced much of the '*roughing* of life.'"

"Well, you know, it is said that honey may be extracted from the bitterest flowers. This is as true in the moral as in the physical world. I found a moral necessity, as well as a moral philosophy, in closing my eyes and seeing only the fair side of the picture; in short of making the best of everything, and waiting the change that was fast developing. And every difficulty and trial surmounted, have but attached me more closely to my adopted home."

"Would you not prefer to remain East, provided you could bring all that attaches you there?"

"My preferences are all Western. No; I can scarcely imagine an inducement sufficient to keep me in the East. My heart is not alienated from my friends: but we can not always be near those we love. The world has claims upon us, which, if we disregard, we forfeit the favor of heaven. I love my native State with the fondness of a first—a girlish love; but my adopted one with the true *devotion of woman's* love. I left the former at the call of duty, and that alone would take me from the latter."

"And you have, really, all the glories and excellencies there that are represented?"

"The half never has and never can be *told*."

"Have you any foreign population?"

"No more than is essential for 'hewers of wood and drawers of water.' There are Germans, Swedes, and Norwegians, many of whom are independent, good, industrious citizens, quiet and law-abiding, such as are no detriment to our population."

"Your territory is reputed healthy, with no ague, and no disease common to the country."

"I know of no disease peculiar to the country. *Bad whiskey* is carrying off its victims by scores; and though the world is better off to be rid of them, and none layeth it to heart when the drunkard is gone, yet others are coming up to take their places; and this will be the case until the liquor trade is suppressed."

"Can nothing be done to stop the abominable traffic?"

"Not so long as the majority of our legislators are men who cater to the public favor, and wink at iniquity—

buying their votes with whiskey, and licensing those places of sin where the vendor of vice, pauperism, and death, is seeking to entrap every youth in a community. I tell you we want men of moral principle—men who shall join the ranks of those who stand up fearlessly in the defense of morality and temperance."

"You hope for the dawning of a brighter day?"

"There is a strong army who will never cease to hope, to fight and pray."

"The magical working of the Maine Law is *felt* in *this* State, and the vender and retailer are made to feel its power, and it *will* yet sweep from this entire nation the drunkard manufacturer.

"God grant it may not be long."

"Well, are you posted in commercial and financial matters? Are there any opportunities remaining for profitable investments?"

"As good as any yet made, and there will be for years to come. I never urge one disinclined to go, for I remember one who came as he said, induced by my representations of the country, through the Press. He landed in a rainy unpleasant day, gazed around, pronounced it all a humbug, and left in disgust. Others, by the same means, were induced to come, arrived under different circumstances, their souls clear from mists and fogs; and yet, rejoice in their decision. But to those predisposed, I say, as I have said to you. "The half never was told, and you cannot regret the change." We want none but sterling, upright men, of strong moral principle who will stand firm on the side of Right—who will build up and not pull down society.

"What is the encouragement to professional men? Any openings for them?"

"Every profession is crowded, and yet there is plenty of room for more. Hundreds of lawyers contrive to find employment. The doctor *lives*, though there should be one to every sick person; merchants in the various branches of trade, all do a thriving business; mechanics are never idle, and have high wages. The milliners and dressmakers even covet rest, but find it not: in short, there is no branch of honest respectable business but meets a sure reward, and is fast leading on to fortune. One of our most wealthy business men, a banker and real estate dealer, went to St. Paul with only six dollars and seventy-five cents in his pocket. He was honest and upright, doing whatever his hands found to do with energy and dispatch; and though he met many reverses during the first few months, in three years he was worth more than a clear hundred thousand dollars, neither obtained fraudulently, nor by a niggardly spirit, but by prudent forethought and a run of 'good luck.' He has merited a reputation for benevolence, and his hand is ever open to the poor, and he is indeed worthy of his 'good fortune.'"

"Such cases are probably rare?"

"By no means. Neither does *every* one meet with the *same* success, but I have in my mind many parallel instances. But money-making is an inferior consideration, though well enough in its place. The well being and improvement of society, should be the predominant aim of every citizen. Money should be sought as a means, not as an end."

"Very true, but is it not the case that the larger proportion of the population have been drawn there by the hope of gain?"

"The majority, no doubt; yet with very many it has

been a secondary object. True, our city could not be built without money, and a vast amount has been expended there, and not only at the Capital but throughout the territory, in an almost incredibly short space of time. We want men of capital, and rejoice that we have them and that others are still going."

"What say you, wife," said he, turning to the lady by his side, "to going to Minnesota?"

"Where thou goest I will go," she replied, "and you are well aware that I have long desired a Western home."

"And ere many months we will have one, if fortune and Providence favor us. I have long desired to *see* the West, with the design of locating if favorably impressed.

"Now allow me to make inquiries relative to the teachers whom the Board of Education has sent to the West? Several hundreds have gone from Yankee land I think?"

"Some four hundred since we met eight years ago, and these are scattered from the shores of the Great Lakes to the Pacific."

"But it is generally believed that Hymen is playing the mischief with them, and that they soon leave the public for *private* schools!"

"So it used to be told in the East, that whenever a boat threw out her plank at any of the Western towns, a score of young men filed thereon, would extend an arm from each side with, '*Have a husband, miss?*' to any young lady who might pass to the shore.

"I am a little incredulous, respecting the truth of this, or the agreeable question has very frequently been answered in the negative. But seriously, only one hundred or thereabouts of the four hundred, have become entangled in the web of matrimony, a number too small rather than too large."

"It is quite desirable, I presume, that all who go should permanently locate West?"

"It is hoped that none will ever return East for a home. Their influence is needed West, which, when concentrated in the domestic circle is, in many instances, even greater than before. But instead of Hymen's playing the mischief with the teachers, as you say, it is rather with the pupils. Why, it was at one time proverbial 'if one wants to get married, attend Miss B's school.' Several of my pupils from thirteen years and upwards, have entered the state of matrimony, and from being trained in a school-room, have begun themselves the training of a household. The wooing in some cases, is done up in quick time.

"The most expeditious case in which I was especially interested, was that of a young miss of fifteen.

"One evening as she left the school-room, I noticed a tall six-footer standing at the corner of a vacant lot, who joined her as she passed along. The following day she was not in her accustomed seat, and on the third day she entered for her books, saying with a happy countenance, that she should 'not be at school any more.' 'Why not?' I inquired. 'O, I was married yesterday!' she replied.

"'Why did you not acquaint me with your intentions my dear? This is altogether too great a surprise!'"

"'I should have done so had I known it myself, but *he* never asked me until yesterday, and we were married last evening.'

"'You have known him well, I presume?'

"'I never saw him until the day before. He asked me, and I didn't like to say No, so I am a married woman.'

"By this time every scholar in the room was choking with suppressed laughter, and I stepped into the porch with the departing pupil, and was there introduced to her husband, who in reply to my regrets said he too was '*sorry to take her away*, but didn't see but he must do so.' They had met for the first time in the street, where he had been awaiting her, having seen her as she entered the school room. A ride was at once agreed on, and as she had no family friends to advise with, the ride resulted in an engagement, and the engagement in marriage of course. He was an honest yeoman of the backwoods, and though never since heard from, they are doubtless enjoying life in a quiet thriving way."

"Death has no doubt diminished the band of teachers?"

"Thirty or more have died; and some, if not all, have left an influence which will tell for the good of future generations. One of my class was first to fall a victim to the destroyer. There were memorable circumstances to render her dear to us all. When we parted, she was full of life and vigor, her great soul fired with enthusiam in her enterprise. She possessed a capacious, well-balanced, thoroughly disciplined mind, which with all her attainments she placed at her Savior's feet.

"At Napierville, Illinois, she entered upon the work assigned her. Here she exerted a great influence, not only with those with whom she was most intimately connected, but with the community around her. She lived not for herself, and yet seemed unconscious of her power over others. 'The true strength and secret of all power!'

"It is the testimony of her pastor, whom I recently met, that the amount of good she accomplished can never be computed in time; that her influence lives to bless the world, though her visible labors closed with her first year West. Never was a young lady more justly and devotedly beloved; and never one more sincerely lamented. The aged felt they had lost a sympathizer and friend, the young, a faithful counselor and guide. 'And,' said one with whom I conversed, 'a revival of religion followed her death, and almost every young person who became a follower of the Savior, attributed her first serious impressions to her faithful teachings and admonitions. So gentle, kind and affectionate had been both precept and example, that all with whom she had intercourse were constrained to admit the loveliness of Christianity, and it seemed that the spirit of Miss Chase was present, and presided over all our meetings.

"How true that the 'memory of the just is blessed,' and it shall live when monuments and crowns have crumbled to decay!

"This is not an isolated case; the same is true of others who are gone. The teachers of course are not *all* of the same stamp, do not all meet with equal success, but are in the main doing an important work."

"Much more important than I had supposed. I know if a man like Governor Slade was devoting his noble energies to the work with such zeal, that it must be of some moment, and I think it is not generally apppreciated."

"Nor can it be, at this distance. I know, sir, that many of these teachers are unostentatiously performing the labor of the Home Missionary, the Sabbath-school Agent, Superintendent and Teacher, besides searching out the cause of the poor, devoting nights to the sick, and attending to many other duties in the community; and no one, it is thought, can attend to it as well as the teacher, '*who has nothing to prevent!*'

"'Their reward is with me,' saith the Lord. And a strong confidence in Him sustains the soul, when sinking beneath a weight of care; yes, the cloud has a 'silver lining.' I have met and conversed with many of these teachers, but never with one who regretted having embarked in the enterprise."

"You have not many of them in Minnesota, I think?"

"Minnesota is too much New England to need them; there are more teachers than schools there. Several have gone to the Pacific coast, and are very successful in Oregon and California. The Board of National Popular Education was a little germ which has expanded into a mighty tree."

CHAPTER LXII.

CLOSE OF 1856.

THE year 1856 has closed! The auspicious dawnings of a new year are welcomed by the people of Minnesota with more than ordinary gratitude, for on no people have the benign smiles of Heaven more signally rested.

We are generously permitted to extract from the New Year's Sermon of Rev. A. M. Torbet, which embodies some ideas on our enviable position and unprecedented prosperity. We preface this, however, with a brief allusion to a "Surprise Party," which ushered in the year 1857.

In order to detain the family at home, it had been intimated that a half dozen friends would spend the evening with them. The half dozen swelled to one hundred, who brought with them a superb set of study furniture, for our pastor, a generous purse to his wife, besides many valuable gifts to both, testimonies of the high appreciation of a generous, loving people to the best of pastors, amounting in all to some two hundred dollars. This had been accomplished with no apparent effort. We have no hesitation in saying that amongst the innumerable social gatherings of that evening, there was not on the broad earth one more agreeable, intelligent and refined, than this, in a young city where savage and civilized life are *supposed* to mingle. We presume that the above incident had some influence on the beautiful and appropriate discourse of the following Sabbath.

Acts, xxviii, 15. *"And from thence, when the brethren heard of us, they came to meet us as far as Appii-Forum, and the three taverns ; whom, when Paul saw, he thanked God and took courage."*

"Another year has kindly approached to meet us. Some it has welcomed at the post of duty; some with the goblet of distilled fire; others, thank God! being caught with guile, it welcomed with the temperance pledge.* To some it will be a year of labor and prosperity, and to others, probably one of dissipation and ruin.

* * * * * *

"As we stand now on its opening period of holy time, may we not thank God for the Past and take courage for the Future? Let us review the blessings of the past year, and from them be encouraged to assume the duties of the coming one.

" We have had many social blessings. God has prolonged to us through the past year the endearments of friendships. Many pleasing interchanges of solitude and society have fallen to our lot. In new homes, when we expected the links of society and social enjoyments to be broken up, we have experienced no want of either. The placid stream on whose bosom we were borne to our present sphere of duty and responsibility, has brought upon its waters many an old familiar face, and put within our grasp the hand of many an old and tried friend and

---

* During the New Year's calls of 1857, some of the ladies had arranged to obtain the autographs of their visitors, when some of the "*fast young men*" found that they had affixed their names to a *temperance pledge.*

fellow laborer with whom we have been associated in other lands. There has been but little to remind us of distance from the home of childhood, and the scenes of other years, except the greeting which these friends have given at their coming and the adieus at their parting. There has been little to make us feel that we were mingling the savage with the civilized life, except the occasional presence of the red man with his war-weapons, his filth and game. We have had our Sabbaths where the social ties of a pure and hopeful religious life have been bound more strongly together by the fact that our outer life was somewhat heterogeneous. The spiritual of Friendship and Society, has made the natural of them to recede among those who were willing and conscientious in its cultivation. And the godly element of our being has been more fervent in its pulsations than in other lands, where it was more mingled with the natural ties that bind man to his fellow. There is no place on earth where the devout and true children of God can find more favorable circumstances for the culture of strong religious affections than here. The bonds of the past are severed; and there is an absence of heathenish customs and rites which do not prevent the full and free admixture in the highest duties and holiest emotions of experimental religion. We can see more fully eye to eye in the providential developments of duty which a new field of enterprise, so full of magnitude and importance as the one we occupy discovers; and realize more strongly the obligations we are under, to establish and sustain the social interests of our holy religion. The winter here, for the present, excludes us to some extent from the rest of mankind, and throws us into more close social relations among ourselves. In order then to make them pregnant with good to our fellow-men; we ought to endeavor to have the religious element pervade them as far as possible. Society may be used to promote the highest spiritual interests of the race, and if by it as a blessing we enjoy, we should seek to confer on others a knowledge of religion, it will be found returning to our own bosom with a ten thousand fold increasing power to encourage our hearts in the discharge of the duties of the coming year and all coming time.

"The past has been a year of unwonted prosperity. From a city of little more than six thousand souls, we have grown in a single year to ten thousand; and *property has grown from a value of hundreds to that of thousands, in almost the same* space of time. The territory has also sustained about the same ratio of increase. From seventy-five, it has gone up to a population of *more than one hundred and fifty thousand.* And where the eye rested one year ago on the wide-spread domain, without a human habitation to disturb the solitude, there now may be seen the smoke curling from hundreds of cabins, filled with gifted, active, and intelligent human beings. It has not been an increase of the rude and uncultivated of the race, but one marked with culture and refinement. It has not been an increase only of the poor without the means of subsistence, but of the sons and daughters of *wealth, worth,* and *distinction.* Nor has the increase been made without the church and the school-house. These have sprung up among the population by the same energy and care that have made the home and opened the farm. An altar at which to worship God, and a place in which to train the mental twig, have been sought and secured by those who have come to make the wilderness and solitary places glad, and blossom as the rose. We have been charmed with the field and the garden, where a year since there was not an appliance of husbandry. We have been astonished at the presence of the cabin, the cottage, the superb dwelling, the brick and stone block, where a year since there were nothing but bluffs or bushes. Confidence and capital have found their way among us, and been used to advantage. Commerce has increased, and business of all kinds has been successfully prosecuted by our increasing number of tradesmen and mechanics. Labor in every department has been rewarded with the unsparing munificence of a divine providence, amid whose indulgences, life, through the past year, has been to us, not only a succession of seasons, but the melody of music, the fragrance of flowers, the blending of colors, and the variety of tastes. God has preserved and blessed our country, notwithstanding our national provocations; and though our territorial relations may be such as to excuse us in some measure from the action of some of the specific national sins of our country, yet they cannot diminish our solicitude, for our weal or wo is interlinked with the general prosperity or adversity. Let us, therefore, repose confidence in God, who omnipotently reigneth, that he will overrule all things for the public good, and be grateful for such public mercies as we do enjoy.

*   *   *   *   *   *

"We have our personal mercies. Life has been preserved. Our Benefactor has made our mornings and evenings to rejoice by his manifold kindness. We have not only had our Sabbaths and sanctuaries, but our eyes have beheld our teachers in the pulpit and the Sabbath-school and Bible-class, and our ears have heard their voices in the language of his Gospel and grace. We have been made glad in the house of prayer, because God in very deed met with our waiting souls, and fed us with the bread of heaven; and shall we not say, with the sweet singer of Israel, 'Bless the Lord, O my soul, and forget not all his benefits?'

"True, we have had our trials, but even these should not check our gratitude. To most of us they have been few, compared with our comforts. They have been light compared with the sufferings of others, and have been variously alleviated. In a measure, when they have shot forth God has debated with them, and stayed his 'rough wind in the day of the east wind.' They have all been founded in our personal good; in a parental regard for our spiritual welfare.

*　　*　　*　　*　　*　　*

"Some of us can recall personal afflictions and bereavements that have fallen to our lot the past year; but are they not offset with personal mercies, the luxury of which is still fresh in our hearts, and produces emotions of gratitude too big for language to express? *And a gratitude is required by your speaker, at least on this occasion, which will not expire with mere acknowledgements, but induce him anew to the Gospel service, and to walk before God and his generous people in newness of life.*

"What then, my hearers, can be more reasonable than to take courage from the past, and press onward? We enter, indeed, on the new year with a confidence in God nourished from the past.

*　　*　　*　　*　　*　　*

"There is nothing left to chance; and you may judge from the past what the future will be. If in it duty and trial have mingled, so will it be in the year to come. If, however, all that the past teaches of God's ways with man, and especially with yourself, is calculated to encourage you to assume the duties of the coming year, with mingled confidence and gratitude, then, let us arise and gird on the armor. A new year welcomes us to the conflict with sin, to the duties of the Christian, and to the crown of glorified saints in heaven. A new year invites you to design and execute something for the good of souls, and the glory of God. It invites you, here, to raise your Ebenezer, and say 'hitherto hath the Lord helped me,' and though 'He slay me, yet will I trust in Him.' We admire confidence, but, in order to be profitable, it must be coupled with fear, lest we offend God.

* * * * * *

"When you are so naturally led to think of the *past* and the *future*, why not, like Paul, when he met the brethren at Appii-Forum, *thank God, and take courage* to perform every other duty which necessity, interest, the salvation of others, the claims of the Savior, and the glory of God require. And if you have not begun a religious life, now is the time. Let the goodness of God lead you to repentance."

CHAPTER LXIII.

CONCLUSION.

In surveying this vast arena—this field for effort, commensurate with the noblest aims and desires of the most disinterested hearts, we cannot but believe that Minnesota has no common part to perform in the drama of events which are to precede the millenial glory. Nor can we but believe, that no small part is assigned to those who were "last at the cross, and first at the grave of our Savior."

Man may bid the tall forest tree to bow; he may make the waste places smile with plenty; he may engage in political strifes, and his eloquence thrill the nation; or he may hold the scepter of power: but to WOMAN a higher, a nobler work is entrusted. It is her province to train the tender twig and to mould the plastic clay. Upon her it depends, whether the individual American citizen shall be a curse or a blessing, and whether the nation shall be rent and prostrated by the feuds of corrupt men, or fulfill the mission of the great Christian republic of modern times.

Hers is no trifling work. The tiny twig is soon to grow into the stately and well proportioned, or gnarled and knotted tree. It is her hand that must give to each expanding leaflet its best position to imbibe the sun's clear rays—to drink the healthful morning dew. It is no trifling work to mould the future destiny of immortal beings. When the child first folds its hands within its mother's, who teaches it to lisp "OUR FATHER," an impression is received which will gather strength with years, and the remembrance of that soft hand upon the head may arrest the wayward youth in his downward career of sin.

We would repeat it: To woman is entrusted the future destiny of Minnesota. Her influence is to determine the predominance of vice or virtue; whether the "powers that be" shall, in the future, be men "fearing God and working righteousness," or men choosing "darkness rather than light," being haters of that which is good. And this influence is not to be wielded by dissension, strife and the ballot-box, but by precept and example. If she frowns upon all that is abhorrent in high places, and encourages virtue, though in the garb of poverty, if she reposes not supinely on the lap of ease—a mere butterfly of fashion, living for display and admiration, but with high and noble aims seeks to answer the great purpose of her existence, she may make the pages of its future history bright with the records of immortal worth. Like the otto of roses, most potent when the flower is crushed, so shall her name and deeds be felt when the soul has escaped from its crumbling casket; sweeter and yet sweeter the fragrance, as the expanding circle of her influence stretches upon the broad ocean of eternity.

We live in an age of enterprise—in an age when progress is on the high pressure principle, and knowledge, all powerful for good or evil, is spreading with wonderful rapidity. Good and evil are intermixed, and yet are so distinct as to be obvious to the most casual observer. Truth and error are engaged in a conflict, but hope is dawning on our moral horizon, and in its westward march will soon shine with all the effulgence of noon-day glory. Truth *will* triumph: "*for the mouth of the Lord hath spoken it.*"

FINIS.

INDEX.

----, Erin 229 Miss 310 Old Betsey 63 Uncle John 63
ALLONG, Claude 22
AMES, A E 209 C G 208 Mr 109 270
ASTOR, John Jacob 161
AYER, Rev Mr 237
B----, Miss 88 323 329
BABCOCK, Rev Dr 89
BAKER, D A J 104
BANFILL, John 235
BARROWS, E G 87
BASS, J W 99
BEACH, Moses Y 289
BEAN, Miss 203 Mr 209
BISHOP, Harriet E 87
BOWMAN, George D 208
BOWRON, Joseph R 101
BRADLEY, Father 117-118 Joshua 116
BRECK, Rev Mr 121
BREMER, Miss 225
BROTHER, Mr 174
BUCHANAN, 175
BULLEN, J A 242
CAMERON, 250-252
CARLIE, Dr 44
CARSON, Kit 231 248
CARVER, 25 32 202 Hartwell 26 Jonathan 24 26
CASE, Mrs 209
CATLIN, John 124
CAVENDER, A H 88 113
CHASE, Miss 331
CHUTE, Mr 201
CLARK, Mrs 33
CLOSE, Rev Mr 113
CRESSEY, E W 230 J R 115 313
DANA, Capt 289
DAVIS, Mr 201
DAYTON, Lyman 236 301
DEMEDICI, Venus 225
DESOTO, 224
DEWEY, Ex-gov 99 John 99
DODD, Capt 307
DOWNING, 222
EASTMAN, Capt 27 161
EWING, Judge 285
FARRIBAULT, Mr 30 284
FORD, 153
FREMONT, 175
FULTON, 19
GEAR, Rev Mr 108 113
GEORGE III, 26

GIBHARD, Mr 201
GOADING, George 34
GOODALE, Jim 248 Mr 249
GOODHUE, 206 James M 125 208
GORMAN, Gov 145 Wm A 126
GRAY, 180
HARRIS, Capt 298-299 D S 289
HASKELL, Mr 133
HAYNER, 111
HENNAPIN, 23 202 282 Father 148 Louis 22
HEZLUP, George 307
HILL, B M 113 301
HOBBS, Miss 289
HOLTON, Mrs 44
HONE, Mr 44
HOPKINS, Mrs 257 Rev Mr 292
HOSFORD, Amanda 103
HOYT, B F 88 113
HURLBUT, Rev Mr 112
HUTCHINSON, 236
HYDE, John 230
HYMEN, 328-329
INDIAN, Bag-on-a-ke-shig 274 Black Whistle 264-265 Dandy 268 276 Hock-e-wash-ta 92 Hocka-wash-ta 63 Hole-in-the-day 274 276-278 Indian John 268 Little Crow 63 265-266 Old Betsey 275 Old Hock-e-wash-ta 269 Old Shackopee 257 Oseola 96 Winona 219
IRVINE, J R 98 John R 50 Mrs 50
JACKSON, Henry 48
JOHNSON, Col 224 Mr 307 P H 292

JONES, Mrs Dr 57
KEENER, Mrs 270
KINGSLEY, 299
LAFRAMBEAU, Joseph 294
LARPENTEUR, A L 50
LASALLE, 23
LASEUR, 20 306
LEAVENWORTH, Col 32
LEE, Minnie Mary 235
LESEUR, 292
LONG, Maj 244 Major 32 Mr 174
MATTOCKS, James 121
MCKUSICK, John 45
MCNEILL, E D 171
MEEKER, Judge 210
MENARD, 21-22
MILLER, J P 207
MILNOR, 250-252
MORRILL, D D 171
MORRISON, Wm 27
MOSS, Mrs 103
MYRICK, Rev Mr 121
N----, Mrs 45
NEIL, E D 88
NEILL, E D 120 171
NORRIS, Mr 133
NORTHUP, Anson 44 200 Mr 45
OGDEN, Maj 39
OWEN, Mr 148-149 289-290
PARSONS, J P 114
PENN, William 60
PERKINS, Judge 182
PHELPS, Rev Dr 157
PIERCE, President 126
PIKE, Gen 27-28
POND, G H 208 256 283 S W 193 301
POPE, Capt 132 234
PRICE, H M 113

INDEX.

PRINCE, Mr 201
PROVENCALLE, Louis 29
PUTNAM, J G 112
RAMSEY, Alexander 124 Gov 126 202 240 276-277 Mrs 278
RENVILLE, Joseph 28 Mr 29
RICE, E 285 H M 202 211 226 273 Mr 109
RIGGS, Mrs 257 Rev Mr 255
RIHELDAFFER, J G 121
ROBEAR, Louis 51
RUSSEL, A A 208 R P 200
S----, James 170 Mrs 36
SABIN, A 111
SANFORD, Mr 201
SCOFIELD, Mary A 104 208
SCOTT, Gen 205
SIBLEY, Henry H 124
SIGOURNEY, Mrs 146
SLADE, Gov 331
SMITH, Capt 185
SNELLING, Col 34-35 38 160 Mrs 34-35 39
SPENCER, Mr 240 Mrs 240
STARR, 299
STEELE, Franklin 43 191 224 Mr 44 199-200

STEPHENS, Col 207 210 John H 205 Mr 149 Simon 148
STEWART, Robert 161
T----, Dr 162
TANNER, James 238 Mr 239
TAYLOR, A W 200
TERRY, Elijah 239 Mr 240
TODD, Col 285
TORBET, A M 115 166 170 301 333 Mr 117
TURNER, Dr 161
TUTTLE, C A 207 M C 171 Mr 149
W----, Miss 75 259 Rev Dr 101
WALKER, Orange 45
WHITNEY, J C 208 Rev Mr 187
WILCOXSON, Rev Mr 121
WILKINS, Capt 188
WILLIAMSON, Dr 20 28 59 65 73-74 259 Rev Dr 52 285 T S 39
WOA-WAN-PA, Wa-ma-da-ka 95 Wa-ma-don-ka Wash-ta 94
ZEE, Harpa 63 Winona 63

www.ingramcontent.com/pod-product-compliance
Lightning Source LLC
Chambersburg PA
CBHW070934230426
43666CB00011B/2430